IMPERIAL RUSSIA IN FRONTIER AMERICA

THE ANDREW H. CLARK SERIES IN THE HISTORICAL GEOGRAPHY OF NORTH AMERICA

Published

CITIES AND IMMIGRANTS: A Geography of Change in Nineteenth-Century America
David Ward

SOUTHWEST: Three Peoples in Geographical Change, 1600-1970
Donald W. Meinig

CANADA BEFORE CONFEDERATION: A Study in Historical Geography
R. Cole Harris and John Warkentin

COLONIAL NEW ENGLAND: A Historical Geography
Douglas R. McManis

ORDER UPON THE LAND: The U.S. Rectangular Survey and The Upper Mississipi Country
Hildegard Binder Johnson

Other volumes in preparation

Imperial Russia
In Frontier America

The Changing Geography of Supply of
Russian America, 1784-1867

James R. Gibson

Cartographer

Miklos Pinther

New York
Oxford University Press
1976

TO MY TEACHERS

Buildings are raised on New World ground,
Now Russia rushes to Nootka Sound,
The Peoples wild are Nature's child,
And friendly now to Russian rule.

Song of Baranov

PREFACE

Russian America (comprising mainland Alaska, the Aleutian, Pribilof, Commander, and Kurile islands, temporary settlements in California and Hawaii, and eventually even Sakhalin) was peripheral not only to the growing Russian Empire but also to the emerging nations of North America. To most Russians, Alaska was even more remote and desolate than Siberia, and it was equally insignificant to most Americans, Canadians, and Mexicans. Nevertheless, for half a century (1790-1840) Russia was a powreful rival of Great Britain, Spain, and the United States for control of the resources of the Northwest Coast, and the Russian effort warrants the attention of anyone interested in the historical geography of the region.

Russian occupancy of Alaska from the late eighteenth century was neither sudden nor novel; it was simply the latest and farthest phase of a protracted and extensive process of eastward expansion that had been launched by Muscovy in the mid-sixteenth century. The advance across northern Asia had been speeded by the taiga's abundance of furs (and monopoly on sables) and by Europe's huge demand for "soft gold," as well as by Siberia's dense network of river roads, weak native resistance, and lack of foreign competition. In 1639, only sixty years after they crossed the Urals, Russian Cossacks and *promyshlenniks* (fur hunters) reached the Pacific. Although for the next half-century this eastward movement was temporarily halted while Russia concentrated on the Amur Valley to the south, by the end of the century powerful Manchu China had blocked the thrust, and the Russian advance resumed its easterly course via Kamchatka.

From this peninsula in 1740 ventured Vitus Bering's second expedition of exploration and discovery. When its survivors returned to Petropavlovsk they brought news of a "great land" across the Eastern (Pacific) Ocean and, more important, numerous samples of sea otter pelts, which were to prove even more precious than sable skins. This discovery prompted a "fur rush" across the Bering Sea via the convenient Aleutian causeway, giving the Russians a half-century head start on foreign competitors; the latter were not alerted until the publication of the findings of Cook's third voyage (1776-79).

So in America as well as in Asia the fur trade remained the basis of Russian eastward expansion. But there were some significant differences. First, the change in fur bearers from sable and squirrel to sea otter and fur seal meant a change in habitat—from continental to maritime—and a change in market from Europe to China. Apart from the concentration of settlement on coasts and islands, the shift also meant greater exploitation of native hunters (Aleuts), more difficult and more expensive outfitting (ship construction and naval training), and more difficult marketing (at Kyakhta on the Russian-Chinese frontier just south of Lake Baikal, the ports of the Celestial Empire remaining closed to Russian ships until the middle of the nineteenth century). Second, Russia moved from the power vacuum of Siberia to the field of international rivalry of the North Pacific, where Russian, Spanish, British, and American imperialism vied for territory and resources, especially on the Northwest Coast, with outright military conflict always a possibility. Here, too, Russia encountered stiff native opposition from the Tlingits. So Russian activity was more circumscribed than in Siberia, although Russia did remain a major force in the evolving political geography of the Pacific Slope until the mid-1800s. Third, Alaska was even more distant from St. Petersburg than was Siberia, and its chilly, damp environment equally uninviting. Russian America was the most remote and raw outpost of the empire; the dreary colonial capital of New Archangel was on the opposite side of the world from the glittering imperial capital of St. Petersburg. Thus, the Russian-American colonies faced an even more serious problem of supply of personnel and matériel, particularly provisions, than did Siberia.

Of all of Russian America's weaknesses—insufficient personnel, uncertain supply, natural severity, Tlingit hostility, strong British and American competition, inadequate transport, depleting fur bearers—probably none was more critical than that of food supply. Actually, this problem did not arise until the beginning of permanent settlement in 1784. Previously the hunting voyages were round trips, and the hunters took enough provisions—mostly dried and salted fish and rye flour—to last the entire voyage. But with the establishment of permanent settlements more and more promyshlenniks stayed in Russian America for longer periods. It was these long-term residents, who were unable to bring enough provisions to last their entire sojourns, who generated the problem of food supply. The fundamental task of provisionment constitutes the subject of this book. Insofar as Russian attempts to solve the problem of food supply generated human settlement, resource development, and regional interchange, the book is a study in human historical geography.

I am grateful to many libraries and archives and to several individuals for assistance. The depositories include the Alaska Historical Library, the Archive of the Foreign Policy of Russia in Moscow, the Archive of the Geographical Society of the USSR in Leningrad, the Baker Library, the Bancroft Library, the British Museum, the Central State Archive of Ancient Acts in Moscow, the Central State Historical Archive in Leningrad, the Helsinki University Library, the Hudson's Bay Company, the Lenin State Public Library and its Manuscript Division in Moscow, the Library of Congress, the Memorial Library of the University of Wisconsin, the Newberry Library, the New York Public Library, the Oregon Historical Society, the Saltykov-Shchedrin State Public Library in Leningrad, the Scott Library of York University, the State Historical Society of Wisconsin, the U.S. Naval Archives, and the Göttingen University Library. The individuals include Academician S. V. Kalesnik of the Geographical Society of the USSR, Leonid Shur and Svetlana Fyodorova of the Institute of Ethnography of the Academy of Sciences of the USSR, Gary Smith of the Canadian Embassy in Moscow, John McKenzie of Fort Ross State Historical Monument, and above all Andrew Clark and Michael Petrovich of the University of Wisconsin for not only tolerating but critically encouraging an impatient student with esoteric interests. I am also indebted to Gail Gibson, Conrad Heidenreich, Betty Melick, and Barbara Ponomareff for translations, to the Cartographic Office of York University, and to Joyce Berry and Lydia Burton for editing.

Finally, I am grateful to the Canada Council for study and research grants, the Ford Foundation for a study grant, the Guggenheim Foundation for a fellowship, the University of Toronto for an exchange grant, the University of Wisconsin for research and travel grants, and York University for research grants.

Transliteration follows the system of the American Council of Learned Societies. Ruble values are expressed as silver rather than paper units, and dates are given in the New (Gregorian) Style, which in Russian America was twelve days ahead of the Old (Julian) Style in the eighteenth century and thirteen days in the nineteenth century.

At the end of the book is a citation of primary and secondary sources, which have been minimized for the sake of the text's readability, and at the end of each chapter is a list of recommended readings in English for those readers who wish to pursue various topics in greater detail.

James R. Gibson

CONTENTS

PART I.   OCCUPANCY
1.   Settlement, 3
2.   Exploitation, 32
3.   Supply, 44

PART II.   OVERSEAS TRANSPORT
4.   Transport from Siberia, 55
5.   Transport from Russia, 73

PART III.   LOCAL AGRICULTURE
6.   Farming in Alaska, 93
7.   Farming in New Albion, 112
8.   Farming in the Sandwich Islands, 141

PART IV.   FOREIGN TRADE
9.   Trade with Boston Men, 153
10.   Trade with Espagnols, 174
11.   Trade with King George's Men, 199
12.   Trade with Kanakas, 209

Afterword, 212
Abbreviations Used in Notes, 218
Notes, 219
Bibliography, 239
Index, 249

LIST OF MAPS

1. Russian Occupation of Alaska, 4
2. Russian Settlements in Alaska, 5
3. The Yakutsk-Okhotsk Track, 58
4. Generalized Routes of Russian Circumnavigation, 82
5. Agricultural Settlements on Kodiak and Adjacent Islands, 97
6. Russian Settlements in California, 114

PART I OCCUPANCY

1 SETTLEMENT

The Russian American Company hardly ever penetrated into the interior of the continent, and, owing to the wild character of its inhabitants, never established there any settlements; only for trading purposes, small factories, called redoubts and odinotshkas, were established along the coast, preferably, near the bays and the mouths of large rivers. These factories generally consist of a roofed yard of moderate size, in which live the clerk of the company, with a few workmen out of the pacified natives, and where is stored a small supply of dried fish and some manufactured goods, wanted for the use of savages.

Sergey Kostlivtsev

First phase

Russian occupation of northwestern America proceeded in four distinct phases (Map 1). During the first or boom phase (1743–99), numerous private companies made long fur-trading voyages, fully exploring and hunting the Commander, Kurile, Aleutian, and Pribilof islands and the coast and islands of the Gulf of Alaska. From 1743 through 1797 forty-two Russian companies made 101 voyages along the Aleutians and obtained nearly 187,000 pelts worth about 7,900,000 rubles; in addition, from 1765 through 1778 five Russian companies made eight voyages along the Kuriles and procured almost 163,000 rubles' worth of furs.[1]

This advance comprised three stages: 1743–54, when 22 voyages were launched, mainly to the Commander Islands and the Near Aleutians; 1756–80, when 49 voyages were made, chiefly to the remaining Aleutians,

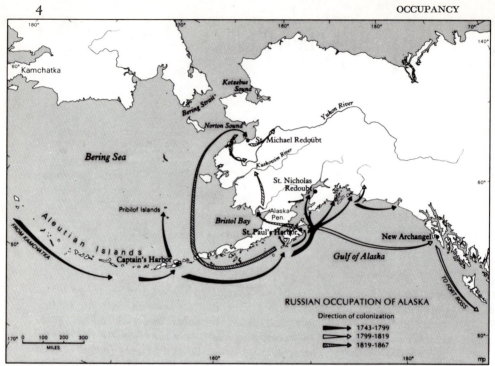

MAP 1

the Alaska Peninsula, and Kodiak Island; and 1781–97, when 21 voyages were made, mostly to the Pribilof Islands and the Alaskan coast.
These shifts followed the declining number and receding range of sea
otters, which had disappeared from the coast of Kamchatka by 1750
and from the shores of the Kuriles by 1780. During the second stage the
volume of returns and the number of companies increased, and the companies themselves became more stable. But by the 1770s the diminishing
rookeries were necessitating longer voyages and better ships and pre-
cipitating fiercer competition, which reduced the number of companies.
Moreover, the warlike Tlingits of the Alaskan mainland were a much
greater obstacle than the passive Aleuts of the Aleutian archipelago.
During the third stage, voyages from Okhotsk or Kamchatka lasted from
two to three times as long as during the first stage. And by 1795 three
companies predominated, whereas in 1781 there had been seven. In
1797 two of these companies—the American Company of Gregory Shelikhov and Ivan Golikov on Kodiak Island and the Irkutsk Company of
Nicholas Mylnikov and his partners at Chuvash [Chugach] Inlet (Prince
William Sound)—amalgamated to form the United American Company.
The latter became the nucleus of the Russian-American Company, which

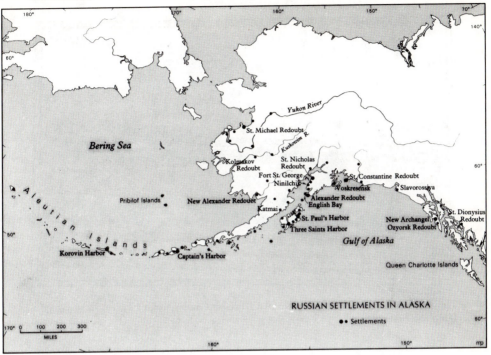

Bering Sea

Yukon River

St. Michael Redoubt

Kuskokwim R.

Kolmakov
Redoubt

St. Nicholas
Redoubt

Fort St. George
Ninilchik

St. Constantine Redoubt

Woskresensk

Slavorossiya

Pribilof Islands

New Alexander Redoubt

Katmai

Alexander Redoubt
English Bay

St. Paul's Harbor

New Archangel
Ozyorsk Redoubt

St. Dionysius
Redoubt

Three Saints Harbor

Aleutian Islands

Korovin Harbor

Captain's Harbor

Gulf of Alaska

Queen Charlotte Islands

RUSSIAN SETTLEMENTS IN ALASKA

•• Settlements

0   100   200   300
MILES

MAP 2

was chartered in 1799 for twenty years to monopolize Russian activity in America.

The first phase of occupation is also distinguished by the establishment of permanent Russian settlements, which were usually sited atop promontories at the mouths of rivers or at the heads of bays along the mainland and insular coasts (Map 2). Such locations reflected the exigencies of maritime hunting and native hostility. A permanent settlement may have been founded on Unalaska Island at Captain's Harbor (Good Harmony or Unalaska) in the mid-1770s, but the first definite year-round settlement was not established until a decade later. The Northeastern American Company differed from its rivals in that it had been formed in 1781 for ten years—not just for one voyage—and that its sponsors, Shelikhov and two Golikov brothers, planned "to establish villages and forts on the American coast and islands"[2] and thereby save time and money on voyages and improve hunting conditions.* In his grandiose

* The Golikov-Shelikhov Company was so successful that during 12 years of operations (1786–97) it procured 88,993 furs valued at 1,479,000 rubles (*Materialy*, IV), which represented nearly a half of the number and almost a fifth of the worth of all Alaskan pelts obtained by Russian companies from 1747 through 1797 (*supra* 3).

Three Saints Harbor, 1790. (*Fyodorova, Russkoye naselenie*, pl. 3, *courtesy Oregon Historical Society*)

schemes Shelikhov, the so-called "Russian Columbus," envisioned Russian settlement and exploitation on both sides of the North Pacific as far as Amuria and California and even Baffin Land. Starting in the summer of 1784, Shelikhov and about 185 men on three galiots established Three Saints Harbor (named after one of the ships) on the southwestern coast of Kodiak Island; by the spring of 1786 there were 113 Russians there. Shelikhov also founded forts on neighboring Afognak Island and Kenai (Cook) Inlet (Alexander Redoubt), but Three Saints Harbor remained his company's chief settlement until 1791, when Alexander Baranov, the new colonial manager, founded St. Paul's Harbor. In 1792 the headquarters were transferred there because of the shortage of timber at the earlier settlement, and St. Paul's Harbor became one of the largest settlements in Russian America. Built on a steep, rocky beach, it consisted of barracks, shops, smithies, and a school within a wooden semicircular stockade and houses, an infirmary, and a church outside the walls.[3]

Other settlements followed. In the fall of 1794 two Shelikhov ships reached Kodiak with 182 reinforcements, bringing the company's total to 331 men.[4] Thus strengthened, the company founded Slavorossiya on Yakutat Bay on the coast of the Gulf of Alaska in 1795. That year Baranov had written Shelikhov that "around Kodiak and in Kenai Inlet sea

St. Paul's Harbor, 1798. (*Fyodorova, Russkoye naselenie*, pl. 6, *courtesy Oregon Historical Society*)

otters are quite extinct, so that I must turn with all my forces to Chugach Inlet, where they are sufficient."[5] The company also settled Atka Island in the Andreanof group of the Aleutians and Urup (Alexander) Island in the Kuriles. Meanwhile, the rival Lebedev-Lastochkin Company had founded Fort St. George (1787) and St. Nicholas Redoubt (1791), both on Kenai Inlet, and St. Constantine Redoubt (1793) on Nuchek (Hinchinbrook) Island on Chuvash Inlet.

Not surprisingly, the Russian population was small and scattered. In 1788 at Unalaska, Captains Martínez and López de Haro learned that there were from 450 to 500 Russian *promyshlenniks* with twenty ships at seven settlements.[6] The concentration of companies halved this total by 1799, when there were no more than 225 Russians, including fewer than 200 promyshlenniks, in Alaska.[7] Most of these men were state (non-serf) peasants from Pomorye in northeastern European Russia.

During the first phase of their occupation, the Russians encountered little resistance from the native occupants of the region. Bearing the brunt of the Russian onslaught were the insular and primitive Aleuts. They were no match for the promyshlenniks, whose firearms were decisive, and their forte—skill in handling the *baidarka* (kayak) and harpoon—was their undoing, for the landlubberish Russians needed such expertise in order to pursue the maritime fur trade. "The love of the Aleuts for catching sea otters surpasses any description and can only be compared to the love of cats for catching mice," observed a Russian naval officer in 1818.[8] Two years later another Russian naval officer remarked: "During our stay here [Unalaska] we noticed that the Russians, going hunting or anywhere else in baidarkas, always knew less about this matter than the Aleuts who live with them here. This is not surprising, for it can be said that the Aleut is born in a baidarka, is gifted at hunting, and is familiar from childhood with winds and currents. . . ." He added: "If the company should somehow lose the Aleuts, then it will completely forfeit the hunting of sea animals, because not one Russian knows how to hunt the animals, and none of our settlers has learned how in all the time that the company has had its possessions here."[9] So the Aleuts were ruthlessly exploited. Half of all males between the ages of eighteen and fifty were forced to hunt under the supervision of Russian *peredovshiks* (foremen) while relatives were held hostage. In 1790 on Kodiak the Golikov-Shelikhov Company, for example, had six parties of some 600 two-man baidarkas hunting at sea and 300 hostages (including 200 daughters of chiefs) at Three Saints Harbor.[10] Such exploitation halved the Aleut population between the middle and the end of the eighteenth century.*

The Russians encountered little foreign competition during most of the first phase. Rival European fur traders did not appear until the middle 1780s, so the Russians monopolized sea otter and fur seal hunting for almost half a century. Moreover, foreign competitors, who lacked Aleuts and posts, had to procure furs indirectly by means of risky ship-side or shipboard barter while at anchor off the coast. But unlike their rivals the Russians were barred from Canton, the best port of entry to the lucrative Chinese fur market. Instead they had to use the inland border town of Kyakhta, which was much more difficult to reach than the seaports of South China.

News of Russian expansion across the far North Pacific periodically reached Spain from its ambassadors in St. Petersburg during the third quarter of the eighteenth century. Partly in order to counter this advance, Madrid extended New Spain's presidios (garrisons) and missions

---

* The decimation of the indispensable Aleuts worried the colonial authorities. When, for example, 622 Aleuts died from all causes in Kodiak Counter from 1825 through 1830, New Archangel reported that "Such a loss of Aleuts is keenly felt by the company, which forms all of its hunting parties from them and cannot replace their peculiar doings with anybody else" (USNA, 33: 169v.).

northward to Alta (Upper) California, founding San Diego in 1769, Monterey in 1770, and San Francisco in 1776. In 1768 a naval base was founded at San Blas, from which twelve naval expeditions reconnoitered the Northwest Coast between 1774 and 1792; several of them went as far as Unalaska.

British interest was spearheaded by Cook's third voyage, which explored the Northwest Coast between Cape Fairweather and Icy Cape. His finding of sea otters subsequently drew British and American traders, who obtained pelts for a pittance from the Indians and exchanged them for a fortune at Canton. The first trading vessel to appear was, appropriately, the *Sea Otter* in 1785 under Captain Hanna, who during five weeks at Nootka Sound on Vancouver Island procured 560 pelts, which he sold at Canton for 20,600 piasters.[11] In 1787 Shelikhov complained to Eastern Siberia's Governor-General Ivan Jacobi that in 1786 the East India Company alone had sent five ships to the Northwest Coast. The clash of English and Spanish interests climaxed in the Nootka Sound Controversy of 1789–90, which removed Spain from this theater of international rivalry. Russian and English interests could also have clashed if the first Russian round-the-world expedition of four warships under Captain Mulovsky in 1787 had not been forestalled by war in Europe.

The British traders ("King George's men") were quickly followed by astute Yankee traders ("Boston men" or "Bostonians"), who linked the Northwest Coast peltry with their China trade so successfully that by the end of the century they had virtually eliminated their British competitors. The "Bostonians" brought millet, flour, sugar, and tobacco, learned which natives needed food the most, and then swapped provisions for furs. In this way in 1800 they were able to obtain 1000 sea otter pelts, whereas in 1790 barely 100 were available. Although the British opponents of the Yankees soon departed, their Russian rivals not only remained but also expanded, even though the American and British traders offered the natives more and better goods, so much so that during the decade of the 1790s they were able to garner 100,000 sea otter skins —one skin every hour.[12]

Second phase

The second, or Baranov, phase (1799–1819) of Russian occupation is delimited by the first charter of the Russian-American Company and the first governorship of the Russian American colonies. It was characterized by southward expansion—as far as California and Hawaii—in the face of stronger native opposition and keener foreign competition. The phase began with the formation of the Russian-American Company, which was empowered by the tsar to monopolize Russian settlement, exploitation, and trade in America. This "Arctic Hansa," which was modeled on the East India and Hudson's Bay companies, was intended to curb foreign expansion on the Northwest Coast. Among its shareholders were high government officials and the tsar himself. Initially headquartered at Irkutsk, the company's head office was moved to St. Petersburg in 1801.*

With these changes Russian America acquired more prestige, more capital, and more men, all of which permitted a policy of southward expansion. Governor Baranov (1799–1818) suggested that Russia occupy the Queen Charlotte Islands and Nootka Sound, an advance forced by the receding range of sea otters. Already by 1789 the animals were rarely seen around the Aleutians, and they soon were scarce in the Gulf of Alaska, too; the catch in Kenai Inlet, for example, fell from 3000 in 1789 to 400 in 1793.[13] Eight hundred baidarkas were sent from Kodiak to the Gulf of Alaska after sea otters in 1794 but only 300 in 1804.[14] The first step southward was the founding in 1799 of New Archangel (Sitka, originally named Archangel St. Michael) on Baranof Island in the "straits" (tidal channels) of the Alexander or King George Archipelago off the Alaska Panhandle. This post was established in order to offset American and English trade with the unruly Koloshes or Sitkans (Tlingits). There was another inducement in the form of abundant timber and suitable tides, which favored the construction of a shipyard. New Archangel quickly became the center of the company's fur trade; in 1800 it accounted for three-quarters of the sea otters bagged in Russian America.[15] In 1807 up to 167 Aleuts were moved there from the Aleutians, and in 1808 New Archangel became the colonial capital, succeeding St. Paul's Harbor. In 1817, 190 Russians, 182 Creoles (métis), and 248 Aleuts lived there— one year before it was viewed by Captain Basil Golovnin:

> The fort stands on a high rocky hill right beside the harbor, and to judge from the purpose of its construction it is the company's Gibraltar, for, standing on a lofty site and being enclosed by a thick palisade with

* The company's dual provenance was politically expedient, for the tsar could disclaim its private actions or the company could invoke state protection, depending upon the circumstances.

wooden towers serving as bastions and being provided with dozens of guns of various kinds and calibers and a sufficient number of small arms and ammunition, it is really awesome and impregnable to the local savages, but it is no fortress to a European power, even to the power of one frigate.

Here is the seat of the governor. He lives in a two-story wooden house [Baranov's castle] built on the fort's highest spot, and he has a splendid view of all of broad Sitka Bay; the nearby green islands with the narrow passages running between them in various directions resemble a spacious garden. On the other side there is a view of high mountains, some of whose peaks are always covered with snow. In the settlement there are a church, magazines, barracks, workshops, and several other buildings, both company and private. The latter, as well as the church, are outside the fort.[16]

The second step in the company's southward march was the founding of Russian California. In 1808 Baranov sent an expedition led by his assistant, Ivan Kuskov, "for settlement in New Albion near the Columbia River."[17] Finding the mouth of the Columbia already occupied by the Astorians but the coast of New Albion vacant, the company in 1812 erected Fort Ross just north of San Francisco Bay as a base for hunting sea otters and raising foodstuffs. Eventually Russian California also included Port Rumyantsev on Bodega Bay, several farms, and a hunting party on the Farallon Islands off the Golden Gate.

Finally, from 1815 to 1817 the Russians pushed as far south as the Hawaiian Islands, where several enterprises were established with halfhearted company support.

Such expansion was reflected in Russian America's population, which became more numerous, more widespread, and more diverse. Already by 1805 the Russians numbered 470,[18] double the 1799 total. By 1817, besides the headquarters at St. Petersburg, branch offices at Moscow, Irkutsk, Kyakhta, Yakutsk, and Okhotsk, and its agencies at Kazan, Tyumen, Tomsk, Gizhiga, and Petropavlovsk, the Russian-American Company had between 450 and 500 promyshlenniks and 26 sailors at sixteen posts in the colonies.[19] The colonies were subdivided into "counters" (higher order units) or districts (lower order units): New Archangel, Kodiak, Unalaska, Atka, Northern, and Ross. Each subdivision contained several ports, forts, redoubts, *odinochkas* (one-man trading posts), or *artels* (hunting parties).

In 1819 in Russian America there were 391 Russians (378 males and 13 females), 244 Creoles (133 males and 111 females), and 8385 natives

Table 1. Population of Russian America, 1818–19

Subdivision	Settlement	Russians	Creoles	Natives
New Archangel	New Archangel	204-222	206	245-346
	Ozyorsk Redoubt	?	?	?
Kodiak	Kodiak and Afognak Islands	73	39	3253
	Ukamok Island	2	0	?
	Katmai Artel	4	0	?
	Sutkhom Artel	3	1	?
	Voskresensk	2	0	?
	Fort St. Nicholas	11	7	?
	Fort St. Constantine	17	3	?
	Fort Alexander	11	0	86
Unalaska	Captain's Harbor	30	?	?
Northern	Pribilof Islands	8-27	0	379
Atka	Korovin Harbor	50	?	?
Ross	Fort Ross	21-27	0	75-78

Sources: Anonymous, "Obozrenie," 49–52, 54, 58–59, 63; AVPR, f. 341, op. 888, d. 284, 1–2 and d. 285, 2–3; Golovnin, *Puteshestvie*, Table B between 316 and 317; Tikhmenev, *Historical Review*, I, 306.

(4063 males and 4322 females).[20] Most of the Russians were *meshcha-nins* (lower- to middle-class townsmen) from Siberia. The Creoles, who were the offspring of Russian fathers and native mothers, formed an important part of the Russian-American Company's labor force, particularly in view of the shortage of Russian personnel.

During the second phase both native opposition and foreign competition increased greatly. The Koloshes tenaciously resisted Russian encroachment. New Archangel was situated in the very midst of the Koloshes, who were more numerous and better organized than the Aleuts, owing mainly to the rich environment of the temperate rainforest. The Koloshes were especially numerous on Baranof Island in the herring (spring) and salmon (summer) fishing seasons; during the 1820s up to 2000 Koloshes assembled in Sitka Bay every spring to fish.[21] In 1851 Governor Nicholas Rosenberg (1850–53) told the head office that "no fewer than 500 well-armed savage Koloshes, who are always ready to take advantage of our negligence, live right by our settlement [New Archangel]."[22] They were also more aggressive than the Aleuts, particularly after they began to obtain liquor and guns, including cannons, from American and British traders from the mid-1790s. The Koloshes even managed to capture New Archangel in 1802, and they prepared to attack the capital in 1809 and again in 1813. As late as 1855 they destroyed

Ozyorsk Redoubt and besieged New Archangel; the Russians suffered some two dozen dead and wounded and the Koloshes up to 80 dead and wounded.* Like the Chukchi, the Koloshes were never fully subjugated to the tsar, and they remained a threat throughout Alaska's Russian period. So it was not without reason that the Russian-American Company classified them as "completely independent." At the same time the company became dependent upon the Koloshes for provisions such as halibut, *yamanina* (wild mutton), potatoes, wildfowl, berries, and roots.

The Koloshes were sometimes incited against the Russians by Yankee skippers, who offered formidable competition during the second phase. Around 1800 Baranov reported to the head office that during the 1790s several American and English ships had been obtaining 2000 to 3000 sea otter skins annually for an average 10,000 to 12,000 pelts per year. They had sold these furs in Canton, he added, for 45 rubles each for a decadal total of 4,500,000 rubles. The Russian-American Company, he estimated, could have procured the pelts for 1,500,000 rubles' worth of trade goods, making a net profit of 3,000,000 rubles.[23] Not only did the American traders outbid the Russians for Kolosh furs, offering them better goods and higher prices, but they also furnished their suppliers with firearms, which were then used against the Russians and other Indians. At the same time, however, the Americans, like the Koloshes, became essential to the Russians, who came to rely upon Yankee supplies, at least until the late 1830s. This same spirit of collaboration was manifested in the joint American-Russian hunting ventures of 1803–13 to the California coast using the company's Aleuts and baidarkas and Yankee ships, with the catch of sea otters being split fifty-fifty.

During the first half of the second phase the Russian-American colonies nearly foundered because of a series of misfortunes. In the very first year the "Okhotsk ship" *Phoenix* sank with over half a million rubles' worth of supplies and ninety new promyshlenniks, as well as the company's best shipbuilder, James Shields, and the head of the Kodiak Mission, Archimandrite Joseph. In the same year the *Northern Eagle* was wrecked en route from Yakutat to Kodiak and 22,000 rubles' worth of cargo was lost.** In fact, owing to unskilled navigators, crude ships, and inaccurate charts, sixteen of the twenty-eight ships bought or built by the

* A government inspector reported in 1863 that every Kolosh had a rifle or a pistol and ammunition and so much liquor that in 1860 they offered to sell rum and vodka to a company steamship in the straits (United States, *Russian Administration*, 65).
** Until the arrival of the *St. Elizabeth* at Kodiak in the fall of 1805, no ship had reached Russian America from Okhotsk for five years (Davydov, *Dvukratnoye puteshestvie*, I, 195; *Materialy*, IV, 63).

company from 1799 through 1820 were wrecked and five were condemned.[24] The frequent shipwrecks caused delays in the execution of orders from the head office and shortages of supplies at a time when the needs of the colonies were growing. In 1805 at New Archangel, for instance, there was only one pound of bread daily for 200 people, and eagles, crows, and cuttlefish were eaten; in that year seventeen Russians and "many" natives died from scurvy.[25] Baranov was forced to turn to American traders for supplies and the head office was induced to launch voyages around the world from St. Petersburg.

The shipwrecks were soon followed by the loss of several settlements. In 1802 New Archangel was attacked by Koloshes armed with American and British guns and, in the words of Kuskov, "the fort and all the buildings were reduced to ashes and the people were annihilated."[26] Twenty Russians and up to 130 Aleuts were killed, as many as 4000 sea otter pelts were taken, and a ship under construction was burned. The post was recaptured by the Russians in 1804 with the help of the sloop *Neva*, one of two ships accomplishing the first Russian circumnavigation. In 1805 the Koloshes burned Yakutat (Slavorossiya), killing and capturing all of the twenty-two Russian families and many of the Aleuts. Also in 1805 the company's settlement on Urup in the Kurile Islands was abandoned.

There were additional difficulties, including the death from mussel poisoning in 1799 of 115 Aleut hunters; conflict between the company and the clergy on Kodiak in 1800; overhunting of fur seals on the Pribilofs from 1800 through 1802 and spoilage of a third of the three-year catch of 900,000 skins; low prices for furs at Kyakhta in 1802 and 1803, because of stiff competition at Canton; a commercial crisis in Moscow in 1804, resulting in many bankruptcies and lean credit; the discarding of 30,000 rubles' worth of furs in 1805 by the *Neva* during a storm; the death in 1807 of Count Nicholas Rezanov, the imperial chamberlain and an influential supporter of the company; an abortive plot against Baranov by nine disgruntled promyshlenniks in 1809; the spoilage of more than 1,000,000 fur seal pelts in 1805–10; and the death of Baranov's two replacements, Johann Koch and Terty Bornovolokov, in 1811 and 1813, respectively, en route to New Archangel. Added to these difficulties were such long-term problems as increasing gun-running and rum-running by American and British skippers and unsuccessful attempts from 1806 to secure a trade agreement with Alta California. No wonder that the company's head office lamented in 1813 that "At the beginning of the glorious reign [1801–25] of the present tsar [Alexander I] . . . the Company found itself in an extremely unstable and difficult position. . . ."[27]

These troubles prompted Rezanov to make a tour of inspection in 1805–6. They also caused a sharp drop in the value of a company share from 3727 rubles in 1799 to 280 in 1805.[28] With the founding of Fort Ross in 1812 colonial fortunes improved, although the company was unceremoniously expelled from the Sandwich Islands in 1817. This incident showed that the aged Baranov was slipping, and in 1818 he was replaced as governor. In the same year there was another tour of inspection, this time by Captain Golovnin, who sharply criticized some aspects of company policy. By 1820 the value of a share had more than doubled.[29]

Third phase

The third or halcyon phase (1819–40) of Russian occupation was distinguished by corporate reorganization, a reorientation of settlement northward and inland, less active native hostility, and more regulated foreign competition. Golovnin's criticisms influenced the company's second twenty-year charter, which was granted in 1821. Gone was the old era of independent management by hardboiled traders, as symbolized by Washington Irving's "hyperborean veteran" and "old Russian potentate," Alexander Baranov, ". . . a rough, rugged, hospitable, hard-drinking old Russian; somewhat of a soldier; somewhat of a trader; above all, a boon companion of the old roystering school, with a strong cross of the bear."[30] Henceforth subordinate and conservative administration by naval officers prevailed. Now employees were paid salaries instead of shares, so that their income became more stable. Now, too, more attention was paid to the needs of the inhabitants with the arrival of more missionaries, doctors, and teachers. Foremost among the clerics was Father Ivan Veniaminov (later Bishop Innocent), whose good works were to earn him the title of "apostle of Alaska" and eventually lead him to the post of Metropolitan of Moscow and Kolomna, the second highest office in the Russian Orthodox Church.

The reorientation of exploitation and settlement to the north and to the interior was prompted by strong American and British competition to the south and on the coast. British competition was rejuvenated in the form of the powerful Hudson's Bay Company, which, benefiting from the merger with the North West Company in 1821 and from the astute direction of George Simpson, resolutely entered the coastal trade in the middle 1820s. The Russian-American Company's shift was also induced by the depletion of fur resources to the south. By the late 1810s sea otters were scarce along the coasts of New Albion and Alta California. As Governor Leon Hagemeister (1818) remarked, "God grant that the north reveals a treasure: the south is not so well off—we have relinquished the Sandwich Islands, and at Ross there are no sea otters and little business."[31] In 1825 former Governor Simon Yanovsky (1818–21) wrote the head office as a shareholder to say:

> The annual decrease in the catch of sea otters, which constitute one of the main revenues of the R.-A. Co., must direct particular attention to the continental interior of northwestern America, which . . . is far from having been penetrated and heretofore has been almost untouched by the company's enterprise, although it is known from the inhabitants that plenty of land fur-bearers, especially beavers, are found there. It can be said that this is the only reserve left for the R.-A. Co. to strongly compensate for the declining catch of sea otters.[32]

And in 1828 the head office itself declared that "it is known to the head office that in the interior of America along the courses of the Nushagak, Kuskokwim, and Kvikpak [Yukon] rivers there is a great abundance of beavers and otters."[33]

So from the late 1810s the company began a series of expeditions along the Bering Sea coast and into the interior of Alaska as well as ventures to the Kuriles in the mid-1820s (Urup Island was reoccupied by fifty men in 1828 and Big Shantar Island in the Okhotsk Sea was occupied from 1830 until 1833), the Kolosh Straits in the mid-1830s, Kamchatka and the Commander Islands in the late 1830s and early 1840s, and the heart of Alaska in the early and mid-1840s—all in search of new or renewed fur resources. In 1818–19 Peter Korsakov led an expedition to the Nushagak River, whose mouth became the site of New Alexander Redoubt in 1819. Two years later Adolph Etholen and Basil Khromchenko headed the "northern expedition" of two ships to Bristol Bay, and in 1829–30 the Northern Land Expedition of a dozen men under Ivan Vasilyev explored the Kuskokwim River with the express purpose of finding sources of land fur-bearers, particularly river otters. There Camp Holitna (Kolmakov Redoubt from 1841) was founded in 1832. Etholen and Michael Tebenkov (both later governors of Russian Amer-

St. Michael Redoubt, 1843. (*Courtesy Oregon Historical Society*)

ica) in 1831 undertook a naval expedition to Norton Sound, where St. Michael Redoubt was established in 1833. In the same year Governor Ferdinand Wrangel (1830–35) founded a settlement on Stuart Island in Norton Sound in order to tap the fur trade of the Alaskan interior and the Bering Sea coast of Siberia. Andrew Glazunov's expedition was launched in 1835 "in order to gradually acquaint us more and more with the interior of the country along the Kvikpak River and to open the richest beaver places."[34] In 1838–40 two more expeditions to the Kvikpak were made by Peter Malakhov, a Creole, like Andrew Glazunov. Another Creole, Alexander Kashevarov, led a naval expedition to Kotzebue Sound beyond Bering Strait in 1838. Finally, the most ambitious expedition of all was undertaken in 1842–44 by Lawrence Zakoskin to the Alaskan interior.

The realignment of occupation was such that during the 1820s the company even considered shifting the colonial capital from New Archangel to the Kenai Peninsula or preferably back to St. Paul's Harbor.* Anticipating such a move, some of New Archangel's residents began to leave, and the population fell from 795 in 1822 to 595 in 1829.[35] In 1830, however, the head office decided to keep colonial headquarters at New Archangel because it was learned that the Hudson's Bay Company intended to establish a post nearby and because the American-Russian convention of 1824 was soon to expire. Furthermore, the colonies lacked sufficient means (including workers) to make such a move.

All this activity required more people and forged new settlements. By 1833 there were seven counters and districts with 627 Russians, 991 Creoles, and 9120 natives (Table 2).

The population now included more seamen and several Finns, who

* Also, operating costs were high and the hostile Koloshes were too close for comfort.

Table 2. Population of Russian America, 1833

Subdivision	Russians males	females	Creoles males	females	Natives males	females	Total
New Archangel	343	36	163	144	60	76	822
Kodiak	90	13	118	121	3282	3325	6949
Unalaska	22	8	113	73	568	714	1498
Northern	6	0	12	22	99	99	238
Atka	40	1	71	75	280	313	780
Ross	45	6	33	44	64	61	253
Kurile	17	0	1	1	109	70	198
TOTAL	563	64	511	480	4462	4658	10,738

Source: Gibson, "Russian America," 8.

were usually skilled workers or naval officers. Again most of the promy-shlenniks were Siberian townsmen from the lower- to middle-classes.

The colonies now comprised five counters: New Archangel, Kodiak, Unalaska, Atka, and Ross, and two districts: Northern and Kurile. New Archangel Counter still predominated. New Archangel itself was the seat of the governor and the entrepôt of the colonies. Concentrated there were colonial administrating, shipping, manufacturing, fishing, and lumbering. Flour milling, sawmilling, and fishing were the functions of neighboring Ozyorsk Redoubt. In 1825, 789 people lived at New Archangel and 24 at Ozyorsk Redoubt; 400 were company employees, including the 309 Russians.[36]

Kodiak was the most populous counter and the second most important counter economically. It included the artels on the islets surrounding Kodiak Island and the settlements on Chuvash and Kenai inlets, the southern coast of the Alaska Peninsula, and Bristol Bay. These were hunting posts, although St. Nicholas Redoubt had a brickworks. Kodiak Island itself was more diversified, with stock-raising, gardening, brick-making, and fishing as well as trapping. The island was Russian America's chief source of "colonial products," including *yukola* (dried fish), *sarana* (dried yellow lily bulb), cowberrries, *burduk* (sour rye flour soup), and blubber. St. Paul's Harbor was still the largest settlement; in 1825 its population comprised 26 Russians, 41 Creoles, and 36 Aleuts.[37]

Unalaska Counter included the Fox chain of the Aleutians, the Shumagin Islands, and the western tip of the Alaska Peninsula. It produced mostly sea otter and fox pelts and walrus tusks, the latter from the

New Archangel, c. 1818. (*Khlebnikov, "Zapiski," 3*)

northern coast of the Alaska Peninsula. Captain's Harbor was the main settlement.

Atka was the bleakest and rawest counter—rocky, windy, rainy, foggy. And provisionment was more difficult here than in any other subdivision. It included the Andreanof, Rat, and Near chains of the Aleutians and the Commander Islands off Kamchatka. Hunting was almost the only function (sea otters and foxes on the Aleutians and fur seals on the Commanders).

The Kurile District, which also specialized in hunting, was centered on Urup Island. In 1830 12 Russians and 60 Aleuts inhabited Urup.[38]

The Northern District comprised Stuart Island and the settlements on the adjacent mainland of Norton Sound. The Pribilof or Fur Seal Islands,* which were under the jurisdiction of New Archangel, produced most of Russian America's fur seal pelts, sea lion rawhides, blubber, whale oil, whalebone, *kamleikas* (waterproof capes made from gut), and salted fur seal and sea lion meat. The whale, fur seal, and sea lion

* The Pribilofs were also known as the New or Northern or Zubov or Lebedev islands.

Captain's Harbor (Unalaska), 1843. (*Oregon Historical Society*)

flesh was a staple food of the company's Aleut and Creole employees. In 1826 there were 130 people on the two largest islands of St. Paul and St. George.[39]

Ross Counter (Russian California) was the most comfortable subdivision in terms of living conditions. It was also the most diversified, with hunting (sea otters, fur seals, and sea lions), farming, shipbuilding, lumbering, manufacturing (tanning, brickmaking), and trading; fishing was negligible.* In the mid-1830s the counter was enlarged by the addition of several new farms. Russian California was the only part of the Russian-American colonies to be claimed by another power (Spain before and Mexico after 1821).

The relative importance of the counters and districts in terms of capital assets toward the end of the third phase is shown in Table 3. New Archangel Counter accounted for half of the total value of Russian America's capital assets, just as it accounted for half of the colonial Russian population.

The company's branch offices (higher order units) and agencies (lower order units) across Siberia were primarily freight depôts, al-

---

* Because of the want of fish, there was more use of beef and grain, so that provisionment was more expensive in Russian California than in any other subdivision of the colonies.

St. Paul Island, 1843. (*Oregon Historical Society*)

though Tyumen was also a recruiting center for Siberian employees. The Irkutsk branch office, for example, handled furs bound for Kyakhta and Russia and Russian goods destined for Russian America. The prime function of the Kyakhta branch office was not transport; rather, it handled the exchange of Russian furs for Chinese products.

The third phase also saw the stabilization of relations with Russian America's adversaries. Company trade with Alta California became more or less regular in 1817, and from 1821 all foreigners were allowed to trade with the *Californios*. Although they were unable to secure a long-term trade agreement, the Russians managed to make transactions nearly every year.

Russian America's relations with the United States and Great Britain, on the other hand, were regulated by formal treaties in the mid-1820s. In 1821 Tsar Alexander I issued a decree that forbade foreign ships to approach within 100 miles of the coast of Russian America north of 51° N latitude (thereby implicitly declaring that parallel the southern limit of Russian territory). This measure had been urged by the Russian-American Company in order to prevent poaching and smuggling by foreign (mainly American) traders. The United States and Great Britain were alarmed by the unilateral Russian claim, particularly since the conservative tsar was thought to be willing to help Spain restore colonial rule over the newborn republics of Latin America (perhaps with Cali-

Table 3. Capital Assets of the Counters and Districts of Russian America, 1836–40

Subdivision	Capital Assets (rubles)
New Archangel Counter (1840)	130,491
Ross Counter (1839)	66,794
Kodiak Counter (1840)	36,748
Unalaska Counter (1839)	20,610
Atka Counter (1839)	6,683
Kurile District (1836)	2,590
Northern District (1839)	1,031

Source: USNA, 14: 344–45v.

fornia as a reward). American feeling was embodied in the even more arrogant Monroe Doctrine, which proclaimed that North and South America were "henceforth not to be considered subjects for colonization by any European power." Discussions among the three powers continued until Russia, which was more concerned about European than American affairs, relented. In 1824 and 1825, respectively, Russia signed conventions with the United States and Great Britain which permitted foreign ships to trade along the coast of Russian America and which fixed the southern boundary of the colonies at 54°40′ N latitude* (thereby ignoring Russian California).

These accords ended Russian expansion in North America by setting the southeastern limits of Russian America. They also legitimized American and British competition in the maritime fur trade. The latter concession was not without benefit, however, for New Archangel still needed the supplies brought by the Bostonians; in fact, even before the signing of the American-Russian convention the head office had petitioned the tsar to permit limited trade with foreigners for this very reason. Both agreements were valid for ten years, and neither was renewed. By the mid-1830s, owing to the scarcity of sea otters and fur seals and the slackening demand for furs, American traders were leaving the maritime fur trade, although the U.S. Government did request renewal of the 1824 accord. British interest remained strong, and during the 1830s the Hudson's Bay Company dominated the trade of the straits by estab-

* This parallel now marks the southernmost point of Alaska's boundary with British Columbia.

lishing several posts and maintaining a couple of vessels along the coast. This policy led to the Stikine or Dryad affair, which stemmed from the refusal of the Russian-American Company in 1834 to allow the Hudson's Bay Company's ship *Dryad* to proceed up the Stikine River to establish a post. The British claimed a breach of the Anglo-Russian Convention of 1825 and demanded 22,150 pounds sterling in damages. The incident was not resolved until 1839.

Russian shipping improved considerably during the third phase, partly because the governors were now required to be officers in the Imperial Navy. This stipulation "brought great benefit: voyages became faster and disasters rarer."[40] Of the 23 ships purchased and constructed by the company from 1821 through 1841, only 4 were wrecked.[41] The company's fleet increased from 10 vessels in 1821 to 5 vessels, including one steamship, in 1842.

The third phase also lacked the numerous misfortunes of the second phase, although there was a smallpox epidemic in the last half of the 1830s. Nevertheless, company profits were somewhat disappointing. The company made small profits in 1820 and 1821 and suffered deficits in 1822 and 1823 because of the loss of the *Elizabeth* in 1821 at the Cape of Good Hope and the temporary prohibition against trade with foreign ships. And then fur returns declined and upkeep costs increased. Annual upkeep of the colonies averaged 150,000 to 175,000 rubles in the first half of the 1820s but 250,000 to 275,000 rubles in the last half of the 1830s.[42] Between 1824 and 1838 colonial expenses rose 91 per cent but colonial revenues rose only 13 per cent.[43] There were several reasons for the increasing expenditures: the extension of hunting inland, the construction of new posts, the depletion of fur bearers near existing posts, the raising of employees' salaries, and the expansion of services such as churches, schools, and hospitals. A remedy was seen in an agreement with the Hudson's Bay Company that would provide goods from England of better quality than those brought by American traders and at lower prices than those shipped from Russia.

Fourth phase

The fourth or waning phase (1840–67) of Russian occupation was one of readjustment, contraction, diversification, and deterioration. The company's charter was renewed in 1841 for another twenty years. The company itself became even more of a government institution controlled by

bureaucrats and officers and even less of a commercial enterprise managed by merchants. Only one member of the new board of directors,
Nicholas Kusov, was a merchant; the rest, including the chairman of the
board, were government officials. Uniforms were worn and the company's
own flag was flown.

The fur trade was also changing. Both supply and demand were dwin-
dling in the aftermath of rapacious hunting and capricious fashion. Costs
had to be reduced and new sources of profit had to be found. Fortu-
nately, the company had some very able managers during this difficult
period—men like Etholen and Tebenkov. Generally, however, the youth-
ful vigor and bold enterprise of the Baranov phase were gone, and, following a string of subservient naval officers as colonial governors and
years of monopolistic special privileges, the company had become a
stodgy, overstaffed, and inefficient concern.

The first and most important measure of readjustment was the conclusion of a ten-year agreement with the Hudson's Bay Company in
1839 whereby the latter was to lease the continental portion of the
Alaska Panhandle for hunting (with the annual rent payable in 2000
river otters) and to deliver goods from England and provisions from the
Oregon Country to New Archangel at moderate prices. In this way the
British gained sole control of the fur trade of the Northwest Coast and
found an outlet for the surplus agricultural output of the Columbia Department, while the Russians secured a reliable source of good supplies.*
This enabled the company to sell Russian California,** which had always been a political problem and never a prolific source of foodstuffs
anyway, and to end trade with Mexican California, which had not been
a steadfast source of provisions on account of periodic crop failures and
the decline of the missions. Besides, it was obvious to the Russians that
California would soon be absorbed by the United States. Finally, the
pact permitted the Russians to end their trade with the Bostonians,
whose presence had always been a mixed blessing. They had not always
been reliable suppliers, and they had been ruthless rivals for furs, not
hesitating to arm and incite the Indians against their Russian customers.
But the company was still not completely rid of American competitors.
No sooner had the Yankee trading vessels disappeared from colonial
waters than they were replaced by Yankee whaling and sealing ships.
By 1842 up to 200 American whalers were plying the far North Pacific.[44]

* This pact also resolved the Dryad affair.
** In 1841 it was sold to General John Sutter of New Helvetia for $30,000.

The withdrawal from California, the near abandonment of the Alaska Panhandle (St. Dionysius Redoubt at the mouth of the Stikine River was vacated), and the reduction of New Alexander Redoubt to an odinochka in 1846 were signs of Russian contraction in North America. This trend was also manifested in greater company activity on the Asiatic side of the North Pacific. From the mid-1840s it reopened business in Kamchatka* and in 1845 transferred its factory at Okhotsk to Ayan.** From 1851 the Company helped to explore and develop the Amur Valley, and in 1853 it was given jurisdiction of Sakhalin—a clear case of the Russian government trying to mask its imperialism in the guise of a "private" venture by an "independent" company. China, beset by internal unrest and foreign intervention, was unable to resist. Also, from 1851 the company began shipping tea directly from Shanghai.† The sale of Alaska in 1867 completed Russia's withdrawal from America and the consolidation of its position in Asia.

The shift to the west reflected the decline of the maritime fur trade. During the fourth phase, sea otters and fur seals were nearly exterminated, despite conservation measures taken by the company. In the spring of 1857 Governor Stephen Voyevodsky (1854–59) reported to the head office that "The hunting of sea otters [in 1856] was fair, despite the fact that the Kurile District obtained only 16 pelts and the Kodiak [hunting] party experienced great difficulty because of strong winds and generally unfavorable weather."[45] Such was the sorry state of the formerly teeming rookeries. The fur market also collapsed. Silk hats replaced felt hats in Occidental millinery fashion, and Chinese demand fell with the disintegration of Manchu rule. The company tried to market furs elsewhere—London, New York, and San Francisco, but with little success.

The decline prompted the company to spread its risk by diversifying its activities. In the early 1850s, besides the Shanghai tea trade, it launched the ice trade with San Francisco, a business that prospered for more than a decade. The company also began selling fish and timber in Hawaii and California; for example, from 1854 through 1858 New Archangel shipped 65,000 feet of sawn lumber, 1665 feet of round timber,

* The Petropavlovsk agency had been closed in 1827.
** The company began the transfer in 1843 but did not finish until 1848; from 1846 freight was shipped via Ayan rather than Okhotsk.
† As early as 1843 the company profited more from the sale of tea than from the sale of furs (Alaska History Research Project, *Documents*, IV, 134).

Table 4. Population of Russian America, 1862

Subdivision	Russians	Foreigners	Creoles	Natives	Total
New Archangel	424	5	485	74	988
Kodiak	85	0	852	5049	5986
Unalaska*	4	0	217	1138	1359
Northern	29	0	110	406	545
Atka	4	0	195	772	971
Kurile	1	0	10	242	253
Kenai Coal Mine	30	1	23	0	54
TOTAL	577	6	1892	7681	10,156

* Including the Pribilofs.
Source: *Doklad komiteta,* I, 130.

and 3024 feet of firewood blocks to California.[46] Starts, too, were made in whaling and coal mining. It was even attempted to sell walrus hides in England. These ventures, plus higher prices for furs, helped to increase yearly dividends on company shares from 15 rubles in the mid-1840s to 20 rubles in the late 1850s.[47] These yields, however, were far below the dividend of 85 rubles of the early 1820s.[48]

All this activity was reflected in the number, location, and population of settlements by 1862 (Table 4).

New Archangel, by now usually called Sitka, was still the colonial metropolis. "Of all the dirty and wretched places that I have ever seen, Sitka is pre-eminently the most wretched and most dirty . . . ," commented Sir George Simpson in 1841.[49] Early that year it contained 983 people (401 Russians, 493 Creoles, 51 Aleuts and Konyagas [Kodiak Eskimos], 18 Koloshes, and 20 Yakuts), who occupied 67 dwellings.[50] In 1845 New Archangel's population totaled 1280.[51] During and right after the Crimean War (1853–55) the town was bolstered by the presence of a Siberian Line Battalion of some 100 men. With the diversification of company activities it became a busy port, with fifty ships calling at New Archangel in little more than a year.[52]

Since 1833 the number of Russians in the colonies had slightly decreased but the number of Creoles had doubled, showing the increasing number of mixed liaisons and marriages and the company's increasing reliance upon Creole manpower. Most of the Russians were still Siberian commoners, who in Governor Tebenkov's opinion were the "best men" in the colonies, despite their "unruly" disposition.[53] The slight decrease

New Archangel, *c.* 1829 (?). (HBC, F.29/2, 254. *By permission of the Hudson's Bay Company*)

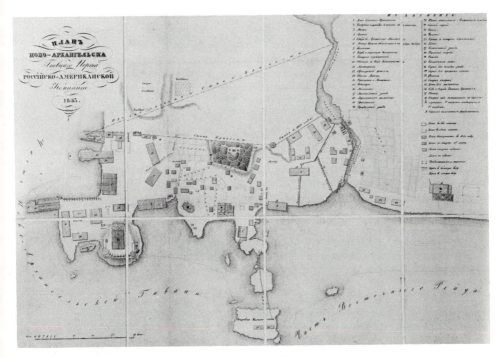

Plan of New Archangel, 1845. (*ORAK, 1845: facing 49*)

in the total population reflected the drop in the number of natives, whose culture continued to suffer from Russian contact.

By the time the company's third charter had expired it was evident that Russian America's prospects were not bright. This outlook was verified by two inspectors, Captain P. N. Golovin for the Naval Ministry and State Councillor Sergey Kostlivtsev for the Finance Ministry. The fur trade had not recovered very much, and the diversification program had faltered.* Both the ice trade and the fish trade had faded. The company's commercial agency (and Russian vice-consulate) in San Francisco was closed at the end of 1861. Coal mining had abated when the coal proved low in quality, and the whaling venture (the Russian-Finnish Whaling Company) was dissolved in 1863. In 1865 Dmitry Nedelkovich, a naval officer in the company's service, observed:

> It is evident from everything that at present the company's business is not in a good state: there is a depression in the main goods, furs and tea, which, I hear, are brought to St. Petersburg by various routes in huge amounts. Consequently, the company is now trying to economize greatly on everything and there is even a head office document that says not to raise the salaries of any employees before the end of their terms, try to collect debts sooner from indebted employees, and as far as possible order fewer goods from Victoria and California, which on account of the [civil] war in America have reached enormous proportions. . . . Here private residents lack everything because of the ruination of property and settled life and, moreover, the stagnation of all domestic production. . . .[54]

Meanwhile, the Crimean War** had depleted the Russian treasury and underlined the vulnerability of Russia's maritime flanks to British sea power. And colonial expenses were mounting. In 1866 the Ministry of Finance told the Naval Ministry that the company's administrative obligations cost the treasury 200,000 rubles annually and that it already owed the treasury 725,000 rubles.[55] Sale of Russian America would replenish the treasury and unload an indefensible and unprofitable colony that the United States might eventually annex anyway, especially in the event of a gold rush. Russia would prefer to have a friend—the United

---

* This decline was reflected in the decrease in the number of company ships to eleven (including 4 steamers) by 1860.
** During the Crimean War the colonial territories (but not the shipping) of the combatants (Russia, Great Britain, and France) were neutral. An Anglo-French squadron did bombard Petropavlovsk, briefly occupy Ayan and Urup Island, and capture the company ship *Sitka*.

States—rather than a foe—Great Britain—in possession of Alaska. And an American Alaska would serve as a buffer between Russian Siberia and British North America. Russia was overextended in America, and her destiny seemed to lie in Asia.

But Russian America's fatal flaws were St. Petersburg's preoccupation with European affairs and the continental character of tsarist colonial policy. The result was a weakness of Russian forces in the North Pacific, particularly in view of the fact that the Russian-American Company was really an arm of the government. By the third quarter of the nineteenth century Russian imperialism's best opportunities were the rich oases of Central Asia and the promising valley of the Amur River, where weak emirs and mandarins could offer little resistance—not faraway and barren Alaska on the doorstep of the expansionist United States. In 1788 Tsarina Catherine II (1762–96) had declared: "Much expansion in the Pacific Ocean will not bring solid benefits. To conduct trade is one thing, to take possession is another."[56] Subsequent Russian rulers seemed to follow this cautious policy. Certainly from 1815 Russia pursued a strictly conservative course in Europe and America in order to preserve the Holy Alliance* and in order to induce the United States to join that coalition. Russia could expand or even consolidate her holdings in America only at the expense of either Great Britain, which she was too weak to oppose, or the United States, which she was too anxious to appease.

These and other considerations led to the Russian decision to sell its colony, a decision that was made easier by the climate of reform in the 1860s in Russia. The American decision to buy was natural in terms of manifest destiny, although many Americans did not welcome the purchase. So Russia's only overseas possession was disposed of for $7,200,000 in 1867, the same year the Dominion of Canada was formed between the two pincers of Alaska and the rest of the United States, and the year before Canada acquired the territory of the Hudson's Bay Company, the Russian-American Company's old adversary.** Since the late 1840s both companies had struggled for survival against changing fashion, encroaching settlers, distracting gold rushes, prying governmental bodies, and the overriding national interests of their mother countries. Within a score of years these circumstances had brought the colonial era of the fur trade in North America to a close.

---

* This alliance was an ineffectual coalition of European monarchs intended to apply principles of Christian morality to foreign relations.
** The Russian-American Company itself was liquidated in late 1881.

Readings

Andreyev, A. I., ed., *Russian Discoveries in the Pacific and in North America in the Eighteenth and Nineteenth Centuries*, trans. by Carl Ginsburg, Ann Arbor, Mich., 1952.

Andrews, C. L., *The Story of Sitka*, Seattle, Wash., 1965 (reprint of 1922 edition).

Chevigny, Hector, *Russian America: The Great Alaskan Venture 1741–1867*, New York, 1965.

Fedorova, Svetlana G., *The Russian Population in Alaska and California Late 18th Century–1867*, trans. by Richard A. Pierce and Alton S. Donnelly, Kingston, Ontario, 1973.

Gibson, James R., "Russia on the Pacific: The Role of the Amur," *The Canadian Geographer*, Spring 1968, 15–27.

Nichols, Irby C., Jr., "The Russian Ukase and the Monroe Doctrine: A Re-evaluation," *Pacific Historical Review*, February 1967, 13–26.

Khlebnikov, K. T., *Baranov*, trans. by Colin Bearne, Kingston, Ontario, 1973.

Krause, Aurel, *The Tlingit Indians*, trans. by Erna Gunther, Seattle, Wash., 1956.

Makarova, R. V., *Russians on the Pacific 1743–1799*, trans. by Richard A. Pierce and Alton S. Donnelly, Kingston, Ontario, 1975.

Mazour, Anatole G., "The Russian-American Company: Private or Government Enterprise?," *Pacific Historical Review*, June 1944, 168–73.

Michael, Henry N., ed., *Lieutenant Zagoskin's Travels in Russian America, 1842–1844*, Toronto, Ontario, 1967.

Nichols, Robert and Robert Croskey, eds., "The Condition of the Orthodox Church in Russian America," *Pacific Northwest Quarterly*, April 1972, 41–54.

Okun, S. B., *The Russian American Company*, trans. by Carl Ginsburg, Cambridge, Mass., 1951.

Pierce, Richard A., "Alaska's Russian Governors," *Alaska Journal*, 1971–73.

Sherwood, Morgan, B., ed., *Alaska and Its History*, Seattle, Wash., 1967.

Shiels, Archie W., *Little Journeys into the History of Russian America and the Purchase of Alaska*, Seattle, Wash., 1964.

Tikhmenev, P., *The Historical Review of Formation of the Russian-American Company*, trans. by Dimitri Krenov, Seattle, 1939–40, I-II.

———, *Supplement of some Historical Documents to the Historical Review of the Formation of the Russian-American Company*, trans. by Dimitri Krenov, Seattle, Wash., 1938.

Wheeler, Mary E., "The Origins of the Russian-American Company," *Jahrbucher für Geschichte Osteuropas*, 1966, 485–94.

Alaska History Research Project, *Documents Relative to the History of Alaska*, trans. by Tikhon Lavrischeff, College, Alaska, 1936–38, I-IV.

2 EXPLOITATION

The Russians did not live here [Russian America] as a people, but as a company of fur-traders only, with a single eye to the getting of skins. . . .

Henry W. Elliott

Hunting

The maritime fur trade was the raison d'être of Russian America. The procurement (by hunting and trading) and exportation of furs remained the principal business of the Russians until the middle of the nineteenth century. Because its extraordinarily glossy and fluffy pelt was much more valuable than that of any other fur bearer (including the precious sable), the sea otter or "sea beaver" was the prime object of the enterprise. This marine mammal was found in rafts (schools) of up to 100 along the coast of the North Pacific from Hokkaido to Baja California— and nowhere else. The animal's habitat, the kelp and shellfish beds of the rocky and shallow coastal waters, was accessible to the baidarka (kayak), a speedy and maneuverable vessel of shallow draft. Parties of one- or two-hatched baidarkas manned by Aleuts, Konyagas (Kodiaks), and Kurilians (Ainus) hunted sea otters under the supervision of Russian foremen. Indeed, the Aleuts and Konyagas were virtually enslaved by the Russians.* The Aleuts, the Russian-American Company's "marine

* In Russian America *yasak* (fur tribute), which had prevailed in Siberia, was expressly banned in 1788, only to be replaced by compulsory labor, albeit without statutory sanction until the third charter (1841) of the Russian-American Company.

Aleuts hunting in baidarkas, *c.* 1828. (*Lütke, Voyage, atlas, pl. 10*)

Cossacks," were the best hunters. "The Aleuts are the only people born with a passion for sea otter hunting," commented a colonial official of the 1820s.[1] In the North Pacific the best time of the year for hunting was late spring and early summer, when fair weather was most probable; then the sea otters swam far asea, where they dozed while floating on their backs. The Aleuts with their baidarkas and harpoons assembled in spring at predetermined locations, and in April or May they embarked in groups of 30 to 100 craft to hunt, sometimes paddling more than 1000 miles during the chase. Sea otters were much harder to catch than clumsier fur seals, sea lions, or walruses; the utmost experience, dexterity, and patience were required. The colonial catch was collected annually at New Archangel and shipped to Okhotsk (to Ayan from 1845) for forwarding to St. Petersburg and especially to Kyakhta, for China was the foremost market. The Chinese upper classes prized the dark sea otter fur for its beautiful appearance and great durability. Among the Northwest Coast Indians, the sea otter symbolized wealth and prestige. The coat is very dense, with thick, soft underfur and long guard hairs; not being warm, however, it was used for trim rather than for whole garments. "A full grown prime skin, which has been stretched before drying, is about five feet long, and twenty-four to thirty inches wide, covered with very fine fur, about three-fourths of an inch in length, having a rich jet black, glossy surface, and exhibiting a silver color when blown open," according to Boston merchant William Sturgis.[2] Sheeny black pelts were the most valuable; southern sea otters were browner, smaller, and fewer. More brown pelts were bagged during summer than winter hunting; winter pelts were also larger and sheenier, for by then the brownish pups had matured. There were four grades of fur: first, Kurilian and Kamchatkan; second, Aleutian; third, Northwest Coast; and fourth, New Albionian and Californian. A California pelt, which was the poorest grade in terms of color, texture, and thickness, brought only one-half to two-thirds as much as a Northwest Coast pelt in Canton.[3] Thus, the Russians not only monopolized until 1785 the two most valuable fur bearers in the world—sables and sea otters—but they also controlled the sources of the two most valuable grades of the latter until 1867.

Sea otters were ruthlessly hunted and quickly depleted. Their depletion was hastened by the use of guns; by 1800, for instance, the Koloshes had discarded bows and arrows for rifles, which they used to shoot animals as well as Russians and other Indians. Also, sea otter dams, whose pelts were more prized than those of their mates or pups, usually bear but one pup every two years, and the pup is quite helpless for one year while it suckles its extremely solicitous mother. "Cod lay eggs but sea otters give birth in ones and twos, and because of this very inequality they could be exterminated,"[4] noted a visitor to Russian America.

The visitor was right. Canton, where American and British traders sold their furs, received 8200 sea otter pelts in 1804 but only 4800 in 1818.[5] In Kodiak Counter the catch fell from not quite 1000 in 1791 to just over 100 in 1830.[6]

In 1828 the head office of the Russian-American Company acknowledged:

> From the beginning sea otters have constituted the primary item of company business, and because of their valuableness they have brought the company its main profits, so that more and more hunting of these animals was attempted, whereby this species has finally been almost completely exterminated, at least along our coast, and now the hunting of sea otters does not bring by far—and henceforth cannot bring—the former profits.[7]

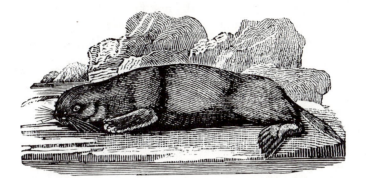

The Sea Otter

By the mid-1850s Russian America was producing only 1000 to 2000 sea otter pelts annually (indeed, none in 1854), and most of the fur catch consisted of fur seals and beavers. And in 1857 the company even began to import fur seal and beaver pelts!

The northern fur seal or "sea bear" or "sea cat" was the second most valuable target of the Russian maritime fur trade. In fact, many more fur seals than sea otters were bagged in Russian America.* Fur seals bred prolifically, mainly on the Pribilof Islands, but also on the Commander Islands, where the young males and pups were hunted with clubs in autumn. Their skins were stretched, dried, and baled; most were sold in Russia, where they were used for clothing by the lower classes. As in the case of sea otters, the northern subspecies was more valuable than the California (Guadalupe) subspecies.

Voracious hunting also rapidly reduced the swarming fur seal rookeries. From 1786 through 1832 there were 3,178,562 fur seals killed (185 daily or one every eight minutes) on St. Paul and St. George in the Pribilofs,[8] but the average annual kill dropped from some 94,000 in 1786–1803 to about 39,000 in 1815–32.[9] During the 1830s Russian America's catch of fur seals averaged but 10,000 to 11,000 yearly.[10]

Sea lions were also hunted on the Pribilofs. Their skin was useful as hide but not fur because it was very thick, with short, taut hair. The Aleuts used the hide for baidarkas, the gut for kamleikas, the flippers for soles, the beard for hats, and the meat (fresh, dried, or salted) for food.

---

* Of all the furs exported from Russian America from 1797 through 1861, 70 per cent were fur seal skins and only 14 per cent were sea otter pelts.

On St. George Island alone during the first half of the 1830s 1500 hides
and nearly 28,000 yards of gut were obtained every year.[11] Until 1844
the supply of sea lion rawhides (*lavtaks*) exceeded demand, but in that
year the Russian-American Company began to ship furs to Russia in
boxes lined with rawhide, and a shortage arose. Harbor (leopard) seals
or "sea dogs" were also hunted; they served the same purposes as sea
lions.

The skins of other animals, as well as beaver castors (castoreum),
walrus tusks, and baleen, were obtained primarily by barter with the
natives at the company's forts and redoubts.* Walruses were speared on
the islands and coasts of the Bering Sea. Walrus hide was not used because it was so thick that it was difficult to cure. But tusks, which measured up to 2½ feet in length and weighed 15 pounds or more, were
prized in Turkey and Persia. In the mid-1810s the company procured
over 7200 pounds of walrus ivory annually on the Pribilofs alone.[12]

Of all Russian America's animal products, sea otter pelts were by far
the most lucrative, bringing, for example, six times as much as fur seal
skins and forty times as much as sable pelts in 1817.[13] By 1834, when sea
otters were selling in Russia for 600 rubles each, fur seals fetched only
twenty-three rubles each. The prized walrus tusks brought less than two
rubles a pound.[14]

Russian America's furs were marketed mostly in China. Until the mid-
nineteenth century, Russian ships were not allowed to enter Chinese
ports, and furs had to be sent to the inland mart of Kyakhta. The long
and arduous route to Kyakhta from New Archangel via Okhotsk (or
Ayan), Yakutsk, and Irkutsk boosted the prices of the pelts, which were
then undersold by American and English pelts at Canton.** At Kyakhta,
Russian furs were exchanged for Chinese products such as porcelain,
cloth, and tea. During the fourth phase, just over a half of Russian
America's output of pelts was traded at Kyakhta (much less from the

*During the second phase, two-thirds of the company's fur catch was obtained
through hunting and one-third through barter with unsubjected natives (Anonymous,
"Obozrenie," 99).
** During the second phase, Baranov was able to ship some furs to Canton in American bottoms. But, as the Minister of Commerce told Tsar Alexander I in early 1805,
"The Russian-American Company cannot uphold the prices on furs because Englishmen and Americans take them from Nootka Sound and the [Queen] Charlotte Islands
to Canton, while the company conveys them via the difficult Okhotsk route to
Kyakhta; consequently, the former will probably always dominate this trade until the
latter opens its own route to Canton" (Ministerstvo inostrannykh del SSSR,
Vneshnyaya politika Rossii, II, 297–98).

early 1850s with the decline of the Chinese market) for more than 3000 cases of tea annually. In fact the Russian-American Company furnished almost one-third of Russia's imports of Chinese tea. The Kyakhta trade was also a source of customs revenue for the Russian government; during the second phase, the company's China trade yielded 2,000,000 rubles in duties.[15]

Russian America's fur catch declined steadily from about the beginning of the 1800s. There were several reasons: overhunting during the first and second phases; conservation measures in the third phase (*zapuskas*, or certain prohibitions against hunting); depletion of the native hunters by disease, liquor, and accidents; and foreign penetration of company hunting grounds by the Hudson's Bay Company in the Alaska Panhandle and the Yukon Valley and by American ships in the straits off the Panhandle and the Bering Sea. Also, because pelts prepared in the colonies were mediocre because of poor curing techniques, company furs did not compete well with Canadian and American furs on the international market. And the company's Russian market sagged when beaver collars were replaced by lambskin collars on Russian Army uniforms. The worst example of overhunting in Russian America occurred at the beginning of the nineteenth century, when some 900,000 fur seals were killed on the Pribilofs in four years. Unable to properly dry so many skins, the Russians shipped only 600,000 of them to Okhotsk and Irkutsk, where they were sold at low prices. Of the remainder, 180,000 were left on the islands and 111,000 were burned; each of these skins could have brought the company four to eight rubles. Owing to the huge slaughter and the incomplete removal of carcasses, other fur seals shunned the islands, and they were not hunted there for five years. It was not until 1810 that the company's catch reached even 150,000 fur seals, whereas it should have been possible to kill 300,000 yearly.[16]

Diversification

The pursuit of the fur trade entailed the development of several supporting activities, such as farming, fishing, lumbering, manufacturing, and mining. All supplies required by the colonies could have been imported, of course, but at enormous cost. Besides, with the decline of the fur trade the company needed other sources of revenue. As early as the beginning of the nineteenth century, Governor Baranov warned that "The company cannot exist by hunting alone . . . the amount of furs is diminishing every year."[17] By mid-century, California and Hawaii were seen as lucrative markets for the concern's new enterprises. In 1852 the head office wrote Governor Alexander Rudakov (1850–53) that "the possibility was developing for the company to gain considerable benefits from trade in California and on the Sandwich Islands and later at other Pacific Ocean ports in the following items: *ice, coal, wood products, and salted fish.*"[18] Certainly such diversification helped the company to weather the demise of the fur trade and also created a wide range of occupations in the colonies. In 1842 at New Archangel, for example, fewer than 200 workers were engaged in a score of trades.[19]

Lumbering provided wood for houses, furniture, implements, barrels,* firewood, and ships. At New Archangel, spruce, larch, and cedar were used for ships and spruce for buildings. The demand for lumber was considerable, as buildings lasted no longer than twenty years and often only ten—partly because of the putrefactive climate and partly because of the fire hazard. In 1826 fourteen to eighteen men constantly employed in sawing timber could meet only the demands of the capital, where the buildings were battered by strong winds and frequent rains.[20] And in 1855, most of the town burned.

The main lumbering centers were Baranof and Kodiak islands and Russian California. At Ozyorsk Redoubt a sawmill produced annually some 6000 planks of various sizes during the last half of the 1840s.[21]

SHIPBUILDING

Shipbuilding was vital to these maritime colonies, where vessels were required for transportation and communication among the far-flung colonial subdivisions and with the distant motherland. During the third phase, the company needed about a dozen ships: one vessel to deliver new recruits and fresh supplies, mainly heavy and bulky items, from Cronstadt (and from 1840 from Finland, Germany, and England, too) to New Archangel and furs and retirees from New Archangel to Cronstadt; two vessels to deliver supplies, including Indian trade goods, personnel, and mail from Okhotsk (Ayan from 1846) to New Archangel and furs and returnees (and from 1840 sometimes salt and flour for Kamchatka) from New Archangel to Okhotsk, perhaps stopping en route at Atka, the Commander Islands, and the Kuriles to deposit supplies and

---

* Flour, fish, and salt were shipped from New Archangel in barrels. From 1854 through 1858, for example, 3500 barrels were made there, of which 2779 were used for exporting salted fish (ORAK, 1859: 103).

load pelts; two or three vessels for shipping supplies, including fish, from New Archangel to Russian California (Port Rumyantsev) and trade goods to Alta California (usually San Francisco) or occasionally Chile (and from 1852 ice and fish from New Archangel and Kodiak to California) and products (foodstuffs, bricks, hides, wool, pitch, timber) and furs from Russian California and provisions from Alta California or Chile (and sometimes salt from Baja California) to New Archangel; one vessel to deliver supplies and directives from New Archangel to Kodiak and Kenai Inlet and furs and products (bricks, potatoes, onions, butter, and beef but especially "colonial supplies"—yukola, blubber, sarana, tendons, burduk, berries) from Kodiak primarily and Kenai to New Archangel; one vessel to deliver supplies, directives, and timber from New Archangel to Unalaska and the Pribilofs* and furs and walrus tusks from Unalaska and skins, hides, blubber, whale oil, and salted meat from the Pribilofs to New Archangel; and one vessel for inspection tours or special expeditions (for example, to the "North" (Bering Sea), the Kolosh Straits, Hawaii, and from 1850 Shanghai and Sakhalin). In addition, the counters of Kodiak, Unalaska, and Atka and the district of the Kuriles each had a small ship for local needs.

All ships were built of larch at Okhotsk or Nizhne-Kamchatsk until the construction of shipyards at Voskresensk (1793), Three Saints Harbor (1793), Yakutat (1796), New Archangel (about 1800), and Fort Ross (1816). In Russian America, shipbuilding cost half as much as at Okhotsk, but initially it was more advantageous to buy used American oak and pine ships, which lasted five times as long as those built at New Archangel of Alaska (yellow) cedar, Sitka spruce, and larch. From 1798 through 1833 the company sent two ships from Russia, bought eight from American skippers, and built a total of forty-one.[22] By 1838 its fleet consisted of ten vessels (4 brigs, 3 sloops, 2 cogs, and one schooner). Four derelicts were used as storehouses. In 1860 the company had 12 ships (4 frigates, 4 steamers, 2 brigs, and 2 barks).[23] The cost of this improvement was considerable. From 1797 through 1818 3,300,000 rubles were spent on the purchase, construction, repair, outfitting, provisioning, and manning of ships;[24] this sum represented 20 per cent of the value of the company's fur catch during the same period.

New Archangel became the center of shipbuilding after 1825; that is, after shipbuilding at Fort Ross had proved unsuccessful because the oak

---

* There was always an extreme scarcity of lumber and firewood on Unalaska and the Pribilofs, despite the use of driftwood.

timber was unsuitable. Larch was used for the outside, spruce for the decking, and yellow cedar for the ribbing. Because of its lightness, dryness, and toughness, yellow cedar was a very suitable material, especially for rowboats, which the company built for itself and for foreign customers. During the fourth phase some two dozen ships were built at New Archangel.

FISHING

Fishing was also a vital activity, for fish was the staple dish of the natives and the Creoles, and to a lesser extent the Russians. And the rich and varied fishery of the Northwest Coast afforded not only an abundant (albeit cyclical) catch but also a year-round catch.* Pacific salmon, California herring, arrow-toothed halibut, and Alaska cod were the main fish caught. Halibut, the most popular fish of the natives, and cod predominated since they were almost always available. The runs did fluctuate, however. Halibut fishing peaked in winter, cod and herring in spring, and salmon in summer. During the 1850s 380,000 dried fish, 114,000 salted fish, and 64,000 fresh fish were stocked annually in the colonies.[25] Company laborers lived on salted fish for four months and on fresh fish for the rest of the year. Shellfish and various sea mammals, especially sea lions, fur seals, and whales, were eaten, too.

Baranof and Kodiak islands were the chief fishing centers. Fish were so plentiful on Kodiak that sometimes they could be caught by hand, and around 1800 more than a half-million fish were cured annually on the island.[26] More fish were dried on Kodiak, where the warm season was sunnier, than on Baranof. Fish salting on both islands lasted from June until September. New Archangel specialized in halibut fishing in winter.

MILLING

Probably the most important manufacturing activity was flour milling. It was cheaper to import whole grain than flour,** and in 1832 at Ozyorsk Redoubt a mill was built that could grind enough flour annually to feed 700 people. By 1843 it was milling about 270 tons yearly. After the mill at Ozyorsk Redoubt was damaged by floodwater in 1840, a new mill with a daily capacity of 2500 to 3600 pounds was erected at New Arch-

* Ross was the only colonial subdivision with few fish.
** Moreover, the flour that the company did occasionally import contained too many impurities.

angel (1841). The Ozyorsk mill was retained, but after 1845 it was con-
verted into a sawmill. By 1846 New Archangel's flour mill could grind
more than 3600 pounds per day, or more than 650 tons per year, enough
to meet the demands of Russian America, Kamchatka, and Ayan.

MINING

Mining was begun late in Russian America, although the digging of clay
for bricks was started early. Bricks were needed for ovens and chimneys.
Around 1800, 3000 to 6000 bricks were fired annually on Kodiak Island,
and more could have been made if better clay, more lime, and skilled ma-
sons had been available. In 1831 Kodiak's brickworks produced 10,000
bricks. There were other works at Fort Ross, New Alexander Redoubt
(Nushagak), St. Dionysius Redoubt (Stikine), and St. Nicholas Redoubt. Fort Ross's brickworks probably produced around 10,000 bricks
annually, and the one at St. Nicholas Redoubt, built in 1841, was expected to make 20,000 bricks yearly. It filled the gaps left by the abandonment of St. Dionysius Redoubt in 1840 and the sale of Fort Ross in
1841 and compensated for the small number and poor quality of bricks
produced at New Alexander Redoubt. In 1847 Governor Michael Tebenkov (1845–50) rated St. Nicholas Redoubt's brickworks the best in the
colonies, for it had the necessary timber, clay, sand, and water nearby.
By 1865 it was producing 30,000 bricks yearly—enough to meet Russian
America's annual needs—but the bricks were high in cost and low in
quality. Bricks from Victoria on Vancouver Island were better and
cheaper. All of these brickworks shipped part of their output to New
Archangel, which needed 12,000 to 15,000 bricks annually in the early
1850s.

In 1848 coal of "fairly good" quality and in "great abundance" was
discovered by Peter Doroshin, a mining engineer, at English (Coal)
Bay on the Kenai Peninsula and at Zakharov Bay on Unga Island in the
Aleutians. In 1856 Governor Voyevodsky reported that the American-
Russian Commercial Company,* which handled the ice trade, hoped to
obtain 10,000 to 12,000 tons of coal annually from English Bay, but by
1858 only 4200 tons had been mined, and that at a "considerable loss."
Most was used by Russian-American Company steamers and blacksmiths,
but some was sold in California. The company's Kenai Mining Expedition produced but 2760 tons from 1857 through 1859 and 850 tons in
1862.[27] The coal was high in cost and low in quality, however, and by

* This American firm was incorporated in 1853 by some San Francisco businessmen.

1864 the company was importing coal from Nanaimo on Vancouver Island.

Several other minerals, such as petroleum, copper, and amber, were found but not developed. Mica was mined on the Kenai Peninsula, where gold was also panned in 1850–51.

The "mining" of ice boomed in the 1850s in response to a large demand in California, where the gold rush and the population explosion had created a sizable and affluent market. With moderate success the company entered this market with timber, prefabricated houses, fish, and ice. It even mined some gold. In 1852 the company established as Russian vice-consul in San Francisco a commercial agent, Peter Kostromitinov, who negotiated a contract with the American-Russian Commercial Company for the delivery of 2000 tons of ice annually to California. This agreement was renewed in 1859 for 3360 tons. Ice was cut in winter from lakes near New Archangel and St. Paul's Harbor and on Woody Island, stored in ice houses, and shipped in spring. Sometimes, as in 1858–59 and 1859–60, mild winters hampered the stocking of ice. From 1852 through 1859 New Archangel produced 17,860 tons and Kodiak 19,260 tons; just over half was exported.[28]

By the mid-1860s virtually all of the company's experiments in diversification were languishing, and with both the fur trade and its alternatives in decline, there was little choice for the Russians but to leave. This decision should not have come as a surprise to anyone aware of Russian America's plight.

Readings

Andrews, Clarence L., "Alaska Under the Russians—Industry, Trade and Social Life," *Washington Historical Quarterly*, October 1916, 278–95.

———, "Russian Shipbuilding in the American Colonies," *Washington Historical Quarterly*, January 1934, 3–10.

Bruemmer, Fred, "Home of the seals: the stormy Pribilofs," *Canadian Geographical Journal*, April 1974, 12–21.

Cohen, Pauline, ed., *The Sea Otter*, trans. A. Birron and Z. S. Cole, Jerusalem, 1962.

Gibson, James R., "Sables to Sea Otters: Russia Enters the Pacific," *Alaska Review*, 1968–69, 203–17.

Golder, Frank A., "Mining in Alaska before 1867," *Washington Historical Quarterly*, July 1916, 233–38.

Howay, F. W., "An Outline Sketch of the Maritime Fur Trade," *Annual Report of the Canadian Historical Association*, 1932, 5–14.

Ogden, Adele, *The California Sea Otter Trade 1784–1848*, University of California Publications in History, XXVI, Berkeley, Calif., 1941.

———, "Russian Sea-Otter and Seal Hunting on the California Coast 1803–1841," *California Historical Quarterly*, September 1933, 217–39.

Rickard, T. A., "The Sea-otter in History," *British Columbia Historical Quarterly*, January 1947, 15–31.

Sherwood, Morgan B., "Science in Russian America, 1741 to 1865," *Pacific Northwest Quarterly*, January 1967, 33–39.

3 SUPPLY

Who can ever have a mind to settle in that country [Russian Amer-ica], where permanent fogs and dampness of atmosphere and want of solar heat and light, leaving out of the question anything like agricul-ture, made it impossible to provide even a sufficient supply of hay for cattle, and where man, from want of bread, salt, and meat, to escape scurvy must constantly live upon fish, berries, shellfish, sea cabbages, and other products of the sea, soaking them profusely with the grease of sea beasts.

Sergey Kostlivtsev

REMOTENESS

The task of supplying the Russian-American colonies with personnel, matériel, and especially food was aggravated by two circumstances. First, the great distance from the mother country made importation a lengthy and costly matter. New Archangel was halfway around the world from St. Petersburg; some 12,000 miles of travel via Okhotsk separated the two capitals.* The oceanic route was twice as long. Russian America was a classic example of remote location. Moreover, transporta-tion and communication over much of these vast distances were im-peded by various obstacles, even in summer, such as the swampy low-land of Western Siberia, the rugged upland of the Russian Far East, the calms of the Horse Latitudes and Doldrums, and the mists and shoals of

* Even from Irkutsk, the capital of Eastern Siberia and the site of the Russian-American Company's headquarters until 1800, it was 6600 miles to St. Paul's Harbor, the company's first colonial capital.

the far North Pacific. Consequently, the delivery of recruits, directives, equipment, and provisions to Russian America and the shipment of retirees, reports, and furs to Russia or Siberia were risky, protracted, and expensive. For example, the head office did not learn of the loss of the *Phoenix* until 1803, four years after the event. As late as 1845 New Archangel received mail from St. Petersburg only once each year by ship from Okhotsk, and an exchange of letters between the two capitals normally took two years, with a special courier taking five months. By contrast, a packet boat with mail reached Vera Cruz in New Spain from Cádiz once each month, and a regular courier journeyed monthly from Mexico to Alta California, taking two months to reach San Francisco with European news that was only six months old; in addition, trading vessels brought news from Spain more frequently than the packet boats, and special messengers brought important news from Mexico more frequently than the regular couriers. Count Rezanov, one of Russia's ablest activists in the North Pacific, fell victim to the hazards of the overextended line of communication between Russia and Alaska. He died at Krasnoyarsk in 1807 from pneumonia aggravated by an earlier fall from his horse on the perilous route between Okhotsk and Yakutsk. Russian America's remoteness even affected the company's first charter. Article 6 states: "In consideration of the distance of the localities where they [company employees] will be sent, the provincial authorities will grant to all persons sent out as settlers, hunters, and in other capacities, passports for seven years."[1] This distance sometimes compelled the colonial authorities to act on their own. Particularly Governor Baranov acted independently, but even Tebenkov wrote headquarters in 1847: "I very much regret and most humbly beg the head office not to blame me if, on account of remoteness and through it the prolonged communication with the head office, I sometimes perhaps dare to act not in accordance with the intentions of the head office. . . ."[2] Colonial officials were especially independent in the matter of trade with foreign ships, which could not afford to dally at New Archangel. With the central authority of the state as well as the company weakened, officials could act even more arbitrarily than usual. "The head office undoubtedly understands the important consequences of the uncontrollability of the conduct of subordinates in a territory so remote from the fatherland. . . ." reported Governor Peter Chistyakov (1825–30) in 1830.[3] Such "uncontrollability" was more common in the outlying parts of the colonies, like the Kuriles and the Pribilofs.

PHYSICAL SEVERITY

Second, the physical and cultural features of the colonies themselves made supply difficult. The physical environment was harsh and the primitive and sometimes hostile native cultures were generally inimical to the local production of materials and foodstuffs required by the Russians—with the notable exception of the prolific fishery. Especially the cool, damp, climate with its frequent fogs and high winds but also the rugged coasts and rocky islands and the thin or infertile soils hampered economic activities and everyday living. Much effort had to be expended on heating and drying. The climate—variable but usually execrable—was particularly forbidding. The records for New Archangel show that the number of clear days from 1828 through 1832 totaled only 348 (1½ per week).[4] It was "always autumn" and "never rainless," according to Cyril Khlebnikov, a company employee who spent fifteen years in Russian America.[5] The raw climate interrupted work; for example, in 1834 a party of eighty baidarkas was absent from Kodiak for four months but hunted only half a day because of stormy weather.[6] The "ruinous" climate wasted sailcloth, rope, and rigging and battered houses and other buildings. It also promoted illness. Earth tremors and tidal waves occasionally worsened matters. "Mild and short" earthquakes occurred "annually and repeatedly" on the Kenai Peninsula, asserted Khlebnikov.[7] Kodiak Island suffered less severe tremors, although one in the summer of 1788 destroyed much Golikov-Shelikhov Company property; in fact, Three Saints Harbor lost its prominence partly because of damage caused by subsidence in the aftermath of the quake.

CULTURAL SEVERITY

The harsh physical environment was only partly alleviated by the Russians and the natives. Although the neolithic Ainus, Aleuts, and Eskimos were skilled at hunting, fishing, and gathering, they had no experience in cultivating or herding.* Thus no native agricultural produce or experienced native agricultural labor was available to the Russians. And the Koloshes were long a threat to any company activity in the Alaska Panhandle. A few natives and Creoles did learn traditional European skills, such as painting, forging, shipbuilding, and navigation, but they were few and late. Besides, not infrequently the natives were decimated by disease—syphilis, German measles, smallpox, influenza, typhoid fever,

* Their only domesticated animal was the dog.

whooping cough. Epidemics raged in 1806, 1808, 1819, and 1824; up to a third of Kodiak's natives were killed by the 1819 epidemic.[8] The number of natives in the colonies fell from more than 6000 in 1796 to fewer than 3000 in 1825.[9] The worst epidemic was the smallpox scourge of 1835–38, when the fatality rate among the natives was 25 per cent[11] and 3000 of them died.[10] Particularly affected were elderly Aleuts and Koloshes; the Aleut population, for example, dropped from about 7000 in 1836 to roughly 4000 in 1840. The epidemics, which particularly impaired the company's hunting capacity, aggravated the chronic colonial labor shortage, which was not relieved (and then only temporarily) until the disposal of St. Dionysius Redoubt in 1840 and Fort Ross in 1841.*

The Russians themselves were handicapped by their small number and limited skill. "There is much work but no men," complained Governor Tebenkov in 1846; three years later he asserted: "The shortage of workers in the colonies greatly affects everything and, incidentally, is very unfavorable."[12] The Russian population of the colonies peaked in 1839 at 823, hardly a large number for such an extensive territory. As the head office told the Minister of Finance in 1824, "It is necessary only to imagine that our settlements comprise no more than 2000 people, including 500 Russians, scattered over an area of several thousand miles to realize whether they are strong enough to resist well-capitalized and numerous Americans acting in concert."[13] The immobility of serfdom (not abolished in Russia until 1861, and even then only halfheartedly) prevented or at least hindered most Russians from migrating anywhere, let alone to Russian America. For those Russians who could move, it was cheaper and easier to migrate to the United States or, within the empire, to Siberia. In 1806 Count Rezanov recommended to the Minister of Commerce that anybody be allowed to go to the colonies, including up to 200 exiles.[14] Two years later the State Council discussed the Minister of Commerce's proposal that "free people, such as merchants, meshchanins, state and economic [church] peasants, tribute payers, retired soldiers, and other serfs with the permission of their landlords, be allowed to settle there," but it was rejected for fear that the state would lose taxes and conscripts.[15]

Russian America's unsavory reputation as a godforsaken wilderness at the end of the earth also discouraged immigration. A deacon remarked that "It is better to go into the army than to go to [Russian] America,"[16]

---

* The shortage of Aleut employees in Alaska was such that in 1838 half of the Aleuts at Fort Ross were transferred to the Aleutians to reinforce sea otter hunting.

and this was said at a time when military service lasted twenty-five years. Tebenkov quipped in 1852 that "A *good* worker not only will not go to the colonies but a good man can get there only accidentally."[17] Consequently, the few that did reach Russian America were often un-educated, unskilled, and undesirable—inept and drunken laborers rather than industrious artisans and farmers. In fact the Commandant of Okhotsk reported in 1815 that most of the company's Russian labor-ers were ruffians and drunkards.[18] They were also often incapacitated by sickness, owing to the hard work, foul climate, and poor diet. For exam-ple, in the late 1820s one-third of New Archangel's company employees (30 to 45 men) were usually sick.[19] In 1832 Governor Wrangel be-moaned the "downright shortage of healthy and competent people, es-pecially sailors,"[20] and the head office admitted in 1842 that most of the company's colonial employees were "decrepit" and "incompetent."[21] To make matters worse, employees occasionally deserted (chiefly in Cali-fornia).

Provisionment

Little wonder, then, that the problem of supply to Russian America, especially of foodstuffs, was critical. For one thing, provisions were ob-viously more vital than other supplies like tobacco, paper, cloth, iron, ammunition, and so forth, which were not absolutely necessary for life. For another thing, food was subject to spoilage in storage or in transit, so greater care had to be taken with it than with inorganic supplies.

Naturally, all employees of the Russian-American Company—mainly Russians, Creoles, and Aleuts, plus a few Finns, Indians, Kanakas (Ha-waiians), and Yakuts and the odd Englishman and American—had to be fed. But it was the whites—overwhelmingly Russians—who demanded "tame" foodstuffs, that is, those derived from cultivated crops and herded livestock. These "Russian supplies," as the company called them, were mainly grain and beef, but included butter, common garden vegetables and tree fruits, sugar, tea, and the like.* The Creoles and natives, on the other hand, ate "colonial supplies"—mostly fish and game and roots and berries. Eventually the Aleuts acquired a liking for flour and the Koloshes for flour and rice. By the early 1860s they were buying these items from

---

* This preference was rudely evinced in the winter of 1793–94, when some rebellious promyshlenniks under Baranov disdained fish and demanded flour (Tikhmenev, *Sup-plement,* 60, 100, 105).

the company; then the Koloshes were procuring some twenty-two tons of flour annually from the company.[22] At that time an inspector reported that the company deliberately limited its sale of grain to the Aleuts so that they would not become too accustomed to it.[23]

The Russian-American Company was bound to meet the food needs of its employees. One of the duties of the governor was "to mind the welfare, food, and health of the employees of the company and of the inhabitants of its possessions."[24] The company's fourth charter required it "to secure provisions for all its employees, crews, and laborers. . . ."[25] And from 1819 employees were guaranteed a monthly food ration by the terms of their contracts. Before 1819 some employees were paid salaries and others were paid half-shares. Those on half-shares had an incentive by virtue of their vested interest but those not directly involved in hunting were shortshrifted; also, even the income of those on half-shares fluctuated with the fur catch. These disadvantages were eliminated by the introduction in 1819 of the universal salary system, which afforded all employees a stable income, regardless of the outcome of hunting. Already in 1816 the company's head office had instructed Governor Baranov "to support each Russian hunter with an annual ration of twelve poods [433 pounds] of breadstuffs (similar to the soldier's ration) in addition to the usual subsistence furnished during the hunting voyages."[26] Henceforth the promyshlenniks served seven years and received 350 rubles a year and thirty-six pounds of flour each month; in times of scarcity they were given five rubles in lieu of the flour. The men could also buy flour and other supplies, such as groats, peas, sugar, tea, and rum, if available, the amount depending upon martial status and family size. Purchases accounted for three-eighths of the capital's grain consumption in the 1820s. The promyshlenniks received and cooked their rations once a day. By the late 1850s, their working day (ten hours a day in summer) and monthly ration (thirty-six pounds of flour) had changed: each man worked a 12-hour day in summer, earning fifty-four pounds of flour and three glasses of vodka a month.

The monthly flour ration was inadequate. In 1820 Governor Yanovsky, Baranov's son-in-law, stated that 36 pounds of flour per month was insufficient for the laborers, and that they had to buy additional flour—up to 145 pounds monthly—from company stock.[27] So the situation must have been worse in 1805, when Baranov asserted that an employee needed only twenty-seven pounds a month.[28] Not only the grain salary but the money salary of the laborers (especially the married ones) was inadequate, so that they were frequently and heavily indebted to the company. Debts incurred by company employees in Kodiak Counter, for instance, rose from 76,531 rubles in 1826 to 104,367 rubles in 1830.[29] Such indebtedness compelled many promyshlenniks to renew their contracts with the company, which sometimes had to use debt cancellations, as well as salary raises and cash awards, as bonuses.

Despite the low level of monthly rations, the total annual food needs of the colonies were considerable (Table 5).

New Archangel Counter was the largest consumer of these provisions

Table 5. Annual Food Needs of Russian America *circa* 1830, 1840, and 1860

	Late 1820s	*Late 1830s–* *Early 1840s*	*Early 1860*
flour	361,130 lbs.*	1,083,390 lbs.	993,108 lbs.
buckwheat	?	5,417	27,085
rice	36,113	?	25,279**
corn	?	5,417	?†
peas	?	5,417	18,056 to
			36,113‡
beans	?	5,417	2,708*†
fish	?	?	558,000 fish
salted beef	10,834 to	?*‡	54,170 to
	14,445		72,226
butter	?	28,891	50,558 to
			54,170
salt	54,170	216,678	361,130 to
			772,260
sugar	45,141	54,170 to	90,283
		72,226	
tea	7,223	?	13,181
coffee	2,709	?	?
rum	3,600 gals.	?	4,830 gals.

* In 1805 152,750 pounds, in 1821 216,678 to 252,791 pounds, and around 1835 541,695 pounds (Pavlov, *K istorii,* 158; USNA, 27: 153; Von Wrangell, *Statistische und ethnographische Nachrichten,* 12).
** In 1856 30,000 pounds (USNA, 60: 92–92v., 116v.).
† In 1856 10,000 pounds (USNA, 60: 92–92v., 116v.).
‡ In 1956 20,000 pounds (USNA, 60: 92–92v., 116v.).
*† In 1856 10,000 pounds (USNA, 60: 92–92v., 116v.).
*‡ In 1834 30,696 pounds for New Archangel alone (USNA, 36: 324v.).

Sources: *Doklad komiteta,* II, 92, 94–95, 97–99, 325, 407–08; Lütke, *Voyage,* I, 124; *Materialy,* III, 163, 169–70; Tikhmenev, *Historical Review,* I, 406, II, 267–68; USNA, 7: 13v.–14, 22, 14: 87v., 31: 303v., 358, 32: 256–56v., 41: 344, 44: 300v., 332, 46: 155v., 361v., 63: pt. 1, 211v.–12, pt. 2, 89, 65: pt. 1, 33.

(75 per cent in 1832). In 1825 and 1860 it accounted for one-half of Russian America's grain consumption.[30]* Kodiak Counter was presumably the second largest consumer. In the mid-1840s its annual grain needs of 108,000 to 126,000 pounds[31] represented 10 per cent of colonial requirements. Not surprisingly, more provisions were dispensed from January through April. During spring and summer higher temperatures reduced appetites and more "wild" foodstuffs were available. At New Archangel around 1825 January's grain rations were double July's.

The increase in Russian America's food needs between the late 1820s and the early 1860s (Table 5) is probably attributable to three factors: the increasing Russian population (from about 500 to about 600);** the increasing use of "tame" foodstuffs by Creole and native employees of the company (the Creole population rose from roughly 900 to 1900); and the increasing shipment of grain and salt to Kamchatka and Okhotsk. As early as 1820 the Russian government had asked the company to supply Kamchatka and Okhotsk with flour and salt, and by 1822 it had proposed that the company annually supply Petropavlovsk and Okhotsk with 362,000 pounds of flour each.[32] But the company was unable to meet such needs until the early 1840s, when it began to obtain ample grain from the Hudson's Bay Company (as well as from Sutter in payment for Russian California) and ample salt from Baja California. So successful was the company that it managed to discourage American ships from trading at Petropavlovsk. In 1851, 13½ per cent (by value) of all of the goods received by Russian America was intended for Kamchatka.[33] In the mid-1850s, however, the Kamchatka trade waned with the abolition of Petropavlovsk port and the transfer of its administration to Amuria.†

Russian America utilized three approaches to supply its colonies with foodstuffs. The earliest approach—the transport of provisions from the motherland—involved shipment by land and by sea from Irkutsk and Yakutsk in Eastern Siberia via Okhotsk and, after 1800, by sea from St.

---

* New Archangel also accounted for the bulk of colonial salaries. In 1830, 37 per cent of the company's 975 employees were stationed at New Archangel, where they earned 61 per cent of the colonial payroll of 388,125 rubles ([Khlebnikov], "Zapiski," 106–7). This disparity reflected the concentration of higher-ranking employees at the colonial capital.
** The number of colonial employees increased even more—from 975 in 1830 to 1200 in 1860 (Doklad komiteta, II, 503; [Khlebnikov], "Zapiski," 106).
† This decline undoubtedly explains the drop in colonial grain needs between the early 1840s and the early 1860s.

Petersburg via Cronstadt and either Cape Horn or the Cape of Good Hope.* Perhaps the least successful approach was local agriculture, which was attempted first within Russian America proper and later (after 1812) in Russian California and Russian Hawaii. The most successful tack—trade with nearby sources—had three variants: barter with visiting ships (primarily American) from 1800, exchanges with foreign colonies (primarily Alta California) from the mid-1810s, and transactions with rival companies (primarily the Hudson's Bay Company) from the early 1810s. All three approaches were flawed: overland-oversea transport by long and difficult routes, local agriculture by forbidding physical conditions, and foreign trade by outside control and international entanglement. Yet the Russian-American Company persisted in all of these modes, perhaps from the hope that eventually one of them would prove successful. Whatever the motivation, the execution of these spatial strategies generated settlement, exploitation, and circulation, three basic geographical ingredients.

Readings

Gibson, James R., *Feeding the Russian Fur Trade,* Madison, Wisc., 1969.

---

* Company documents variously refer to the first variant as coastwise (*beregom*) supply, overland supply, supply through Siberia or via Okhotsk; and to the second variant as oceanic supply, overseas supply, supply around the world, or supply via Cronstadt.

PART II OVERSEAS TRANSPORT

4 TRANSPORT FROM SIBERIA

*Hitherto they [the Russian-American colonies] had always been pro-
vided with necessaries through Jakutzk and Ochotzk. The great distance, and the extreme difficulty of conveying goods and necessaries,
for which purpose upwards of 4000 horses are annually employed,
increased the price of every article, even in Ochotzk, beyond measure.
. . . Difficult and expensive as was this mode of conveyance to
Ochotzk, it was equally so, and the risk much greater, from thence to
the islands and the coast of America. The wretched construction of
the vessels; the ignorance of most of their commanders; and the navigation of the stormy eastern [Pacific] ocean, which throughout the
year was attended with danger to vessels of this description, were the
causes of many of them, together with their valuable and necessary
cargoes, being lost almost every year. . . .*

Captain A. J. Von Krusenstern

"Siberian Deliveries"

The transport of provisions from Siberia to Russian America via Okhotsk
(via Ayan from 1845, when the Russian-American Company's factory
was moved there) was essentially an extension of an old system of supply called the "Siberian deliveries," whereby grain was conveyed from
Pomorye across the Urals to Siberia. This system was begun in the late
1500s to meet the food needs of the early Siberian colonists; it was ended
in 1686, for by then Western Siberia was producing its own foodstuffs. In
Eastern Siberia, the Russian Far East, and Russian America, however,

Table 6. Origin, Kind, and Amount of Freight Sent to Russian America from Siberia, 1857

Source	Item	Quantity
Moscow	Circassian tobacco	21,668 lbs.
	dried mushrooms	72
	vegetable seeds	?
Tyumen	woolen mittens	1,500 prs.
	sheepskin gloves	1,500
	inner mittens	800
	pressed caviar	361 lbs.
	vizigas (dried spinal chords of fish)	181
Tomsk	tallow candles	18,057
Irkutsk	rye flour	361,130
	salted beef	36,113
	peas	21,668
	melted cow's butter	10,834
	[stone pine] nut oil	361
	sugar candy	181
	hops	36
Yakutsk	melted cow's butter	54,170
	cleaned cattle tallow	36,113
	cedar [stone pine] nuts	36,113
	Yakut knives	1,000 units
	Yakut and Buryat kindling steels	200
	Yakut axes	200
	Chukchi spears	50

Source: USNA, 22: 15–15v.

where the land was more rugged and infertile and the climate more severe, agriculture was less productive, and some provisions still had to be imported. Thus, the Siberian deliveries continued east of the Yenisey River, and even as far as Alaska—their latest and farthest stage known as the "American delivery."

The American delivery consisted largely of provisions from several sources. Circassian tobacco, Chinese tea, and sugar probably predominated, followed by flour, butter, and beef.* Also, most of the personnel and mail bound for Russian America went via Okhotsk. An inventory for 1857 is shown in Table 6.

* Tobacco was one of the chief trade goods used by the Russian-American Company in its dealings with the natives. Around 1820 tobacco, tea, and sugar constituted from a third to a half of all freight going from Yakutsk to Okhotsk (Anonymous, "Vzglyad," 34).

Sources and Lines of Supply

The two prime sources of provisions were Baikalia and Yakutia. Baikalia, centered on Irkutsk, was mainly a source of flour, plus beef and butter, which were produced by both Russian settlers and native Buryats in the wooded steppe on both sides of Lake Baikal. The Buryats had been chiefly cattle herders before the arrival in the late seventeenth century of Russian peasants, from whom they adopted cultivation. Yakutia was principally a source of butter and beef, which were produced by Yakut cattlemen in the lush grassland of the "big bend" of the Lena River around Yakutsk. The Yakuts also borrowed cultivation from the Russians, but it remained a minor occupation. Few Russian peasants settled among them. Around 1820 there were 125,000 cattle and 100,000 horses in the Yakutsk District alone.[1]

FROM IRKUTSK TO YAKUTSK

Baikalian provisions were packed at Irkutsk in winter and carted in spring 150 miles on the Yakutsk Track across the Bratsky Steppe to Kachuga Landing at the head of navigation on the upper Lena. An observer remarked in 1815 that "many necessities are sent from here to Okhotsk and Kamchatka by the state, as well as necessities for its North American settlements by the [Russian-American] company."[2] At Kachuga Landing the provisions were transferred to flat-bottomed and single-decked river vessels propelled by oars and sails; steamboats did not appear on the "Volga of Eastern Siberia" until 1856. The local historian-geographer Nicholas Shchukin asserted that the "Lena River is in all respects the national road to Yakutsk, Okhotsk, Kolyma, Kamchatka, and America."[3] (The Yakutsk Track did continue along the Lena, but the river passage was faster and cheaper.) The barge-like riverboats left in late spring at high water in strings of two to four vessels, taking from two to six weeks to navigate the 1500 miles downstream to Yakutsk, depending upon the depth of the water, the strength of the current, and the skill of the boatmen. The number of craft varied, of course, from year to year; in 1830 Shchukin counted 40 riverboats hauling 1800 tons of flour from Kachuga Landing to Yakutsk.[4]

FROM YAKUTSK TO OKHOTSK AND AYAN

Yakutsk was a sizable regional capital on the left bank of the Lena's big bend; in 1784 it contained 69 storehouses for provisions alone, besides 357

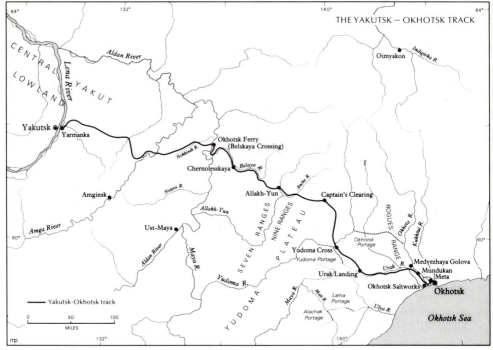

MAP 3

dwellings, 100 shops, a bazaar, and 21 other establishments.[5] There the provisions from Baikalia and Yakutia were ferried across the Lena to the rendezvous of Yarmanka, where there were several hundred tethering posts and extensive meadows with ample grass for the herds of pack horses and the droves of beef cattle. In the spring and summer, the animals proceeded to Okhotsk via the Yakutsk-Okhotsk Track (Map 3). This irregular and indefinite trail, whose importance dated from Bering's Second Kamchatka Expedition (1733–42), stretched 600 to 750 miles in a southeasterly direction. Its route varied in accordance with the vagaries of the weather and the memories of the Yakut guides and lead horses. Yet it was preferred to the indirect and upstream Lena-Aldan-Maya-Yudoma-Urak river route, a more difficult and costly passage. Cattle were driven by hired Yakuts; upon arrival in Okhotsk two to four months later the animals were killed, salted, and barreled. Flour was packed in rawhide bags (*sumas*) and butter in birchbark satchels; two of these containers, which weighed roughly 100 pounds each, were carried by a stocky and shaggy Yakut horse (the best pack horse in Siberia).

Convoys consisted of 100 to 150 animals; they were grouped in strings of 10 to 12 horses with one conductor and took from one to two months to make Okhotsk, depending upon the condition of the trail. During the first half of the nineteenth century 10,000 to 15,000 pack horses were employed annually on the Yakutsk-Okhotsk Track to convey state and private freight. Probably about a sixth of that number transported company freight, which on the basis of 200 pounds per horse would have totaled 165 to 250 tons.

From 1845 company provisions were forwarded from Yakutsk to Ayan. This route comprised three sections: a 250-mile vehicular road to Ust-Maya, a 400-mile river passage to Nelkan, and for the last 150 miles to Ayan, a horse trail. When Russian America was sold in 1867, the route was abandoned.

FROM OKHOTSK AND AYAN TO NEW ARCHANGEL

At Okhotsk (or Ayan), which was reached between mid-June and mid-August, the flour, butter, and beef were put aboard company vessels for trans-shipment to New Archangel. In 1790 the Golikov-Shelikhov Company reported that "ships are dispatched every two years to our American colonies to take out the furs, bring over a new lot of workmen, and a supply of provisions and goods."[6] Under the Russian-American Company a ship usually left New Archangel in the middle of May and reached Okhotsk in late June or early July,* standing there until late August, when the last pack trains and cattle droves arrived from Yakutsk. The furs from Russian America, which had been packed in 90-pound boxes lined with rawhide (to prevent wetting), as well as colonial reports and discharged employees, were unloaded and replaced with supplies, dispatches, and recruits from Russia and Siberia. The ship left Okhotsk in late August or early September and, sailing under favorable northwesterly winds, it usually arrived at New Archangel in October. The route lay across the Okhotsk Sea, through the First or Lopatka Channel between the southern tip of Kamchatka and the Kuriles, along the southern side of the Aleutians to Kodiak, and across the Gulf of Alaska to the colonial capital.

---

* However, if the ship stopped en route at Atka or Urup, it reached Okhotsk so late that its cargo had to be forwarded to Irkutsk by the winter (fall) route (which cost from 69 kopeks to about one ruble per pound) rather than by the summer route (19 kopeks per pound), and the furs reached market at Kyakhta and Moscow so late in the trading season that they fetched lower prices (USNA, 7: 293–93v.).

Amounts and costs of transport

Figures on the amount of supplies in general and of provisions in particular received by Russian America from Siberia are fragmentary but
enough to indicate the volume of traffic. For example, in 1787 the Golikov-Shelikhov Company sent a supply ship from Okhotsk to Kodiak
with 9 tons of flour and over 5 tons of rigging; in 1799 the United American Company packed 1496 horses with 54 tons of grain and over 23
tons of other freight and drove 118 bulls from Yakutsk to Okhotsk; in
1843 the Russian-American Company's brig *Constantine* left Okhotsk
for New Archangel with 32 passengers and 32 tons of cargo; and during
the early 1840s about 45 tons of butter, groats, tobacco, and candles were
sent annually from Okhotsk to New Archangel.[7]

Shipment of foodstuffs was very costly. The long and difficult route
raised the cost of Irkutsk flour sixfold at Okhotsk in 1804 and nearly
doubled the cost of Yakutsk butter at New Archangel in 1842.[8] The supply line was so expensive that in 1842 freightage across Siberia to
Okhotsk cost seven times as much as that from England to New Archangel.[9] As early as 1813 the company's headquarters had complained that
"supply of the colonies with all necessities via Okhotsk . . . has required
a disproportionate expenditure of the company's resources."[10] And in
1837 the head office declared that it was "almost impossible" to transport
Russian America's grain needs via Okhotsk, mainly because the high
freight charges made the grain "very expensive."[11]

Problems

The costly transport resulted primarily from the difficulty of conveyance
between Yakutsk and Okhotsk. Cartage from Irkutsk and Kachuga Landing and shipping down the Lena to Yakutsk was not very difficult. Sometimes low water impeded navigation on the Lena, but with its wide
channel and moderate current the river generally facilitated traffic. Peter
Dobell, an American adventurer and entrepreneur who spent several
years in Eastern Siberia and the Russian Far East, considered the Lena
"one of the safest navigable rivers of its size in the world."[12]

The Yakutsk-Okhotsk Track, however, was such a hellish obstacle
course that the hardy Yakut pack horses could only cover 10 to 15 miles
per day. More than a thousand torrential river crossings, most of them

along the Aldan-Okhota stretch, often claimed horses, cattle, and packs; and in the extensive bogs along the Lena-Aldan stretch animals were often mired or smothered. Attempts to use corduroy failed because its surface soon became slippery and uneven. Owing to the long winter and the late spring there was little forage along the trail; the pack horses weakened and often collapsed, and the beef cattle grew thin. East of the Aldan thick brush, dense forest, and stony potholed ground slowed and injured the animals. Steep slopes and snowy, icy summits had to be overcome, as well as bold predators—bears, wolves, and dogs—who attacked the convoys and droves. Swarms of mosquitoes and midges tormented both the animals and conductors, and the emaciated animals were subject to disease, chiefly anthrax, which killed as many as 6000 yearly during the 1820s.[13]* Furthermore, settlement along the trail was sparse, so that little help was available en route for stricken convoys and droves. Added to all of these impediments were escaped convicts from the saltworks near Okhotsk, who raided traffic; unreliable Yakut conductors, who pilfered or abandoned freight; corrupt Russian officials and contractors, who cheated Yakut outfitters and embezzled company goods; and indifferent and incompetent workers who repaired the track. Travelers commonly judged the Yakutsk-Okhotsk Track to be the worst in the empire, if not in the world. Wrangel remarked in 1830 that the difficulties of the trail were embodied in a popular comment: "in Siberia the Okhotsk Road means the most fatiguing and the most dangerous journey."[14] No wonder that many of the animals and provisions that left Yakutsk failed to reach Okhotsk, and many of those that did arrive were maimed or spoiled. Sometimes packs had to be cached en route and were not retrieved until the following year; meanwhile, of course, they

---

* Up to half of the horses perished every year from all causes. During rainy summers or anthrax outbreaks the toll was higher. So great were the losses that the trail was strewn with horse carcasses and skeletons. Governor George Simpson of the Hudson's Bay Company, who traveled the track in the summer of 1842, exclaimed that "When compared with this corner of the world, England, which is sometimes said to be the hell of horses, must be contented with the secondary honour of being their purgatory. The unfortunate brutes here lie down to die, in great numbers, through famine and fatigue; and this road is more thickly strewed with their bones than any part of the plains on the Saskatchewan with those of the buffalo" (Simpson, *Narrative*, II, 264–65). Consequently, Yakut horses were sometimes scarce, and the impoverished Yakuts became reluctant to lease them. Alarmed by the heavy loss of pack horses, Siberia's Governor Michael Speransky recommended around 1820 that the Russian-American Company use the oceanic route from Cronstadt instead of the Siberian route (Vagin, *Istoricheskiya svedeniya*, II, 5–7 and supp., 404).

were damaged by rain, frost, and scavengers. Goods often reached Okhotsk too late for the annual ship to New Archangel.

The track's eastern terminus was located on Okhotsk Spit, a sandy and soggy tongue of land at the mouth of the Okhota River; in 1815–16 the town was moved to Tungus Spit at the mouth of the adjoining Kukhtui River. In the early 1820s, when Okhotsk had some 1000 residents, the town impressed the English traveler Captain John Cochrane as being one of Siberia's neatest, cleanest, most regular, and most pleasant towns.[15] Yet almost every year several buildings were destroyed and several persons were drowned in the cresting river and the swelling seas. In the fall of 1830, for example, all of the buildings of the company factory were inundated by high tides driven by a strong wind.[16] Flooding and attendant erosion gradually reduced the townsite; between 1827 and 1838 the distance from the factory's fence to the sea shrank from 240 to 32 feet and that from the warehouse to the river from 160 to 108 feet.[17]

The harbor's navigable channel was narrow and shallow, as was the channel from the harbor to the sea; the latter, moreover, shifted every year. Ships drawing more than eight feet of water had to await high tide before entering the harbor, which was 75 per cent dry at low tide. As Russia's Minister of Finance complained, "large ships can neither stand in Okhotsk's roadstead nor enter the mouth of the Okhota River because of the shallows and shoals."[18] So only small ships, mainly brigs of 150 to 200 tons, could use the port. In 1830 Governor Chistyakov told the head office:

> apart from its expensiveness, I consider it my duty to remark that the continental system of coastal supply of the colonies with all necessities will prove very inconvenient; I am not referring here to goods that are suitable for coastal transport, such as silks, woolens, and the like, but to the annual delivery besides them of up to 15 thous. poods [271 tons] of provisions, which, although found to be advantageous by the head office, will be very difficult to transport from Okhotsk, for the two ships that are now always sent from the colonies [to Okhotsk] will be inadequate for that, and larger ships, like the sloops *Urup* and *Baikal*, which, because of their size and draft, are very unsuitable for the narrow and shallow entrance to Okhotsk, have to be loaded or at least fully loaded not in the harbor but in the open roadstead, whereby they are subject to no little danger.[19]

Furthermore, ships were also endangered by shifting sandbars, contrary winds, and strong tides. Consequently, company ships were often delayed up to a month or more and occasionally damaged or destroyed while entering and leaving the so-called port. Shelikhov lamented in 1794 that virtually half of each voyage from Okhotsk to Kodiak was spent leaving Okhotsk.[20] Lieutenant Nicholas Khvostov, who accompanied Count Rezanov to Russian America in 1805–6, denounced the port of Okhotsk as "one of the most unfortunate in the world."[21] And in 1842 the head office summarized its dissatisfaction with Okhotsk:

> Many years of experience have shown that the present site of the Okhotsk Factory is very inconvenient. The river's entrance is narrow and surrounded by sandbars, so that company ships bringing precious cargo from the colonies are annually exposed to innumerable dangers while entering the port; and while leaving, which is also accompanied by appreciable difficulties, they lose much time in awaiting a wind, without which departure from the port is impossible. The supply of the factory with wood and especially with fresh water, which must be brought to the spit daily, is also attended with great difficulties and often with danger for the residents because of the strong current and rough sea during ebbtide and floodtide. Moreover, the factory's buildings—the office, warehouses, etc.—are situated on a narrow spit washed by the river and the sea. The spit's soil consists of pebbles or fine gravel, which is why it is impossible to guarantee the safety of the company's buildings and property that constitute the counter, for the spit is threatened by flooding and beach erosion. With every strong wind from the sea, especially in the fall, part of the beach is removed, and the area of the spit is diminishing with frightening rapidity. In eleven years—from 1827 until 1838—the width of the spit decreased by 260 feet, and now it is only 24 to 45 feet from the factory's fence to the shoreline. The danger threatening the factory is all the more inevitable in that during a heavy storm communication with the town is halted because the adjoining part of the spit is flooded, and consequently the rescue of the residents and the company's property would be quite impossible in case of a washout of the shores of the spit.[22]

The trans-shipment of company provisions from Okhotsk to New Archangel was also hampered—at least until the third phase—by unsound ships and incompetent seamen. In 1804 Khvostov listed the following prerequisites for the improvement of Russian seafaring in the North Pacific: better ships, proper equipment, experienced officers, and diligent sailors.[23] During the first half of the first phase Okhotsk's vessels were extremely crude and flimsy because shipwrights were rare and materials scarce at this remote outpost. Single-decked and single-masted, these short and broad ships had flat bottoms, wooden anchors, and hide sails;

their sideboards were attached with osiers or thongs for want of nails or pegs and chinked with moss for want of caulking. These were called *shitiks* ("sewn ones") and carried fewer than twenty tons. During the last half of the first phase shipbuilding at Okhotsk improved slightly in response to the longer voyages to the Gulf of Alaska, and larger and stronger vessels—galiots (50 to 100 tons) and brigs (150 to 200 tons)—were built. The Golikov-Shelikhov Company hired an English shipwright, James Shields, whose craftsmanship during the 1790s considerably improved the company's fleet. Thanks to Shields, and an American shipwright named Lincoln, by the turn of the century ships were being built in Russian America three times as quickly and two times as cheaply as Russian government ships at Okhotsk. Writing the head office from New Archangel in 1805, Rezanov noted: "Over there [Okhotsk] the ignorance of the shipbuilders and robbery without shame by men representing the company, produce worthless ships that cost more than ships built anywhere else."[24] Rezanov insisted that the company further improve its ships by not only building more in Russian America and fewer at Okhotsk but also by buying superior foreign ships, and in 1806 he expressly authorized Governor Baranov to buy American vessels, ". . . paying even more than they cost when forced to do so by critical circumstances."[25] From 1799 through 1820 the company bought thirteen ships from foreigners (eight for deployment in colonial waters and five for voyages around the world) and built fifteen of its own in Russian America.[26] With the training and hiring of more shipwrights (like the Creole Netsvetov, the Russian Grudinin, and the Finn Johanson) the quality of company ships became adequate during the third phase.

Until then the company's seamen were not much better than its ships. During the first phase sailors were as rare as ship's carpenters at Okhotsk, and the crews of the hunting vessels were "all better hunters than seamen,"[27] for most of them had never before even seen a sea or a ship! Gregory Shelikhov's widow Natalia admitted to a high Russian official in 1795: "At [the] present time we have five ships in America and only one skipper, and even he is in poor health. We have great need for trained seamen for further exploration, discoveries, surveying and transportation. . . ."[28] Shelikhov himself had petitioned the Russian government shortly before his death in 1795 for permission to engage officers of the Imperial Navy on leave of absence as commanders of his trading vessels, but such permission was not given until the first charter of the company was granted in 1799. In 1801 two pilots and two second mates from the Siberian Flotilla at Okhotsk and two naval officers were hired. They remained until 1808, training men in rigging and gunnery and demonstrating faster runs between Okhotsk and New Archangel. In 1804 the company engaged two more naval officers, and shipbuilding and seamanship in Russian America continued to improve.* Nevertheless, from 1799 through 1820 sixteen ships were lost ". . . as a result of accidents, and especially because of carelessness and lack of skill on the part of the Okhotsk pilots."[29] Rezanov told Baranov in 1806 that the "Insufficient number of ships, their poor construction, inadequate training of the crew and insubordination of the enlisted officers bring nothing but harm to the company."[30] But the regular appointment of naval officers from 1818 as governors of Russian America and as commanders of company ships greatly improved the situation.** By 1835 Governor Wrangel was able to report that all twelve of the company's vessels were well built, well equipped, and well manned.[31]†

* It should be mentioned, however, that at first such hiring was also disadvantageous in that some of the naval officers, disdaining the merchant class, proved intractable (e.g., Tikhmenev, *Supplement,* 309–16). The worst such conflict occurred in 1816 between Baranov and Lieutenant Michael Lazarev of the *Suvorov,* which left New Archangel under threat of shelling by Baranov.

** In 1827 Captain-Lieutenant Frederick Lütke found at New Archangel that all of the company's ships were commanded by officers of the Imperial Navy and that the company's best ships were those that had been purchased from Americans (Lütke, *Voyage,* I, 107–8).

† In the same year, however, Richard Henry Dana found at San Francisco that the company's brig *Polifem* left something to be desired: "The second day after our arrival, we went on board the brig, it being Sunday, as a matter of curiosity; and there was enough there to gratify it. Though no larger than the 'Pilgrim,' she had five or six officers, and a crew of between twenty and thirty; and such a stupid and greasy-looking set I certainly never saw before.

"Although it was quite comfortable weather, and we had nothing on but straw hats, shirts, and duck trousers, and were barefooted, they had, every man of them, double-soled boots coming up to the knees, and well greased; thick woolen trousers, frocks, waistcoats, pea-jackets, woolen caps, and everything in true Nova zembla [Novaya Zemlya] rig, and in the warmest days they made no change.

"The clothing of one of these men would weigh nearly as much as that of half our crew. They had brutish faces, looked like the antipodes of sailors, and apparently dealt in nothing but grease. They lived upon grease; ate it, drank it, slept in the midst of it, and their clothes were covered with it.

"To a Russian, grease is the greatest luxury. They looked with greedy eyes upon the tallow bags as they were taken into the vessel, and, no doubt, would have eaten one up whole, had not the officer kept watch over it. The grease seemed actually coming through their pores, and out in their hair, and on their faces. It seems as if it were this saturation which makes them stand the cold and rain so well. If they were to go into a warm climate, they would all die of the scurvy.

The sounder ships and abler sailors, however, could not completely overcome conditions in the far North Pacific—shallow and uncharted waters, powerful tides, strong and changeable currents, thick fogs, and alternating high winds and dead calms. The currents and fogs of the Kurile Straits were especially perilous, as were the fall gales in the Bering Sea. The safest time for sailing these waters was from May through August. Thus, around 1800, when the round trip between Okhotsk and New Archangel took at least six months, ships had to leave Russian America in April and return in September, risking ice floes in late spring (Okhotsk usually became ice-free in early June) and heavy gales in early fall. By about 1840, however, the one-way run between Okhotsk and New Archangel had been reduced from three months to one and one-half months, and it was possible to make the round trip more safely in one season (summer).

Until the third phase such difficulties caused frequent groundings and founderings of vessels. Alexander Rowand, Governor Simpson's traveling companion, learned at Okhotsk in 1842 that "out of 80 or 90 vessels that have been built here, scarcely one has escaped shipwreck, and this occurrence has generally happened on the neighboring sand bars."[32] There were so many derelict state and private vessels at Okhotsk in the early 1800s that Commandant Michael Minitsky (1809-16) was able to convert many of them into magazines, thereby forming "a complete *museum* of vessels, presenting curious specimens of antique ship building, from the commencement of the enterprises of the first Russian traders to the north-west coast of America, down to modern times."[33] Indeed, shipwrecks of state vessels were so common that the wrecks were salvaged to build and equip private vessels. Private ships, however, fared little better than state ships. All seven vessels used by the Golikov-Shelikhov Company in the 1790s were wrecked; on the average they made only two round trips between Siberia and Alaska and

---

"The vessel was no better than the crew. Everything was in the oldest and most inconvenient fashion possible; running trusses on the yards, and large hawser cables, coiled all over the decks, and served and parceled in all directions.

"The topmast, topgallant masts, and studding-sail booms were nearly black for want of scraping, and the decks would have turned the stomach of a man-of-war's man.

"The galley was down in the forecastle; and there the crew lived, in the midst of the steam and grease of the cooking, in a place as hot as an oven, and as dirty as a pigsty. Five minutes in the forecastle was enough for us, and we were glad to get into the open air [Dana, *Two Years Before the Mast*, 241–42]."

lasted but six years.[34] At the beginning of the 1800s Captain Ivan Kruzenstern, commander of the first Russian circumnavigation, noted that
"Up to this time the ignorance and inexperience of the masters of the
[private] ships were the reasons why one of three ships was usually lost
every year."[35] At this time Russian America's very existence was threatened by frequent shipwrecks; by 1819 eighteen company vessels had
been lost.[36] Of these costly mishaps the head office complained in 1813:
"Frequent losses of ships from their bad construction and bad management have aggravated these [excessive] expenditures . . . [on] the
supply of the colonies with all necessities via Okhotsk. . . ."[37] The situation improved markedly with the reorganization of the colonies in
1818, for from 1821 through 1833 the company lost only one vessel.[38]

The horrendous difficulties of transport on the Yakutsk-Okhotsk Track
and the Okhotsk-New Archangel seaway caused much loss, spoilage,
and delay of supplies, particularly provisions.* The time required to ship
foodstuffs from Irkutsk to New Archangel—up to two years—was alone
enough to cause some deterioration; spoilage caused by alternate wetting and drying and heating and chilling was especially problematical.
Dobell decried the handling of flour between Irkutsk and Okhotsk:

> There is also much to be altered in the manner of transporting the flour
> on the Lena and to Ochotsk. Flour is generally sent down the Lena in
> large square flat-bottomed vessels called barques, in bulk; and, as it is
> often badly dried, it heats, becomes bitter, and loses much of its nutri-
> tious quality. When it arrives at Yakutsk it is thrown into magazines,
> also in *bulk*, where it becomes further heated, and is more or less
> spoiled. If it were sent in bags from Irkutsk it would be much better
> preserved, and the additional cost would be trifling, as the bags would
> serve many years in succession. At Yakutsk the flour is packed into
> leathern bags, called sumas, made of ox-hides untanned, but dressed
> white, and the hair taken off. To pack the flour into them tightly, so
> that each suma shall contain two poods and thirty-five pounds [107
> pounds], it is necessary to wet them; the flour that adheres to the wet
> suma dries and becomes as hard as a stone, and is thus rendered im-
> penetrable to all sorts of weather; so that if the suma be good there
> cannot be a safer mode of conveying the article; but unfortunately the
> sumas that are now contracted for at about two roubles and a half

---

* Provisions, of course, were vital, but other supplies were also important; for example, in 1787 Eastern Siberia's Governor-General Ivan Jacobi reported to Catherine
II that the promyshlenniks in Russian America could not arm themselves as well as
their English and American competitors because of the difficulty of supply via
Okhotsk.[39]

a-piece, are so thin and bad, that the flour often spoils, and the sumas only serve for a season or two, instead of lasting four or five years, as was formerly the case. It would be cheaper to pay five roubles for a good strong suma, that would last several years, than to buy such trash because it is cheap. However, it would of course prove less profitable to the parties concerned, if the sumas were good and the contracts fewer.[40]

Sumas were especially vulnerable during fordings and downpours on the Yakutsk-Okhotsk Track; soaked flour, groats, and biscuit became hard and moldy and tasted bitter and horsy. Salted beef and boiled butter were perhaps even more susceptible to spoilage than breadstuffs. The Yakut cattle were usually driven to Okhotsk or Ayan before the snow melted, so that there was little forage during the long drives. At the port the thin animals could not be rested and fattened but were slaughtered immediately and hurriedly salted in barrels in order to make the waiting company ship, which had to embark no later than August. Consequently, the meat was spare, tough, and expensive.[41] It was also often putrid by the time it reached New Archangel, owing to improper salting as well as the long voyage. In 1832 Governor Wrangel reported that the salted beef received from Okhotsk was always spoiled.[42] All the more than 5 tons of beef sent from Ayan in 1850–51 and 90 of the 96 barrels sent in 1853 were unfit to eat.[43] Often supplies from Okhotsk were so damaged that they could not be used at all; Governor Etholen, for example, reported in 1843 that many of the Okhotsk supplies were "quite worthless" and that there were so many unusable goods at New Archangel that it was difficult to find storage space for them.[44]

Reactions

The problems of the Siberian supply line eventually prompted both the Russian-American Company and the Russian government to seek some solutions. The sea route to New Archangel could not be improved; only the ships and the sailors could be bettered. With this done by the second quarter of the nineteenth century, attention was concentrated on the supply line's main bottlenecks—the Yakutsk-Okhotsk Track and Okhotsk itself, both of which had been periodically remodeled and were to be eventually relocated.

Ever since Bering's First Kamchatka Expedition (1725–29) attempts had been made to find a better route to the Okhotsk Sea and a better port on its coast. The usual suggestions were the Uda, Aldoma, Ulya, or Urak rivers and their mouths; Shelikhov even suggested twice, in 1788 and 1794, that Okhotsk be replaced by a new port at the mouth of the Uda.[45] Meanwhile, the track continued in use with occasional reconstruction, as in the mid-1750s and mid-1780s and in the 1810s. Okhotsk itself was shifted from the Okhota to the Kukhtui side of the joint river mouths in 1815–16 but the new site proved no better than the old one.

It was left to the Russian-American Company to take decisive action. In 1828–29 it investigated the Yakutsk-Udsk route and the mouth of the Uda River, finding that the river mouth was a satisfactory port site but that the track was unusable, and in 1840–41, Ayan Bay and the Yakutsk-Ayan route were examined. As early as the 1780s this harbor and route had been found superior to either Okhotsk or Udsk and the other tracks. Road and port construction had actually been started jointly by the Russian government and the Russian-American Company in 1801, but when costs began to mount the company withdrew its support and work stopped. By the 1830s, however, the decline of Alta California and American trading vessels as sources of supply (as well as the mediocre performance of agriculture in Russian California) had enhanced the role of a Siberian supply line. Moreover, the drawbacks of the Yakutsk-Okhotsk Track and Okhotsk had become even more apparent after shipping was improved between the Siberian port and New Archangel.

In 1831 reconnaissance confirmed the merits of Ayan (a "convenient and safe" harbor with plenty of pasture, timber, fish, and game) and of the Yakutsk-Ayan route, and the head office declared its "firm intention" to transfer its Okhotsk factory southward. The company conceded that the Yakutsk-Ayan route had two disadvantages: the shallowness of the Maya River and the unsuitability of the Maya's banks above the Yudoma River for tracking (towing). "The Maya River is not, of course, the most suitable for navigation," understated the head office, but it could accommodate boats carrying five and a half tons; besides, that part of the route from Yakutsk to Ust-Maya was "the most convenient of all the routes from Yakutsk to the Okhotsk Sea."[46] But it was not until April 21, 1842 at a meeting of company shareholders in St. Petersburg that it was decided to move the Okhotsk factory to Ayan, provided that Ayan proved "a good harbor and suitable for the establishment of a port, and [that] the transport of freight from Ayan to Yakutsk [would] not be slow or costlier."[47] It had been determined in the 1840–41 reconnaissance that, although timber for shipbuilding and fish were scarce at Ayan, its har-

Russian-American Company factory at Ayan, 1846. (*Oregon Historical Society*)

bor was deeper and the climate milder. Dark soil and pasture were also available. Furthermore, ships could enter the harbor regardless of wind; this constituted its main advantage over Okhotsk, where ships had to wait in an exposed roadstead for a fair wind before entering the harbor.

Governor Etholen confirmed these observations when in 1843 he advised the head office that "the coming and going of ships in Ayan Bay [would] be incomparably more advantageous than at Okhotsk."[48] In 1844–45 it proved one-third cheaper and eight days faster to transport freight to Ayan than to Okhotsk. So in 1845 the factory with 135 persons was transferred to Ayan, and logways, boats, ferries, stations, and settlers were established on the Yakutsk-Ayan route. In 1846 it cost the company 600 rubles less to transport goods over the new route than it would have cost on the old. Etholen, an experienced seaman, summed it up: "In short, in terms of all conveniences—with respect to both life (for man living in Ayan) and the navy—Ayan Bay cannot be compared at all to Okhostk Port, which can be called a coffin for human life and for ships."[49] Bishop Innocent also noted that the Yakutsk-Ayan route was "much better" than the Yakutsk-Okhotsk Track; he wished that "the Crown had paid attention to Ayan and to the Ayan Road and had transferred to it the stations from the Okhotsk Road."[50] The Bishop's wish was soon fulfilled. In 1849 an Imperial decree abolished Okhotsk Port, and from 1850 through 1852 the Siberian (Okhotsk) Flotilla transferred all state property from Okhotsk to Ayan and Petropavlovsk.

Ayan and the new route, however, were only relatively better than their predecessors and remained the weak links in the Siberian supply line. At Ayan there were no suitable timber stands or fishing grounds. Half of the route, which measured 925 miles, was river passage, which meant mostly upriver transport, since there was more west-east than east-west traffic. It took up to twenty-three days to go downstream to Yakutsk but as many as forty days to go upstream to Ayan. In 1846 transport accounted for thirty-five per cent of the cost of goods received by Russian America from Siberia via Ayan.[51] Some freight was still hauled to Ayan over the Yakutsk-Okhotsk Track because tracking up the Maya and Aldan rivers was severely hampered by trees, boulders, and bogs along their banks. The Yakutsk-Ayan route, however, remained in use until it was closed in 1867.

By then Russian interest in the North Pacific had shifted from Alaska and Kamchatka to Amuria. Russia's seizure of the valley of the Amur River (called by Prince Kropotkin the "Mississippi of the East") in the mid-1850s during the downfall of Manchu China fulfilled an old Russian dream that envisaged the river as a busy commercial artery between the Siberian interior and the Pacific and the valley as a fertile granary and a prolific sable reserve. The Russian-American Company, which participated in the acquisition of Amuria and Sakhalin, tried to provision its colonies with grain and beef from Transbaikalia and Preamuria via the Amur in the hope that this route would prove easier and cheaper than the Yakutsk-Ayan route.* Russian America received many supplies, mostly provisions, via the Amur from 1855 through 1859; in 1858, for example, more than 451 tons of flour, 36 tons of beef, and 27 tons of butter were shipped to New Archangel over that route.[52] In addition the company procured up to 2000 sable pelts annually in Amuria during the last half of the 1850s. However, although the Amur did prove to be a less difficult and less expensive route than the Yakutsk-Ayan route, it was

---

* The Amur route also had the advantage of relieving the Yakuts, who usually regained less than half of the horses that they leased for transport from Yakutsk to Okhotsk. As the sea lion was to the Aleuts, so the horse was to the Yakuts; they made *kumiss* of its milk, meat of its flesh, apparel from its hide, netting from its hair, and money from its sale or lease.

far from ideal. Blind channels, shifting sandbars, shallows, snags, boulders, ice floes, rapids, and head winds impeded traffic. Navigation of the shallow estuary was especially hazardous.

Thus, Russian America's continental or coastal supply line from Siberia remained quite inadequate, in spite of the replacement of the disastrous Yakutsk-Okhotsk Track initially by the Yakutsk-Ayan route and ultimately by the Amur River route. Count Mordvinov, an official of the Russian-American Company, declared in 1824 that provisionment of Alaska via Okhotsk was almost the same as no provisionment at all.[53] Only one alternative route for the delivery of supplies to the colonies was left—shipment by sea from European Russia via the Horn or the Cape.

Readings

Cochrane, Capt. John Dundas, *Narrative of a Pedestrian Journey through Russia and Siberian Tartary*, Philadelphia, 1824.

Collins, Perry McDonough, *Siberian Journey: Down the Amur to the Pacific, 1856–1857*, ed. by Charles Vevier, Madison, Wisc., 1962.

Dobell, Peter, *Travels in Kamtchatka and Siberia*, 2 vols., London, 1830.

Gibson, James R., *Feeding the Russian Fur Trade*, Madison, Wisc., 1969.

Gibson, James R., "Russia on the Pacific: The Role of the Amur," *The Canadian Geographer*, January 1968, 15–27.

Markoff, Alexander, *The Russians on the Pacific Ocean*, Los Angeles, 1955.

Simpson, Sir George, *Narrative of a Journey Round the World, During the Years 1841 and 1842*, London, 1847, II.

5 TRANSPORT FROM RUSSIA

The Russian American Company, having experienced great difficulty in supplying their colonies on the north-west coast of America with all kinds of provisions and necessaries, on account of the length and tediousness of the journey by land to Ochotsk, resolved to try if the conveyance by sea would not prove more favourable to their views.

Yury Lisyansky

Motives

With the formation of the Russian-American Company in 1799 it was decided to try to deliver supplies by ship from European Russia via the naval base of Cronstadt on the Gulf of Finland. This decision was prompted mainly by the difficulties of supply from Siberia via Okhotsk. In the words of a Russian local historian: "After futile attempts to find a suitable communication [from] Yakutsk to the coast of the Okhotsk Sea, the Russian-American Company decided to establish intercourse with its colonies on the Eastern Ocean by the round-the-world route."[1] This route was also intended to supply the Okhotsk Seaboard and the Kamchatka Peninsula, for these areas, too, suffered from the drawbacks of the Siberian supply line. Michael Buldakov, a company director and one of Shelikhov's sons-in-law, declared in 1803 that the company "devised a new method of supplying foodstuffs to Eastern Siberia, Kamchatka and Okhotsk; and this method is now used by our [first round-the-world] expedition."[2]

Supply (particularly of foodstuffs) was the main but not the sole purpose of oceanic transport from the Baltic Sea to the Bering Sea and back.
After delivering supplies the ships, it was hoped, could convey company
furs quickly and cheaply to market at Canton on the return voyage. Such
marketing would circumvent not only the longer and harder overland
route from Okhotsk to Kyakhta in the Asian interior but also any sus-
pension of trade at Kyakhta, as occurred from 1785 to 1792.* The delivery of furs to Kyakhta took up to two years, and not a few pelts were
spoiled and stolen en route. English and American traders shipped their
furs to Canton, which put the Russians at a disadvantage in the Chinese
market. Captain Ivan Kruzenstern, one of the promoters and leaders of
the first Atlantic-Pacific voyage, stated the matter this way:

> I knew that my countrymen carry on a considerable trade in furs with
> China, which they bring from the islands in the eastern ocean, and the
> coast of America; and that they are first obliged to carry their skins to
> Ochotzk, from whence they send them to Kiachta, which occasions a
> loss of two years and often more; that every year several vessels with
> their rich cargoes are lost during their voyage across the eastern ocean
> was likewise well known to me; and it therefore appeared to me that
> the advantages would be infinitely greater, if the Russians were to
> bring their goods to Canton direct from the islands or the American
> coast.[3]

Count Nicholas Rumyantsev, Minister of Commerce, concurred; in
1805 he wrote Tsar Alexander I that the Russian-American Company
could not "uphold the prices on furs, for Englishmen and Americans
take them from Nootka Sound and the [Queen] Charlotte Islands to
Canton, while the company conveys them by means of the difficult Okhotsk route to Kyakhta; consequently, the former will probably always
dominate this trade, until the latter opens its own route to Canton."[4]

Another motive was the desire to show the flag in the North Pacific
colonial arena and to defend the company's colonies against the hostile
Koloshes and audacious foreign rivals—the British, Americans, and Spaniards. The Americans especially were brazenly poaching in Russian-
American waters and, what was even more sinister, were trading firearms
and spirits to the Koloshes, who succeeded in capturing New Archangel
in 1802. Such ruthless competition was threatening Russian America's
very existence, and the company felt that a show of force by Russian

* During this interregnum fur prices at Canton jumped 20 per cent, much to the de-
light and benefit of English and American traders (Tikhmenev, *Supplement*, 206–7).

warships would safeguard the colonies. As it turned out, the *Neva,* one of two ships to accomplish the first Russian circumnavigation, did help Governor Baranov regain New Archangel in 1804.

Two additional motives caused the Russian government to support the new system of colonial supply. First, the state saw the voyages as excellent training exercises for seamen for its budding navy. Second, Russia wished to gain international prestige through the discovery and exploration of uncharted waters and unmapped islands and the investigation of native cultures and natural phenomena—just as England had benefited from Cook's voyages. This aim was exemplified by the discovery of Antarctica by Captain Bellingshausen and Lieutenant Lazarev in 1820.

Origins

Russian voyages from the North Atlantic to the North Pacific were first proposed by Admiral Golovin in 1732. He suggested the annual dispatch of two frigates via Cape Horn to protect the Second Kamchatka Expedition. Golovin believed that the principal benefit would be the practical training of Russian sailors, who, he asserted, would learn more seamanship on one such voyage than in ten years on Baltic cruises.[5] But no action was taken for half a century, that is, until there were permanent Russian settlements in North America. In 1786 Gregory Shelikhov learned at Petropavlovsk from Captain William Peters of the East India Company that foreign vessels were seeking furs on the Northwest Coast. Angered by what he considered to be an infringement of Russian sovereignty (and perhaps fearful of additional competition), Shelikhov complained in 1787 to Governor-General Jacobi, who reported the matter to St. Petersburg. At the beginning of 1787 an imperial edict ordered the outfitting of four navy ships under Captain Mulovsky to protect Russian interests in the North Pacific (that is, to prevent foreigners from trading and hunting in Russian waters), to supply the Okhotsk Seaboard, to open maritime trade with China and Japan, and to make geographical discoveries. Late in the same year, however, the expedition was canceled on account of "current circumstances"—imminent war with Turkey and Sweden, for which Russia would need all her ships and sailors at home.[6]

But the idea of overseas supply remained alive. Around 1790 Shelikhov proposed that Russian America be supplied by sea from Archangel on the White Sea or from St. Petersburg. In 1800 and in 1802 Lieutenant

Kruzenstern, who had served under Mulovsky, submitted to the Admiralty College (Naval Ministry) a plan to send ships with supplies via Cape Horn to Russian America, whence they would take furs to South China and the East Indies, where they would buy oriental goods for Russia and Western Europe, returning via the Cape of Good Hope. He too felt that the voyages would serve to train Russian seamen. And in 1802 Captain Commander Gabriel Sarychev, who had been a member of the Billings Expedition (1785-94) to northeastern Siberia and northwestern America, recommended supplying the Okhotsk Seaboard and the Kamchatka Peninsula from Cronstadt via the Cape of Good Hope. Four vessels, he estimated, could transport 722 tons of supplies to Okhotsk at a cost of 30,000 rubles, whereas the transport of the same tonnage from Irkutsk would cost 289,000 rubles, or ten times as much.[7] Meanwhile, Shelikhov's proposal was adopted by his influential son-in-law Nicholas Rezanov, who may have been inspired by the large profits being made on furs by English and American traders at Canton. Rezanov's report on the subject was approved by Rumyantsev and presented to the tsar, who granted the company permission to undertake a circumnavigation. The company decided to outfit two ships in order to provide more safety and to transport more supplies. The vessels *Leander* (430 tons) and *Thames* (373 tons) were bought in England for 172,000 rubles and renamed *Hope* and *Neva*.[8] Captained by Kruzenstern and Yury Lisyansky and accompanied by Rezanov, they left Cronstadt in 1803. The mission was, typically, multipurpose—delivery of supplies, marketing of furs, safeguarding of Russian waters, and opening of trade with Japan.

Voyages

So began a series of voyages between the Baltic and Bering seas. From 1803 through 1864 at least 65 such voyages were launched by the Russian government (33), the Russian-American Company (19), and other Russian owners (13), or roughly one every year (Table 7).

Three of these voyages were abortive: those of the *Elizabeth* and *Ayaks* in 1821 and the *Silent* in 1824. Not all of the remaining 62 successful voyages were complete circumnavigations; 13 remained in the North Pacific (6 in Kamchatka, 4 in Alaska, and 3 in Amuria) to bolster the company's fleet or the Siberian Flotilla, seven went forth and came back by the same route (6 via Cape Horn and one via the Cape of Good

Hope), and 19 are uncertain. At least 23 voyages were genuine circumnavigations.

Thirteen of these known circumnavigations proceeded eastward via the Cape of Good Hope and returned via Cape Horn (Map 4). This route had two advantages: the winds were more favorable, and there were more unvisited and uncharted islands in the western Pacific. Ten voyages proceeded westward via Cape Horn and returned via the Cape of Good Hope. But strong westerly winds around Cape Horn often delayed ships several weeks, sometimes forcing them to change course and to proceed eastward via Cape of Good Hope (for example, the voyage of the *Diana* in 1807–9). Another disadvantage of the westward route was that ships had to sail the little-known waters of the northern Indian Ocean (ships following the eastward route, on the other hand, could ply the southern Indian Ocean, rounding Australia on the south).

Most of these voyages were multipurpose ventures, although they usually had a dominant aim. The voyages of the *Rurik* (1815–18), the *East* (1819–21), the *Peaceful* (1819–21), the *Discovery* (1819–22), and the *Loyal* (1819–22) were made primarily for scientific purposes. The rest were made mainly to supply Russian America and to protect the Russian-American Company's business. The exceptions were naval voyages from 1840, which were undertaken to supply Russian warships stationed at Petropavlovsk and Nikolayevsk (lower Amur) and to hound foreign ships (chiefly American whalers) in the Okhotsk and Bering seas. Thus, most of the voyages—46 of 65—were essentially voyages of supply to Russian America.

Owing to the very high cost of acquiring and outfitting a vessel, the number of voyages undertaken by the company amounted to only about a third (19 of 65) of all the voyages; similarly it made but 19 of the total of 46 supply voyages. The imperial navy made 14 supply voyages (carrying, of course, some company supplies), and the rest of the supply voyages were made by other Russian ships. In addition foreign vessels chartered by the company made at least 18 voyages to Russian America, mostly via the Horn, from 1842. The foreign ships became especially necessary from the late 1840s, when the Hudson's Bay Company stopped shipping provisions to Russian America, and from the early 1850s, when many navy ships were assigned to the Russian Far East to supply and defend Russia's new Amurian territory—particularly during the Crimean War, when both Petropavlovsk and Ayan were attacked by enemy warships. Heretofore the company had few ships to spare for

Table 7. Russian Voyages from European Russia to Russian America and the Russian Far East, 1803–64

No.	Ship	Commander	Route	Date	Value of Cargo (rubles)
1.	Company ship *Hope*, 430 t.	Capt.-Lt. I. F. Kruzenstern	Cronstadt-Cape Horn-Petropavlovsk-Cape of Good Hope-Cronstadt	1803–6	260,510*
2.	Company ship *Neva*, 370 t.	Capt.-Lt. Yu. F. Lisyansky	Cronstadt-Cape Horn-Kodiak-Cape of Good Hope-Cronstadt	1803–6	
3.	Company ship *Neva*, 370 t.	Lt. L. A. Hagemeister	Cronstadt-Cape of Good Hope-New Archangel	1806–7	131,593
4.	Navy sloop *Diana*, 300 t.	Lt. V. M. Golovnin	Cronstadt-Cape of Good Hope-Petropavlovsk-New Archangel-Petropavlovsk	1807–9	?
5.	Company ship *Suvorov*, 335 t.	Lt. M. P. Lazarev	Cronstadt-Cape of Good Hope-New Archangel-Cape Horn-Cronstadt	1813–16	246,476
6.	Navy brig *Rurik*, 180 t.	Lt. O. Ye. Kotzebue	Cronstadt-Cape Horn-Petropavlovsk-Unalaska-Cape of Good Hope-Cronstadt	1815–18	?
7.	Company ship *Suvorov*, 335 t.	Lt. Z. I. Ponafidin	Cronstadt-Cape Horn-New Archangel-Cape Horn-Cronstadt	1816–18	184,385
8.	Company ship *Kutuzov*, 525 t.	Capt.-Lt. Hagemeister	Cronstadt-Cape Horn-New Archangel-Cape of Good Hope-Cronstadt	1816–19	426,566**
9.	Navy sloop *Kamchatka*, 900 t.	Capt. (2nd rank) Golovnin	Cronstadt-Cape Horn-Petropavlovsk-New Archangel-Cape of Good Hope-Cronstadt	1817–19	?
10.	Navy sloop *East*, 900 t.	Capt. (2nd rank) Bellinghausen	Cronstadt-Cape Horn-Port Jackson-Cape Horn-Cronstadt	1819–21	?
11.	Navy sloop *Peaceful*, 530 t.	Lt. M. P. Lazarev	Cronstadt-Cape Horn-Port Jackson-Cape Horn-Cronstadt	1819–21	?
12.	Navy sloop *Discovery*, 900 t.	Capt.-Lt. M. N. Vasilyev	Cronstadt-Cape of Good Hope-Petropavlovsk-Cape Horn-Cronstadt	1819–22	?
13.	Navy sloop *Loyal*, 530 t.	Capt.-Lt. G. S. Shishmarev	Cronstadt-Cape of Good Hope-Unalaska-Petropavlovsk-Cape Horn-Cronstadt	1819–22	?
14.	Company ship *Borodino*, 600 t.	Lt. Z. I. Ponafidin	Cronstadt-Cape of Good Hope-New Archangel-Cape Horn-Cronstadt	1819–21	798,927

No.	Ship	Commander	Route	Years	Value
15.	Company ship *Kutuzov*, 525 t.	Lt. P. A. Dokhturov	Cronstadt-Cape Horn-New Archangel-Cape Horn-Cronstadt	1820–22	441,215†
16.	Company brig *Rurik*, 180 t.	Navigator (12th class) Ye. A. Klochkov	Cronstadt-Cape of Good Hope-New Archangel	1821–22	142,741
17.	Company ship *Elizabeth*	I. M. Kislyakovsky	Cronstadt-Cape of Good Hope	1821	89,674
18.	Navy sloop *Apollo*, 900 t.	Lts. S. P. Khrushchov and I. S. Tulubyev	Cronstadt-Cape of Good Hope-Petropavlovsk-New Archangel-Cape Horn-Cronstadt	1821–24	?
19.	Navy brig *Ayaks*	N. I. Filatov	Cronstadt-Holland	1821–22	?
20.	Navy sloop *Ladoga*	Capt.-Lt. A. P. Lazarev	Cronstadt-Cape of Good Hope-Petropavlovsk-New Archangel-Cape Horn-Cronstadt	1822–24	?
21.	Navy frigate *Cruiser*	Capt. (2nd rank) M. P. Lazarev	Cronstadt-Cape of Good Hope-New Archangel-Cape Horn-Cronstadt	1822–25	?
22.	Navy sloop *Enterprise*, 750 t.	Capt.-Lt. O. Ye. Kotzebue	Cronstadt-Cape Horn-Petropavlovsk-New Archangel-Cape of Good Hope-Cronstadt	1823–26	?
23.	Navy sloop *Silent*	P. A. Dokhturov	Cronstadt-?	1824–25	?
24.	Company ship *Helena*, 400 t.	Lt. P. Ye. Chistyakov (outbound) and Capt. (2nd rank) M. I. Muravyov (inbound)	Cronstadt-Cape of Good Hope-New Archangel-Cape Horn-Cronstadt	1824–26	462,004‡
25.	Navy transport *Gentle*	Capt.-Lt. F. P. Wrangel	Cronstadt-Cape Horn-Petropavlovsk-New Archangel-Cape of Good Hope-Cronstadt	1825–27	?
26.	Navy sloop *Moller*	Capt.-Lt. M. N. Stanyukovich	Cronstadt-Cape Horn-Petropavlovsk-Cape of Good Hope-Cronstadt	1826–29	?
27.	Navy sloop *Senyavin*	Capt.-Lt. F. P. Lütke	Cronstadt-Cape Horn-New Archangel-Petropavlovsk-Cape of Good Hope-Cronstadt	1826–29	?
28.	Company ship *Helena*, 400 t.	Lt. V. S. Khromchenko	Cronstadt-Cape of Good Hope-New Archangel-Cape Horn-Cronstadt	1828–30	458,276
29.	Navy transport *Gentle*	Capt.-Lt. L. A. Hagemeister	Cronstadt-Cape of Good Hope-Petropavlovsk-New Archangel-Cape Horn-Cronstadt	1828–30	?
30.	Navy transport *America*, 655 t.	Capt.-Lt. V. S. Khromchenko	Cronstadt-Cape of Good Hope-Petropavlovsk-New Archangel-Cape Horn-Cronstadt	1831–33	467,505
31.	Navy transport *America*, 655 t.	Capt.-Lt. I. I. Shantz	Cronstadt-Cape of Good Hope-Petropavlovsk-New Archangel-Cape Horn-Cronstadt	1834–36	435,000

No.	Ship	Commander	Route	Date	Value of Cargo (rubles)
32.	Company ship *Helena*, 400 t.	Lt. M. D. Tebenkov	Cronstadt-Cape Horn-New Archangel	1835–36	350,000*†
33.	Company ship *Nicholas*, 400 t.	Capt.-Lt. Ye. A. Berens	Cronstadt-Cape Horn-New Archangel-Cape Horn-Cronstadt	1837–39	400,000
34.	Company ship *Nicholas*, 400 t.	Lts. N. A. Kadnikov and S. V. Voyevodsky	Cronstadt-Cape Horn-New Archangel-Cape Horn-Cronstadt	1839–41	560,000
35.	Company ship *Alexander's Heir*, 300 t.	Capt.-Lt. D. F. Zarembo	Cronstadt-Cape Horn-New Archangel	1840–41	122,580
36.	Navy transport *Abo*, 655 t.	Capt.-Lt. A. L. Yunker	Cronstadt-Cape of Good Hope-Petropavlovsk-Cape Horn-Cronstadt	1840–42	?
37.	Navy transport *Irtysh*, 450 t.	Capt. (1st rank) I. V. Vonlyarlyarsky	Cronstadt-Cape of Good Hope-Petropavlovsk-Okhotsk	1843–45	?
38.	Russian ship ?	?	Cronstadt-?-New Archangel-?	1846–?	131,151
39.	Russian ship ?	?	Cronstadt-?-New Archangel-?	1847–?	part of 147,145
40.	Russian ship ?	?	Cronstadt-?-New Archangel-?	1848–?	part of 95,109
41.	Navy transport *Baikal*, 477 t.	Capt.-Lt. G. I. Nevelskoy	Cronstadt-Cape Horn-Petropavlovsk-Okhotsk	1848–49	?
42.	Russian ship ?	?	Cronstadt-?-New Archangel-?	1849–?	part of 162,832
43.	Russian ship ?	?	Cronstadt-?-New Archangel-?	1850–?	78,225
44.	Navy corvette *Olivutsa*	Capt.-Lt. I. N. Shushchov	Cronstadt-Cape Horn-Petropavlovsk	1850–51	?
45.	Company ship *Sitka*	?	Cronstadt-?-New Archangel-?	1851–?	105,448
46.	Russian ship ?	?	Cronstadt-?-New Archangel-?	1852–?	12,123
47.	Navy transport *Dvina*, 640 t.	Capt.-Lt. P. N. Bessarabsky	Cronstadt-Cape of Good Hope-Petropavlovsk	1852–53	?
48.	Navy frigate *Pallas*	Capt. (2nd rank) I. S. Unkovsky	Cronstadt-Cape of Good Hope-Imperial Harbor	1852–54	?
49.	Navy frigate *Aurora*, 1,947 t.	Capt.-Lt. I. N. Izylmetyev	Cronstadt-Cape Horn-Petropavlovsk	1852–54	?
50.	Russian ship ?	?	Cronstadt-?-New Archangel-?	1853–?	244,691

No.	Ship	Captain	Route	Dates	Value (rubles)
51.	Navy schooner *East*	Capt. (2nd rank) V. A. Rimsky-Korsakov	Portsmouth-Cape of Good Hope-De Castries Bay	1853–54	?
52.	Navy frigate *Diana*	Capt.-Lt. S. S. Lesovsky	Cronstadt-Cape Horn-De Castries Bay	1853–54	?
53.	Navy frigate *Aurora*, 1,947 t.	Capt. (2nd rank) M. P. Tirol	Cronstadt-?-De Castries Bay-Cape of Good Hope-Cronstadt	?–1857	?
54.	Navy transport *Dvina*, 640 t.	Capt.-Lt. I. I. Butakov	Cronstadt-?-Amur River-Cape Horn-Cronstadt	?–1857	?
55.	Navy corvette *Olivutsa*	Capt. (2nd rank) V. A. Rimsky-Korsakov	Cronstadt-?-Imperial Harbor-Cape of Good Hope-Cronstadt	?–1857	?
56.	Russian ship ?	?	Cronstadt-?-New Archangel-?	1856–?	75,621
57.	Russian ship ?	?	Cronstadt-?-New Archangel-?	1857–?	86,518
58.	Russian ship ?	?	Cronstadt-?-New Archangel-?	1858–?	100,677
59.	Company ship *Nicholas I*	?	Cronstadt-?-New Archangel-?	1859–?	122,473
60.	Company ship *Kamchatka*	?	Cronstadt-?-New Archangel-?	1860–?	65,700
61.	Russian ship ?	?	Cronstadt-?-New Archangel-?	1861–?	72,105
62.	Navy transport *Gilyak*, 897 t.	Capt.-Lt. A. I. Enqvist	Hamburg-Cape of Good Hope-De Castries Bay-Imperial Harbor-Cape of Good Hope-Cronstadt	1861–63	?
63.	Russian ship ?	?	Cronstadt-?-New Archangel-?	1862–?	76,498
64.	Russian ship ?	?	Cronstadt-?-New Archangel-?	1863–?	7,359
65.	Navy transport *Gilyak*, 897 t.	Capt.-Lt. A. I. Enqvist	Cronstadt-Cape Horn-De Castries Bay-Vladivostok-Cape of Good Hope-Cronstadt	1864–66	?

* Another source states that the total value of the cargo of the *Hope* and *Neva* together was more than 600,000 rubles, almost half of which consisted of presents for Japan (Tikhmenev, *Historical Review*, I, 129–30).

** Another source states that the total value of the cargo of the *Suvorov* and *Kutuzov* together was more than 1,000,000 rubles (Tikhmenev, *Historical Review*, I, 242).

† Another source states that the value of the *Kutuzov's* cargo was 1,109,369 rubles (Tikhmenev, *Historical Review*, I, 245).

‡ Another source states that the value of the *Helena's* cargo was 500,000 rubles (Tikhmenev, *Historical Review*, I, 407).

*† Another source states that the value of the *Helena's* cargo was 493,617 rubles (USNA, 39: 186v.).

It is possible that the above discrepancies represent the (higher) value of cargo leaving Cronstadt and the (lower) value of the same cargo reaching New Archangel or Petropavlovsk.

Sources: Ivashintsov, "Russkiya krugosvetnia puteshestviya," 163–90; Ministerstvo Oborony Soyuza SSR, *Morskoy atlas*, III, Map 25; ORAK, 1846: 18, 1847: 18, 1848: 18, 1849:18, 1850: 7, 1851: 8, 1852: 7–8, 1853: 9, 1856: 8, 1857: 12, 1858: 10, 1859: 8, 1860: 11, 1861: 10–11, 1862: 12, 1863: 13; Tikhmenev, *Historical Review*, I, 407–11; Zubov, *Otechestvennie moreplavateli-issledovateli*, 446–51; Gibson, "Russian America," 13.

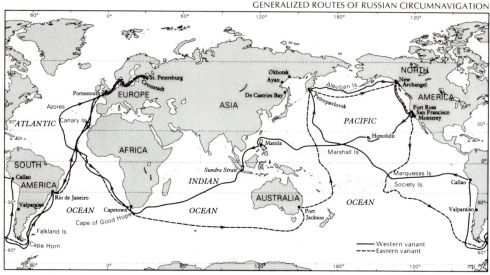

GENERALIZED ROUTES OF RUSSIAN CIRCUMNAVIGATION

MAP 4

oceanic supply, but between 1850 and 1853 it acquired seven vessels. Thereafter supplies were shipped on company and chartered vessels.[9] Unlike the company and navy ships, which carried supplies from European Russia, the other Russian ships and the chartered ships brought freight from Finland, Germany, and England.

CARGO

The company and navy supply ships generally transported items that were too bulky, heavy, or fragile to be packed from Yakutsk to Okhotsk —manufactures such as ship materials, metal goods, textiles, leather goods, glass and earthenware utensils, and instruments and provisions such as flour and sugar.* The proportion of provisions, however, remained small until the late 1840s. Sometimes the ships stopped in England to obtain additional manufactured goods. Occasionally, too, the ships called at South American ports (usually Rio de Janeiro or Valparaiso) for tropical foodstuffs such as sugar and coffee. Returning from the colonies the ships carried, besides stone ballast and some passengers, part of the fur catch—black bear, blue fox, marten, and wolverine pelts

---

* On the Yakutsk-Okhotsk Track, heavy goods often had to be dismantled and conveyed in pieces, for each pack horse could carry no more than 250 pounds; upon arrival at Okhotsk the pieces were reassembled by welding, splicing, and so forth.

—and whalebone and walrus tusks. Other furs—sea otter, fur seal, white fox, river otter, beaver, and lynx—were shipped via Okhotsk.

TRENDS

During the first and second phases, when Russian America relied upon American traders and Alta California for provisions, oceanic voyages were moderately important as a means of supplying the colonies. From 1808 through 1818, for example, when Governor Baranov accumulated supplies worth 928,000 rubles at New Archangel by other means, the company sent 2,817,319 rubles' worth to New Archangel via Cronstadt and Okhotsk. (Only 884,224 rubles' worth, however, actually reached the colonial capital.)[10] So, during the first phase, Russian America received perhaps a half of its supplies from Siberia and Russia. In 1819 the head office wrote the tsar:

> Four repeated attempts have convinced the Russian-American Company that it is much more helpful and convenient to send to its American colonies all goods that are needed both for shipbuilding and navigation and for the maintenance of personnel and the safeguarding of fortresses on ships around the world from Cronstadt than to send freight there via Okhotsk, whither the delivery of goods, especially heavy ones, is accompanied by extreme difficulty and much loss because of the unsuitability of the road.[11]

However, the losses of the *Elizabeth* (1821), the *Ayaks* (1822), and the *Silent* (1825) depreciated oceanic supply. Moreover, regular trade with Alta California from 1821 furnished considerable foodstuffs, and after 1824–25, when conventions were signed with the United States and Great Britain, there was no longer a need for Russian ships to patrol colonial waters. These treaties delimited Russian America at 54°40′ N and prohibited the trading of firearms and spirits to the Indians of the Northwest Coast. Oceanic supply slackened further with the signing in 1839 of the Russian-American Company-Hudson's Bay Company agreement, which assured the colonies sufficient supplies. But after ten years the Hudson's Bay Company refused to renew the provisionment clause of this agreement, and this refusal, together with the scarcity and dearness of foodstuffs in California during the gold rush, prompted the regeneration of oceanic supply, which then became extremely important. The Russian-American Company reported to its shareholders in 1850 that the colonies would be provisioned from Europe until there was a "change of circumstances" in California and in other Pacific Coast lands

(Oregon Country) that had been sources of provisions.[12] Experience had proved that a ship could reach New Archangel from Cronstadt quickly enough to serve in Russian America for four or five months before leaving in the fall, returning to Cronstadt at the beginning of the navigation season and departing for New Archangel in the same year. By the late 1840s Russian America was receiving most of its supplies by sea from Europe, largely on chartered foreign vessels now that navy ships were no longer available. The remaining colonial supplies came mostly from Siberia via Ayan. This pattern continued until 1867.*

RESULTS

The voyages between the Baltic Sea and the Bering Sea did more than deliver supplies. For one thing, they made discoveries, especially in the Okhotsk and Bering seas, the tropical waters of the Pacific, and the Antarctic Ocean. The most notable discoveries were those of Antarctica by Captain Bellingshausen and Lieutenant Lazarev in 1820 and the navigability of Tatar Strait and the Amur estuary by Captain-Lieutenant Nevelskoy in 1849. For another thing, hundreds of naval officers and thousands of crewmen received invaluable practical training in oceanic seamanship during the formative period of the imperial navy. Such prominent naval figures as Admiral Kruzenstern and Naval Minister Wrangel perfected their sea legs on voyages between Cronstadt and the North Pacific. Also, some Decembrist revolutionaries had been exposed to radical ideas while serving as volunteer apprentices on British and Dutch ships and later while visiting foreign ports as officers on Russian ships sailing to the North Pacific; for example, Torson on the *East* (1819–21), Kuchelbecker on the *Apollo* (1841–44), and Zavalishin on the *Cruiser* (1822–25). Many useful maps and charts were compiled, meteorological and oceanographic observations recorded, and ethnographic, zoological, and botanical descriptions and collections made. And informative journal accounts, including a gem of Russian literature, Ivan Goncharov's *The Frigate Pallas*, were written.

In terms of supply, however, the voyages did not prove very successful. In fact, the first one was a disappointment. Although the leaders were rewarded by the tsar with promotions, medals, cash, and pensions,

---

* Some provisions, however, were shipped from Amuria in 1854 and 1855, when the "usual supply of the colonies from Europe" was prevented by the Crimean War (ORAK, 1859: 82).

conflict between Rezanov and Kruzenstern had marred the expedition. Rezanov also failed to open trade with Japan, and low prices were received for furs at Canton, where the Russians had hoped that they would be paid 57 rubles for sea otters and 2 rubles for fur seals.* (The skins, however, fetched only 32 and 1½ rubles, owing to the glutting of the market by 14,000 sea otter and 90,000 fur seal pelts brought on American vessels.) At Canton the *Neva* had to pay customs duties of 7500 rubles, and the two ships barely missed being seized by the Chinese, who had been angered by the behavior of a Russian ambassadorial mission in 1805.** And at home only small profits were realized on the cargo of china, nankeen, and tea (which proved inferior to the "caravan" tea brought overland via Kyakhta), despite the exemption of these goods from import duties. In 1824 Captain Peter Rikord, onetime commandant of Kamchatka (1817–22), opined that oceanic provision was beset by "insurmountable inconvenience" (meaning possible shipwreck and wartime disruption) and by the fact that grain would "cost very dearly and [could] spoil en route."[13] Actually, remarkably little inconvenience arose; only four ships were wrecked and voyages were halted for only two years during the Crimean War. Also, surprisingly few crewmen were lost; the only disaster was the death of about 40 of the *Borodino's* complement of 112 to 123 men in 1819–21. Much more telling were spoilage and expense. Indeed, the company in 1821 cited these factors as the principal disadvantages of oceanic supply.[14]

PROBLEMS

As mentioned earlier, spoilage of foodstuffs during the long voyage through tropical waters was common. Besides heat and moisture, rats were a major problem; for example, after the frigate *Cruiser* was unloaded and fumigated at New Archangel in 1823, more than 1000 dead rats were found on board. In 1824 the Ministry of Finance asserted that the oceanic shipping of grain was unsatisfactory because on long voyages it became musty and caught fire. Shipping flour was also unsatisfactory because barrels were costly and occupied much valuable space.[15] The company acknowledged that grain could turn sour or catch fire

* En route to Canton the *Neva* threw overboard some 32,000 spoiled pelts valued at 80,000 rubles (nearly a fifth of its fur cargo).
** The *Neva* was also prevented from returning to Cronstadt in 1810 by the Napoleonic Wars and from returning to Canton because of its closure (Alaska History Research Project, *Documents*, III, 201).

(through spontaneous combustion of green or damp grain) and that it could be spoiled by dampness from leaks sprung during storms.[16] ". . . Experience has already shown," it was admitted, "that whole grain cannot be transported on ships through the equatorial zone without harm."[17] Flour fared little better, and non-foodstuffs could also be damaged—metal rusted and cloth and leather mildewed. Hence the complaint of Governor Kupreyanov (1835–40) in 1837 that many of the items received on the *Helena* in 1836 were very low in quality.[18] Such items undoubtedly contributed to the stockpile of unusable goods at New Archangel. Governor Chistyakov recommended in 1827 that only less spoilable cargo like sailcloth, sackcloth, rope, and rigging be shipped from Cronstadt.[19]

For the same reasons colonial products—mainly certain furs—were subject to spoilage on the return voyage. The company's head office told Governor Wrangel in 1833 and again in 1834 that repeated experiments had demonstrated that the shipment of furs by sea from New Archangel to Cronstadt was disadvantageous for two reasons: (1) sea otter, fur seal, and black and silver fox pelts changed color and became drier and less soft from passage through the equatorial zone; and (2) furs destined for Kyakhta—fur seals, river otters, red and white foxes, and beavers—arrived too late for prime marketing, having first reached St. Petersburg in the late fall or early winter. It was better to ship these pelts via Okhotsk.[20] Thus, whereas the demand for supplies warranted the dispatch of two or more ships to New Archangel, the fur catch justified the return of but one ship to Cronstadt, and voyages were sufficiently profitable only when a full cargo returned from New Archangel.[21]* Recognizing this fact, Governor Chistyakov in 1827 advised that the company dispatch a ship only once every three years or even less frequently.[22] The head office, realizing that there would be enough returnable cargo at New Archangel every three years only, concurred.[23]** The less frequent voyages, however, brought fewer supplies.

Like all wooden sailing ships, the company vessels constantly required repairing and overhauling and depreciated rapidly. Furthermore, nobody would insure the ships because of the great distance of the voyages, the uncertain deployment of the ships in Russian America, and the lack of official witnesses in the colonies.

---

* A ship returning to Cronstadt from New Archangel normally needed about 10,000 tons of ballast.
** Incidentally, colonial products were landed duty free at St. Petersburg.

COSTS OF TRANSPORT

Little wonder, then, that every voyage entailed "considerable" outlay and incurred "irreparable" loss.[24] Expenses were such that the company had to increase the selling price of the imported goods at New Archangel by 50 per cent over their cost, but even this markup barely covered the cost of transportation.[25] By 1860 the markup had risen to 77 per cent (42 per cent for handling, packaging, and hauling and 35 per cent for profit).[26]* But losses still occurred. Three voyages in 1819–22 on the *Borodino, Kutuzov,* and *Rurik,* for example, cost 2,400,000 rubles; that of the *Kutuzov* alone cost 700,000 rubles and returned cargo worth only 200,000 rubles.[27] Again, the company lost over 225,000 rubles on the two voyages of the *Helena* (1824–26 and 1828–30).[28]

In fact, transport from Cronstadt was more expensive than any other form of supply save that from Okhotsk or Ayan.** It was considerably cheaper to buy from the Hudson's Bay Company. In 1842 the delivery of supplies to New Archangel cost 180 rubles per ton on navy ships from Cronstadt and up to 630 rubles per ton from Siberia via Okhotsk but only 114 rubles per ton on Hudson's Bay Company ships from England[29]—a saving of as much as 516 rubles per ton! By 1860 shipment from England was even cheaper (at least for non-provisions)—up to 94 rubles per ton, compared with up to 254 rubles per ton from Russia.[30] Supply by American trading vessels was also substantially cheaper, the company reporting that in the early 1810s American seaborne supplies cost

* In 1834 the state charged the company 30 per cent for freightage on the navy ship *America* (USNA, 9: 386–86v.).
** In the late 1810s it was four times cheaper to ship heavy goods (anchors, cannons, iron, copper, rigging, sails) to New Archangel via Cronstadt than via Okhotsk (Anonymous, "Obozrenie," 102). Around 1860 it cost the company up to 630 rubles per ton to transport freight overland to Okhotsk but only up to 254 rubles per ton on company ships (180 rubles per ton on navy ships) from Cronstadt to New Archangel, mainly because supplies could be conveyed in a greater volume and in a more intact state by sea than by land (Tikhmenev, *Historical Review*, I, 437). Transport via Ayan was no cheaper; in 1848 the company's net profit at New Archangel on supplies from Cronstadt was 42 per cent but on those from Ayan only 19 per cent (USNA, 55: 130). It did prove cheaper, however, to ship via Amuria. In 1857 the transport of rye flour from Cronstadt cost twice as much as from Amuria (*Doklad komiteta*, II, 93, 323).
Supply from Siberia and Russia together consumed not a small part of the company's income. For instance, the sale value of supplies sent to New Archangel via both Okhotsk and Cronstadt from 1808 through 1818 totaled 2,817,319 rubles, which represented 18 per cent of the value of the company's colonial fur catch during the same period (Anonymous, "Kratkaya Istoricheskaya Zapiska," 3v.).

half as much as Russian ones.[31] By 1826 the head office had decided to ship from Cronstadt only those supplies that American ships sold at unreasonable prices or did not carry at all.[32] Governor Chistyakov was told:

> the head office considers it proper to change its opinion regarding the further supply of the colonies with necessities from Russia. The experience of previous years has shown that the company can no longer provision its colonies by delivering necessities there around the world from either Russia or via Okhotsk. But in order to harmonize political and practical considerations the company's head office does not intend to completely abandon these expeditions but to send them as infrequently as possible.[33]

Thus, by 1826 the company had begun to reduce oceanic supply (but not to abandon it completely, thanks to "political" considerations; that is, the necessity of showing the Russian flag and protecting Russian interests). Thereafter shipments from Cronstadt consisted largely of cheap Russian manufactures. When oceanic supply was revived in the late 1840s, victuals were again shipped in quantity from Cronstadt, but this resurgence was short-lived. In 1861 the head office informed Governor Ivan Furguhelm (1859–63) that it intended to "halt the shipment of rye flour from Russia, and that in all probability it would be sent there for the last time this year."[34] Oceanic supply, like the Siberian supply line, was simply too problematical. The company had been aware of this fact much earlier and had tried its hand at other more reliable and less expensive means of provisionment. One of these alternatives was local agriculture. If foodstuffs produced in Russia and Siberia could not be readily transported to Russian America, perhaps the difficulty of transport could be avoided by producing them in the colonies themselves.

Readings

Lisiansky, Urey, A Voyage Round the World in the Years 1803, 4, 5, & 6, trans. by the author, London, 1814.

McCartan, E. F., "The Long Voyages—Early Russian Circumnavigation," Russian Review, 1963, 30–37.

Nozikov, N., Russian Voyages Round the World, trans. by Ernst and Mira Lesser, London, n.d.

Von Kotzebue, Otto, *A New Voyage Round the World, in the Years 1823, 24, 25, and 26,* London, 1830, 2 vols.

Von Krusenstern, Captain A. J., *Voyage Round the World in the Years 1803, 1804, 1805, & 1806,* trans. by Richard Belgrave Hoppner, London, 1813, 2 vols.

Von Langsdorff, G. H., *Voyages and Travels in Various Parts of the World . . . ,* London, 1814, 2 pts.

PART III   LOCAL AGRICULTURE

6 FARMING IN ALASKA

The islands lying near the American coast and stretching from Kyk-tak [Kodiak] toward its Eastern side and to Northeastern America are stonier and mountainous, but nevertheless there is good, suit-able land for grain cultivation, to which I attested with my own ex-periments, having sown Barley, Millet, Peas, Beans, Pumpkins, Car-rots, Mustard, Beets, Potatoes, Turnips, *and* Rhubarb. *All grew in the best way, except that* Millet, Peas, Beans *and* Pumpkins *did not bear fruit, and then only because the time at which they should have been sown was missed. For haymaking there are suitable meadowy places and fairly suitable grasses, and in places livestock can live all winter without hay.*

Gregory Shelikhov

Beginnings

Agriculture was begun in Russian America by the farsighted Golikov-Shelikhov Company in 1784 when, at the founding of Three Saints Har-bor, Shelikhov, hoping to set an example for the onlooking Konyagas, called their attention to his men as they worked at "digging, and sowing and planting the ground for kitchen-gardens."[1]* Initially, wheat and bar-ley, peas and beans, turnips and beets, mustard and parsnip, potatoes and gourds, and rhubarb were planted; later, buckwheat, spelt (German wheat), and millet were sown. The soil was spaded, not plowed, for want of draft animals. In May of 1787 Shelikhov instructed his manager Yev-

* The rival Lebedev-Lastochkin Company, characterized by its network of perma-nent settlements, may have undertaken agricultural experiments before 1784.

strat Delarov to take to Kodiak "two pairs of year-old steers and calves, as well as a pair of pigs and goats," keeping an eye on "the economy of the farm by the sowing of grain and planting of garden-produce."[2] In 1789 the Billings Expedition observed that "Several of the Russians have their wives with them, and keep gardens of cabbages and potatoes, four cows and twelve goats."[3] By 1790 Shelikhov was able to report to Governor-General Pil of Eastern Siberia:

> We have already seen the first results of my efforts along this line: the harvest of the various types of grain sown while I was there [1784] has already been gathered in. Besides, the yield is increasing and the cattle brought there is also multiplying. In addition I intend to send over there next summer a breed of horses, a few pairs of the best stallions and mares, and some horned cattle.[4]

Kodiak Island thus became the center of agriculture in Alaska from the beginning of Russian settlement.

Shelikhov's agricultural operations, however, were not confined to Kodiak. He informed Pil in 1790 that already "the lands [of the Aleutian Islands and the Alaskan coast] suited for cultivation or for cattle-breeding have been noted and explored for future settlement"; "I hope to introduce farming and cattle-breeding there," he added.[5] Shelikhov believed that the coast and the islands of the Gulf of Alaska were well suited to the growing of grain and the keeping of livestock, especially the stretch from Unalaska Island to Kenai Inlet, which he considered even more favorable for agriculture than Kodiak Island because it had more arable land and more shipbuilding timber. So in 1793 he asked Pil to seek on his behalf royal permission to send ten peasant families as well as some artisans to the colonies—"for the establishment of grain cultivation in suitable places in the Great American Land and on the Kurile Islands."[6] The tsarina consented[7] and in May 1794 Shelikhov was assigned ten families of peasant exiles and twenty families of craft exiles "for the construction of a wharf near Cape St. Elias and for the introduction of agriculture at proper places on the American mainland and on the Kuril Islands, at your own expense."[8] Shelikhov's instructions were:

> To develop agriculture, to raise grains and vegetables for your own consumption and for export to Okhotsk and Kamchatka. To build a reserve for grain and vegetables for emergencies. To encourage agriculture by payment to the settlers for products sold to the Company and to encourage the use of local foodstuffs; such as fish, game and roots. To raise cattle and poultry.[9]

On August 24, 1794 twenty-five peasants and twenty shipwrights with cattle,* poultry, seed,** implements, and other supplies, plus personnel (sailors, promyshlenniks, missionaries), left Okhotsk on two company ships, the *Three Saints* and the *Catherine*. Four of the peasant families (six individuals) remained at Okhotsk; with up to thirty-two promyshlenniks, grain, and cattle they were sent to Urup in the Kurile Islands. The group's leader, Basil Zvezdochetov, was instructed "to pay his attention to agriculture and to start hunting only after every settler will have a house of his own, a vegetable garden and a field to raise grain."[10] Shelikhov also felt that "The Kurile people [Ainus] should be enticed to settle on Urup Island and to engage in agriculture."[11]

Meanwhile, the other exiles arrived on Kodiak, from which they were sent in 1795 on the *Three Saints* to Yakutat (Bering) Bay. Baranov, Delarov's successor, believed that an agricultural settlement could not be established closer to Kodiak on account of the high latitude, mountainous terrain, and unsuitable soil around Kenai and Chuvash inlets.† The settlement, named Slavorossiya, was founded on Yakutat Bay in the summer of 1796. At the same time cattle were sent from Kodiak to Unalaska.

Company Operations

Such were the beginnings of Alaskan agriculture. This foundation was broadened by the United American Company in 1798 and by the Russian-American Company from 1799. One of the goals of the former was to organize agriculture and cattlebreeding in America and on the islands.[12] And one of the duties of every Russian-American Company factory was "To mind the stocking of various vital supplies for Russians

* Shelikhov sent 7 sheep, 7 goats, 4 heifers, one mare, and one colt, which were to be shipped to Cape St. Elias, along with all livestock on Kodiak (except one pair of each kind, to be left for breeding). More livestock were not sent because of insufficient room on the two ships (Andreyev, *Russkie otkrytiya*, 343–44, 354).

** Shelikhov sent 2166 pounds of fall rye, 393 pounds of wheat, 375 pounds of spring rye, 298 pounds of peas, 264 pounds of barley, 76 pounds of oats, 30 pounds of hemp, and 21 pounds of buckwheat, plus radishes, carrots, turnips, rutabagas, beets, cabbage, cucumbers, muskmelons, watermelons, lettuce, spinach, purslane, parsley, celery, parsnip, onions, and many other vegetables. Half of the seed was to be used for the first sowing and the other half was to be saved in case the first sowing failed. The seed was to be planted at the first suitable opportunity; the manager was "to act in this important matter with all care and the best method," using the economic manuals on Kodiak and his own experience and that of the missionaries and colonists (Andreyev, *Russkie otkrytiya*, 343).

† Actually, Yakutat Bay is higher in latitude and more mountainous than parts of Kenai Inlet.

and Aleuts, as well as agriculture and the cultivation of garden vegetables . . . and the propagation of domestic cattle and poultry."[13] Almost every post had small gardens and several cattle, pigs, chickens, and
ducks and perhaps some sheep and goats. The main farming districts
were Kodiak Island, Kenai Inlet, and Baranof, Unalaska, and Atka islands. On the Kenai Peninsula St. Nicholas Redoubt had gardens of
"considerable size" as well as cattle. At New Archangel there were also
cattle but mostly gardens, which formed a narrow green strip along the
beach. Cattle herding and vegetable gardening were also important on
Unalaska. On Atka "special attention" was paid to gardening because it
was very difficult to stock supplies there.[14] The island was a promising
locale for livestock: "No other place in the colonies except Ross is so
suitable for the breeding of cattle and swine as Atka and the islands adjoining it; there is lush grass everywhere in summer, and the moderate
cold and light snowfall save the work of making a winter supply [of
hay], and the cattle always have pasturage," Governor Wrangel told the
head office in 1832.[15] Not even remote Bering Island in the Commanders
escaped the company's agricultural attention; in 1848 seven or eight
head of cattle were placed there.[16]

Kodiak Island, however, remained the focus of company agriculture in
Alaska (Map 5). In 1805 Count Rezanov ordered that farming be extended throughout Kodiak Counter, that horses and bulls be maintained
for plowing, and that an agricultural school be founded under the direction of the missionaries.[17] About this time one of the missionaries, Father
Gideon, recorded: "At every artel there are, besides livestock, gardens
where only potatoes and turnips are planted."[18]* He added that the
island's chief agricultural settlement was Chiniatsk (Sapozhnikova**),
located on the coast from eight to nine miles southwest of St. Paul's Harbor. More cattle were kept there than anywhere else on the island, and
wheat and barley were grown. In fact cattle raising was Kodiak's principal agricultural activity.† The company even pastured cattle on the
"good grass" of some of the neighboring islets—Spruce, Woody, Marmot,
and Long—at least until 1825. Initially, however, cattle raising was centered at Igatsk (Orlovsk), situated on a bay of the same name some

---

* In 1847 every house at St. Paul's Harbor had a garden containing mostly potatoes
and turnips (USNA, 54: 244v.).
** This settlement was named after a successful farmer called Sapozhnikov, who may
have been one of Shelikhov's colonists. A bay and a river also bore his name.
† Cattle raising (for fresh meat) was more essential on Kodiak than at New Archangel because fresh fish were available throughout the year at the colonial capital but
not on Kodiak.

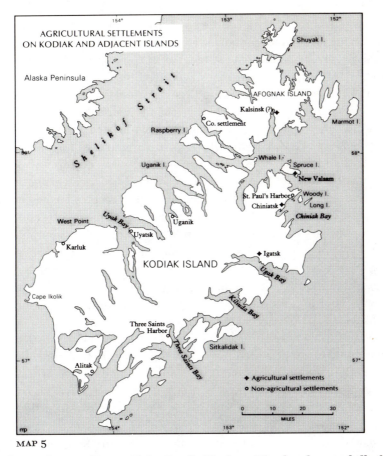

MAP 5

sixty-five miles southwest of St. Paul's Harbor. The locale was hilly but
there were many grassy ravines. This artel, where twenty-two Aleuts and
two Russians lived in 1825,[19] also raised better vegetables, particularly
potatoes, than any other settlement in the counter. In 1832 Wrangel
made Chiniatsk and Kalsinsk the island's main cattle centers in place of
Igatsk, where losses of cattle had always been considerable.[20] Finally, in
1843 all company cattle on Kodiak were consolidated into three herds
totaling no more than 250 head at Chiniatsk, Kalsinsk, and Igatsk.[21]

Private Operations

Besides company agriculture, which was conducted by employees (both
promyshlenniks and native hands, chiefly Aleuts), private agriculture
was also undertaken by promyshlennik wives and Creoles, who often had

their own few animals (mostly cows and pigs) and small gardens. Indeed, whereas most of the cattle in Alaska belonged to the company, most of the vegetable gardens were private.* Their output was consumed largely by their owners, but any surplus was purchased by the company, which in the mid-1830s even restricted its own gardening on Kodiak in order to assure a market for private gardening. This measure was especially designed to encourage the agricultural efforts of the "colonial citizens," who came to dominate private farming by the middle of the century. Colonial citizens were superannuated Russian employees who had married Creoles or natives and who, because of old age, poor health, long residence, or absence of close relatives in the motherland, had remained in Russian America. They received land, housing, cattle, poultry, grain seed, farming and hunting implements, and a one-year supply of food, and in return sold their agricultural output to the company. Imperial permission to form this class was requested and received in 1835, but it was not until 1842 that the first colonial citizens were settled. In 1858 they numbered 240 souls, living mostly in Kodiak Counter,[22] but by 1861 only 94 were left—50 on Afognak, 10 on the Kenai Peninsula, 10 at New Archangel, and 9 on Bering Island.[23]

Private farming was also undertaken by natives, although they were few and late to adopt agriculture. Only the Koloshes took much interest; by 1820 they had many pigs at New Archangel and in 1824 it was noted that potatoes were "raised even by the Koloshes, who have learned from the Russians the manner of cultivating them, and consider them as a great delicacy."[24] From the 1830s the Koloshes had enough potatoes, ducks, and geese to sell to the company. In 1843 the Kaigansk** Haidas accepted Etholen's offer to bring potatoes to New Archangel every fall; in 1845 160 to 250 boats of Indians, many from as far away as the Queen Charlotte Islands, arrived at the colonial capital to sell potatoes.[25] All the Northwest Coast Indians seem to have readily adopted the starchy food.

The Aleuts were slower to accept agriculture. In 1843–44 the sixty-five Aleut settlements of Kodiak Counter were consolidated into seven settlements totaling 1375 souls, who were given cattle and potatoes (for

---

* Land occupied by the houses and the gardens of private individuals could be privately operated but not privately disposed of without the company's permission (USNA, 38: 55v.–56).

** Kaigansk (Kaigani, Kaigahnee, or Kigarnie) was a Haida village on Dall Island in Dixon Entrance.

propagation) to supplement their fish diet and to help settle them.[26] By 1847 Governor Tebenkov was able to report: "Many Aleuts have their own small gardens, and some even keep cattle. Bread, tea, and sugar have become deeply rooted."[27] By 1860, however, Alaska's natives were neglecting agriculture. During an inspection tour in that year Governor Furguhelm found native gardens only at St. Nicholas Redoubt and on Kodiak and Unga islands.[28]

Finally, missionaries also farmed. They conducted agricultural experiments on Kodiak as early as 1795, when Father Herman wrote: "We grow turnips, potatoes, and all garden vegetables, but cucumbers, as well as grain, are not tried."[29] Father Gideon reported that in 1805–7 the missionaries kept gardens where they grew plenty of potatoes, turnips, and radishes; the potatoes were ground into flour and the turnips were eaten fresh in summer (in place of cabbage) and pickled in winter.[30] The center of mission agriculture was Father Herman's station of New Valaam on Spruce Island, where he grew 150 to 180 beds of potatoes in 1825.[31] New Valaam was so successful that in 1831 Wrangel believed that it could serve as a "seedbed of gardening" for the entire counter.[32] After Herman's death in 1837, however, the establishment decayed.

Production

Despite widespread and persistent efforts, farming did not prosper in Alaska. Shelikhov had been optimistic about the agricultural potential of the coast and the islands of the Gulf of Alaska, declaring that, although they were "for the most part stoney and naked mountains, yet among them is very good land, extremely fit for cultivation; of which I thoroughly convinced myself by my own experiments." He added: "For hay there are plenty of meadow-lands, which produce excellent grass; and in many places the cattle will do very well without hay the whole winter through."[33] His hopes, however, were soon dashed. His own first effort at Three Saints Harbor failed; almost the entire planting of wheat, barley, and peas was destroyed by mice (who ate the roots) and by birds (who ate the ears). The crop was also flooded by sea water. Similarly, Baranov reported in 1795 that at St. Paul's Harbor, "Carrots, potatoes, radishes, and turnips are grown. No luck with cabbage and barley. . . . The peas and cucumbers do not ripen."[34] Shelikhov's efforts elsewhere were even less successful. In 1805 Slavorossiya was destroyed by the Koloshes. And about the same time his agricultural settlement on

Urup Island, called New Russia, was abandoned. The settlement's over-seer, Zvezdochetov, had been instructed to pay special attention to farming and to begin hunting only after each settler had a house, a garden, and some pasture. But after the wheat, rye, oats, and flax that he had planted in 1796 failed to ripen, he neglected agriculture. He also mistreated the settlers. In 1798 fourteen settlers fled to Kamchatka; seven more followed in 1803 or 1805. The rest, not receiving any supplies from Okhotsk, became sick and eventually perished.

Farming was not much more fruitful under the Russian-American Company. Virtually no grain was grown. Occasionally barley succeeded but wheat, buckwheat, rye, oats, and millet consistently failed. The grain usually blossomed and eared but rarely kerneled and ripened. Nevertheless, by order of the head office wheat and especially barley were sown every year. On Kodiak barley planted by the peasant Sapozhnikov yielded 54-fold in 1794, and in 1806 along the Sapozhnikov River barley yielded 18-fold and oats 12-fold and wheat yielded "well."[35] But these results were atypical. More typical was the description of grain growing at St. Nicholas Redoubt: "Wheat and barley grow well but do not have time to ripen and kernel."[36] As the company told its shareholders in 1860, "repeated attempts again and again at sowing rye and barley . . . were, unfortunately, always unsuccessful."[37]

Vegetable gardening was more successful. Especially roots and tubers like potatoes, turnips, rutabagas, carrots, radishes, and beets, which were less exposed and less sensitive to the elements, did well, although they tended to taste watery. Leafy vegetables did poorly, usually failing to head. Cabbage, lettuce, and cucumbers succeeded only under glass at New Archangel but at Unalaska failed even under glass. The most successful vegetables were potatoes and turnips, which grew large and tasty at almost every post. On Kodiak Island "No grain grows because of the wet weather, but garden vegetables . . . grow well," reported Governor Yanovsky in 1819.[38] Occasionally there were surplus potatoes; for example, in both 1858 and 1859, 35 barrels were even shipped to New Archangel.[39] At St. Nicholas Redoubt potatoes, turnips, radishes, beets, cabbage, lettuce, onions, and garlic were grown. About fourteen tons of potatoes were produced annually in the mid-1830s,[40] and a "considerable quantity" of potatoes and turnips was sometimes shipped to New Archangel. At New Archangel potatoes and turnips and occasionally radishes and cabbage grew well; in fact, potatoes grew better there than anywhere else in Russian America, yielding from 12-fold to 14-fold at best and from 6-fold to 8-fold at worst in the mid-1820s; then the annual harvest reached 1000 barrels (seventy-two tons), 100 of which were sold to visiting ships.[41] In the mid-1830s, 530 barrels (44 tons) were grown annually, with the yield sometimes reaching 10-fold or 12-fold.[42] By contrast, at Unalaska, where vegetables were allegedly grown "in abundance," potatoes yielded 6-fold on the average, with as few as three potatoes to one pound.[43] New Archangel's superiority, however, was only relative. In 1830 Governor Chistyakov bemoaned: "with what incredible labor and expenditure of time is this spot of sandy and stony ground cultivated, and the fruits of this ungrateful soil now serve as an important confirmation of the meager subsistence of this country!"[44]

Stockbreeding was not so successful as gardening. Most settlements could keep no more than a couple of cattle, a few pigs, and perhaps several sheep and goats, plus some chickens. In 1817 there were only 636 cattle, 339 pigs, 108 sheep, 65 goats, and 16 horses in Russian America,[45] and most of the pigs, sheep, and horses were at Fort Ross. Pigs multiplied quickly, but their flesh smelled and tasted fishy because they were fed fish. Chickens, though sufficient in number, were likewise tainted from eating fish. Goats multiplied slowly; on Kodiak they increased by no more than thirteen within five years around 1800.[46] The propagation of cattle was especially disappointing. Their number decreased from 310 in 1818 to 220 in 1833 and 218 in 1860.[47] These totals could have met the company's annual beef needs in 1833 (50 to 67 beefs) but certainly not in 1860 (250 to 333 beefs), for these needs would have required the keeping of 188 to 251 head in 1833 and 938 to 1249 head in 1860.[48]* In 1860 the company admitted to its stockholders that "The rearing of cattle also does not present that degree of success which would be expected in the colonies from this branch of the economy."[49]**

---

* These requirements are based upon Khlebnikov's figure of 217 pounds of dressed beef from each animal and the head office's estimate of a ratio of slaughtered animals to total animals of 4 to 15. The head office calculated a requirement of 400 beefs for 1860 (*Doklad komiteta*, II, 503).

** As with vegetable gardening, there is some evidence that private cattle raising was more successful than company cattle raising. In 1818 the head office ordered that some cattle be given to deserving promyshlenniks and Creoles and some be auctioned to other promyshlenniks in the hope that they would be more successful than the company (Anonymous, "Obozrenie," 116). Similarly, in 1865 Governor Dmitry Maksutov (1863–67) recommended that company cattlebreeding be decreased, since it incurred more loss than gain, and private cattlebreeding be increased (USNA, 65: pt. 1, 113v.). Private livestock comprised mostly pigs and chickens, which were ample in number.

Only on Kodiak Island did stockbreeding meet with any success. "For stock raising pasture is very extensive and abundant" noted Captain Golovnin in 1818, when there were 500 cattle, 100 pigs, and 100 sheep belonging to the company in Kodiak Counter."[50]* But in the last half of the 1850s there was a considerable decrease in the number of cattle; at St. Nicholas Redoubt, for example, the number dropped from sixty to two.[51] Around 1860 on the Kenai Peninsula there were no more than fifty head, which were maintained at a loss.[52]

At New Archangel, there were usually less than a dozen head of cattle, and at the end of 1860 an inspector found only five to six cows and four horses on all of Baranof Island.[53] Cattle were equally scarce at other settlements. Even Unalaska, the second-ranking stockbreeding district in Alaska, had few cattle—only twenty in 1824, seventeen of which were at Captain's Harbor.[54]

Not only were there few cattle, but their flesh was greasy and tasted watery. They also gave little milk and butter. Kodiak Counter produced just over 1000 pounds of butter in 1832 (enough to meets its own needs) and just under 2000 pounds in 1834.[55] Only occasionally was there a surplus of butter for shipment to New Archangel.

Stockbreeding in Alaska was so unproductive that the company had to substitute fish for meat and to rely on imported beef and butter. At New Archangel it even had to buy from the Koloshes: wild sheep, grouse,** ducks, geese, and halibut. As early as 1830 Wrangel complained that "We buy much of our food every year on the Kolosh market, in spite of the ever-increasing prices, which are now extremely high."[56] Such reliance upon disaffected natives was indicative not only of the unproductive state of Alaskan agriculture but also of the precarious nature of colonial supply.

Problems

Agricultural production was limited by an inimical physical environment and by a deficient labor force. The main physical obstacle was the shortness and the rawness of the growing season. The frost-free period was

---

* Horses, introduced in 1794, had failed. They were reintroduced in 1842 from Russian California but by 1860 only one old mare remained. For hauling ice 12 more had to be imported. (USNA, 63: pt. 1, 192v.).
** In 1860, for instance, 1000 grouse were brought from Koloshes at New Archangel (*Doklad komiteta*, II, 95, 148).

barely long enough for the maturation of northern cereals and vegetables. Nowadays it lasts 180 days on the southern Kuriles (Urup Island), 170 days on the eastern Aleutians (Unalaska Island), 160 days
at Kodiak (St. Paul's Harbor), and 159 days at Sitka (New Archangel);
during the Russian period the frost-free period may have been even
shorter.* This meant late frosts in spring and early frosts in summer,
which were especially harmful to grain. In 1860 Governor Furguhelm
noted that on the Kenai Peninsula "at Ninilchik [a settlement of colonial
citizens] and St. Nicholas Redoubt trial sowings of rye and barley have
been made two or three times, but unfortunately they did not succeed.
The late spring, which usually begins in the middle [at the end**] of
May, and the overly early fall constitute insuperable obstacles to the
development of this important activity."[57] The company acknowledged
in 1860 that repeated attempts at growing rye and barley along Alaska's
coasts and rivers had failed because of the late spring, the early fall,
and the frequent rain and snow.[58] For example, in 1839 on a small
island near New Archangel the company made experimental sowings of
wheat, barley, and oats, which proved "very unsuccessful"; half of the
crop was rotted by the incessant rain and damp soil, and the remaining
half had to be harvested prematurely in order to avoid the fall frosts.[59]

But the rawness and wetness of the growing season was more damaging than its shortness. Owing to the high latitude, the proximity of the
Aleutian low pressure system, and the nearby mixing of cool and warm
ocean currents, most of the frost-free days were cloudy or foggy and
cool, so that crop growth was slowed, despite the long days in summer.†
Harvesting especially was thwarted by wet weather. Archmandrite Jo-

* Evidently the climate of Alaska between the mid-seventeenth century and the mid-
nineteenth century was colder and wetter than before and after, for notable glacial
advances, accompanied by lower temperatures and higher precipitation, occurred in
the early 1700s, at the end of the 1700s and the beginning of the 1800s, and in the
second quarter of the 1800s. So agriculture probably faced cooler and damper conditions than those that limit farming today. Although any climatic changes would have
been minor, they would have particularly affected marginal agriculture.
** In Russian America in the nineteenth century the Julian calendar (Old Style) was
13 days behind the Gregorian calendar (New Style) until the delineation of the International Date Line in 1869; thereafter the difference was 12 days, as in Russia,
until 1900.
† Nowadays the northern margin of significant agricultural settlement approximates
the isoline of 120 to 130 degree months (Fahrenheit). Sitka averages 145, Kodiak
116, Yakutat 103, and Dutch Harbor (Unalaska) 103 degree months. The water bal-
ance in these places is adequate, being 100 per cent at all except Dutch Harbor,
where it is 98 per cent.

seph reported in 1799 that on Kodiak it was impossible to grow grain, which always sprouted but never ripened because of excessive moisture.[60] Lisyansky observed in 1805 that "the air is seldom clear, and even in summer there are few days which may be called warm,"[61] and Golovnin noted in 1818 that the "fogs and rains, which are very frequent and occur two and three days of every week, would always interfere with agriculture."[62] Nevertheless, fair weather occurred more often and lasted longer on Kodiak than at New Archangel, especially in summer, because of Kodiak's slightly less maritime climate.* Visiting New Archangel (where between 1847 and 1862 the month of August averaged more than seven inches of rain scattered over 23 days) Golovnin remarked: "Grain cannot ripen there, where even common, coarse garden vegetables do not fully ripen in the open air . . . on account of the frequent or almost incessant rains."[63] At Unalaska, where between 1827 and 1834 there was an average of only four clear days each August, surface vegetables could not even be grown under glass because of the lack of sun in summer.[64] Little wonder that vegetables tasted watery.** But at least the plants bore fruit, whereas grain did not. In 1860 the company admitted in its annual report: "The late spring, which usually begins in the middle of May, and the premature fall, the frequent rain and fog, and other unfavorable characteristics of the climate constitute insurmountable obstacles to the development, to any degree, of this important article [grain] for the provisionment of the settlers."[65]†

Limited and mediocre soil, resulting from the rugged terrain and widespread glaciation, was the other major physical obstacle to agriculture. Baranov discovered early that there was little good soil and that it was found in patches only.[66] This lack was particularly felt at New Archangel, where in 1820 a Russian naval officer wrote: "near the fort there is so little space that it is insufficient for the necessary vegetable gardens," adding: "This lack of land deprives the local inhabitants of the cultivation of vegetable gardens and the keeping of cattle.†† In

* Kodiak's superiority was only relative, however. The summer of 1826, for example, was so wet that no hay or fish could be dried on the island (Khlebnikov, "Zapiski," 114v.).

** In 1860–61 Golovin wrote that on the coasts and islands, berries were watery and flavorless and flowers were odorless, also owing to the abundant rainfall (*Doklad komiteta,* II, 282).

† The overcast summer weather also hampered the drying of pelts, which were stretched on poles in the open air. Many pelts were spoiled by inadequate drying.

†† He also observed that there were several exiles who had been sent from Siberia for farming but were working for wages for want of land (Lazarev, *Zapiski,* 239).

1823 another Russian naval officer, Dmitry Zavalishin, noted that gardening was "very difficult because of the complete lack of earthy soil, which therefore had to be created artificially."[68] In 1845 this dab of garden was reduced by more than half by the construction of new buildings.[69] Elsewhere, too, farmland was inadequate. In Kodiak Counter most colonial citizens eventually abandoned agriculture partly on account of the shortage of fertile soil. An inspector concluded in 1861 that the soil of Alaska's islands was "perfectly barren, and unfit either for agricultural or grazing purposes."[70] Pests were another problem, at least at first. Shelikhov's initial plantings were ravaged by mice and birds. The latter devoured peas in particular. "Nature herself," an anonymous observer remarked, "at every step presents insurmountable obstacles to agriculture here."[71]

Stockbreeding's nemesis was insufficient hay. There was no shortage of grass for pasture and hay, especially on Kodiak Island,* but often it could not be made into hay, owing to many difficulties. First, the foul weather impeded cutting and drying. For example, at New Archangel, where haymaking took place between late July and early October, rain frequently lodged standing hay and soaked mown hay, and most of it was ruined. Second, haymaking required many hands on short notice, for sunny spells were brief and fields were scattered. But most hands were busy with other more important tasks. This was especially so in Kodiak Counter, where in 1834 it was reported that because of the "shortage of men and the dispersion of fields, and despite the abundance of grass, it is so difficult to stock hay for cattle for the winter that it is impossible to increase stock raising; consequently, it remains almost at the same level as 10 years ago."[72]** Furguhelm reported in 1860 that in Kodiak's rainy climate many hands were needed to make hay quickly but that they were occupied hunting sea otters or loading ice on ships or catching and salting fish or hauling supplies to outlying settlements.[73] So hay was usually not made until the middle of September, when it was too ripe (less nutritious) and the weather was rarely fine.

The shortage of hay was critical for livestock, who needed much fodder for the long and cold winter. On the Kenai Peninsula and Unalaska,

* The grass of the Aleutians, however, while abundant and succulent, was not very nutritious; moreover, unless it was manured it soon deteriorated under regular mowing, being replaced within three to five years by ferns, bunchgrass, and wormwood (Veniaminov, *Zapiski*, I, 55–56).
** It was added that the dearth of hay prevented the keeping of horses on Kodiak Island.

hay was required for up to eight months;* on the latter not only was
there no time for making hay, there was no wood for shelter.[74] Thirty-
two of the fifty cattle starved in 1830 and nineteen the following year.[75]
On Kodiak many young cattle perished during the long and severe winter of 1854–55, and the rest of the decade saw a "considerable decrease"
in the number of cattle in Kodiak Counter, thanks to the shortage of
feed.[76] As early as 1831 Wrangel had reported that the scarcity of hay
prevented Kodiak's cattle from meeting the beef needs of company employees,[77] although there were enough cattle to do so. And in 1832 he
rightly declared that "the difficulty of preparing hay for a large herd for
the whole winter will always be an obstacle to the multiplication of cattle to such a number that Kodiak could prepare enough salted beef for
the needs of the colonies."[78] At New Archangel the feed situation was
even worse. Rarely was enough hay made here to feed ten cattle.** Hay
was so scarce in the mid-1820s that the cattle were fed grain; it cost as
much to keep one animal as it did to keep one worker.[79] Sometimes hay
was brought from Kodiak and later was even imported from California—
up to 300 tons annually in the early 1860s.[80]† At this time the head office
estimated that a ration of one pound of beef per day for six months for
each of its 1200 colonial employees would total 108 tons of beef, which
would entail the slaughter of 400 head and the maintenance of 1500
head annually, which in turn would require, besides much pasture, some
3600 tons of hay for at least six months.[81] But the company could not
even begin to produce that much hay in Alaska.††

Livestock also suffered from inadequate supervision. On Kodiak in
1821 Governor Matthew Muravyov (1821–25) noted that cattle raising
was in poor condition because of poor supervision, and in 1832 Wrangel
was informed that untended cattle were being killed by falls from
cliffs.[82] On the Fox Islands pigs roamed almost at will and became half
wild. Predators killed many animals; on Kodiak, at least at first, calves,
sheep, and goats were devoured by dogs, and at New Archangel pigs

* Father Veniaminov, however, stated that hay was required for at least six months
on the Fox Islands (Veniaminov, *Zapiski*, I, 71).
** New Archangel's hay crop was "limited" in 1836, "Normal" in 1837, "sufficient" in
1838, "very meager" in 1839, "extremely poor" in 1840, and "very poor" in 1841.
The hay crop of 1840 was so poor that it had to be supplemented with dried potato
plants (USNA, 39:246, 40:291v., 42:306, 43:220v., 45:274, 46:266).
† In 1839 New Archangel imported hay from Fort Ross for Governor Kupreyanov's
two cows (Sutter, "Personal Reminiscences," 25).
†† There was also a shortage of feed for pigs. In summer they rooted at large, and in
winter they ate fish, which gave their flesh a loathsome taste.

and chickens were slain by large birds. Sometimes herds were decimated by disease; for instance, from October 1829 through April 1830, Kodiak suffered a "painful loss" with the death of sixty-two cattle from an infection and starvation.[83] Over-slaughtering likewise reduced the herds. The plight of cattle breeding on Kodiak was summarized in 1848 by Governor Tebenkov:

> It is necessary to maintain stock raising on Kodiak only because without it the economy of the colonies would be incomplete; there is no better place for it in the colonies. For all the efforts of my predecessors and of the managers of Kodiak Counter, stock raising never justifies the expenses that are required for its feeding, guarding, and other operations. A small amount of butter from it, and occasionally some meat—this is, as it were, a reminder that there are cattle on Kodiak. The manager of the counter, Murgin, surmising that the scarcity of milk cows and the generally small increase of cattle stemmed from the disproportionate number of bulls, ordered that all spare bulls be separated into one herd and removed. I sanctioned this measure but for all that I do not think that it is the cause. The cause lies in the climate, which is too severe to obtain as much milk from the cows as ought to be obtained; to this must be added the complete ignorance of cattle raising on the part of the natives, and no less so on the part of the Russians. These are the two main reasons for the slight success of our cattle raising. An attempt was made to import Yakuts; but this measure did not prove as successful as expected. To this must be added the production of hay, which was not always successful, as well as other more or less unforseen circumstances. All this leads to the conclusion that the cattle on Kodiak will never reach the point where they will justify their expense and trouble.[84]

The loss of livestock meant fewer draft animals and less manure—crucial shortages in view of the scarcity of manpower and the mediocrity of the soil. For want of oxen on Kodiak plows were drawn by Aleuts in 1806. And land travel was curbed by the lack of horses; instead sea travel by *baidarka* (kayak) and *baidara* (umiak) prevailed. Animal manure was so scarce that seaweed (especially sea cabbage) was used as fertilizer, and at New Archangel the gravelly soil was also fertilized with herring roe, fish remains, ground mussels, chopped twigs, and leaves.

Farming was further retarded by a shortage of implements and workers. In 1795 the missionaries of Kodiak tilled with sharp sticks for want of plows; by 1806 there were plows on the island but they were "very wretched."[85] More critical, few Russians were attracted to Alaska, thanks to its distant location and primitive state, including low wages, high prices, poor food, squalid housing, rampant disease, hazardous labor, mistreatment, and the like. Most of the few Russians who did come did not stay long (usually no longer than their five-year terms, unless they were indebted to the company), and few hands were available for long-term farming. Of a group of 175 Russians (thirty-five families) brought by Shelikhov in 1794, only four (three men and one woman) remained in 1820.[86] The heavy labor turnover was a major problem. From 1819 through 1831, 648 Russians (mostly promyshlenniks) arrived (largely via Okhotsk) and 403 Russians (mostly promyshlenniks) departed for a net influx of 245 persons in thirteen years or nineteen persons per year.[87] "The Russian population of America is so small that it not only stands in the way of expansion but prevents holding even the places which are now occupied," Rezanov declared in 1806.[88] Such holding included agricultural settlement. For the small labor force there were simply too many chores—trapping, fishing, building, hauling, repairing—most of which were deemed more important than farming as long as provisions could be obtained elsewhere without too much difficulty. Seldom were there enough men left for the day-to-day tasks. By 1825 cattlebreeding at Katmai and on Kodiak's nearby islands of Spruce, Woody, Marmot, and Long had to be discontinued because of the shortage of men.[89] For the same reason on Unalaska in the late 1820s and early 1830s few turnips were grown.

Not only were the Russians who practised agriculture scarce, they were often unskilled. In 1795 Archimandrite Joseph of Kodiak wrote Shelikhov that he would like "to start the raising of potatoes, cabbage and other vegetables here, but the main obstacle is that nobody knows anything about it."[90] A decade later the German naturalist George Von Langsdorff noted that Kodiak still needed persons well acquainted with husbandry.[91] Father Veniaminov, who spent a decade (1824–34) on Unalaska, wrote that at first "many of the Russians . . . did not even know how to plant potatoes."[92] Often promyshlenniks had no knowledge of gardening, according to Wrangel.[93] And even some of the colonial citizens lacked agricultural experience. Moreover, by definition most of them were old, sick, or incompetent. In 1847, after inspecting their settlement of fourteen families on Spruce Island, Governor Tebenkov reported that it could not exist without regular company assistance. The Russian fathers, he noted, were too old and too weak and their children could no more be taught agriculture than "wild birds" could be so taught; the climate and the soil were inimical to farming, even gardening; there was not enough pasture for cattle (which also needed hay six months of the year); and there was no fish or game on the island.[94]

The Russian farmers could not expect much help from the natives, since few Aleuts or Konyagas adopted agriculture wholeheartedly. In 1790 Shelikhov, hoping that the natives would follow the agricultural example of the Russians, wrote: "Within a short time it will be possible to train and utilize volunteers from among those savage tribesmen in agriculture, shipbuilding, and navigation."[95] This expectation was not realized, however, perhaps partly because of the atrocious example set by the Russians and probably partly because of the strong attachment of the natives to their traditional occupations of hunting, fishing, and gathering; these pursuits alone satisfied their food needs. A member of the first Russian circumnavigation observed in 1804 that the Konyagas ignored agriculture, and in 1835 Wrangel reported that the Aleuts showed "no inclination to begin farming at their homes, not even for their own use."[96] But by 1860 the Aleuts were raising some vegetables, fewer livestock, and no grain; in other words they were farming about as much as the Russians themselves. Of the Aleuts on Kodiak, Governor Chistyakov reported in 1828 that they did not know how to handle cows at all, owing to their untidiness, laziness, and perhaps disinclination; through negligence or ignorance, he went on to say, most calves died.[97]* And in 1865 Governor Maksutov noted that cattle rearing on the island was in "somewhat of a decline" because of the feed shortage at St. Paul's Harbor and because, for want of Russians at outlying settlements, Creoles were used as herders. Unfamiliar with cattle raising, the Creoles handled livestock so ineptly that the cows usually gave little milk, and often the cattle perished.[98]

The Koloshes were more successful agriculturalists, and particularly their output of potatoes aided the company. But they remained hostile, and this hostility hampered Russian activities, including farming. In 1802 they destroyed New Archangel and in 1805, Yakutat. In 1806 Rezanov reported that at New Archangel, which had been regained in 1804: "Our men do not go to the shipyard, nor to the forest to cut timber or burn charcoal, without loaded guns. At all other kinds of labor similar precautions are taken."[99] A company report of 1823 complained that foreign seafarers (Americans) incited all the native tribes against the Rus-

* In late 1828 two married Yakuts were sent to Kodiak to tend cattle; in 1829 Chistyakov reported that they had proved "much better" than the Aleuts and asked that fifteen more be sent to Kodiak as cattle herders (USNA, 31:192, 353v.).

sians and that many Kolosh chiefs had cannons. The armed Koloshes, the report added, were good marksmen.[100] As late as 1861 an inspector reported that "no Russian dared to go 50 paces from the fort of New Archangel" for fear of the Koloshes, who allegedly numbered 25,000 in 1841.[101] The Russians could not let their pigs feed in the woods lest the Koloshes kill them.

Finally, Russian occupation followed the eastern Siberian (fur trade) rather than the western Siberian (agricultural settlement) model; this meant that the fur trade pre-empted all other activities. Unlike Siberia, however, where agriculture and the continental fur trade conflicted spatially but not temporally, in Alaska agriculture and the maritime fur trade competed for the same time but not, of course, for the same space. In this competition agriculture was the loser, for it was not the raison d'être of the company, which naturally favored lucrative hunting over marginal farming—particularly when more bountiful sources of provisions were available. If expensive, these sources were made affordable by the high profits of the fur trade.* In 1805 Rezanov noted that "because of the lack of horses and the absence of men in summertime while hunting, grain cultivation cannot be pursued on Kodiak."[102] And in 1861 an inspector concluded that the principal obstacle to stockbreeding in Alaska was the company's preference for employing its insufficient workers in more profitable pursuits like hunting.[103] This point was reiterated by the *New York Herald* on April 29, 1867, when it informed its readers that the policy of the Russian-American Company had been "steadily opposed to directing the attention of its employes away from their lucrative fur trade, and for this reason agriculture has been discouraged."[104]

Farming and fishing also clashed, and again farming was the loser, for fishing's return was more reliable and more abundant. Again Rezanov noted on Kodiak in 1805: "Hunting and fishing occupy everyone from spring until fall: sick oldsters, wives, and children remain, so that the land is never plowed."[105] And in the same year an anonymous observer remarked:

---

* Alaskan agriculture was certainly costly and uneconomic. For example, in 1835 it was reported that company gardening on Unalaska was completely useless because it was done by 15 to 20 free Aleuts, who worked from mid-April until the end of May for 50 kopecks each per day plus food, which amounted to some 700 rubles, whereas only 20 to 30 barrels of potatoes were produced, and some of these had to be saved for seed (USNA, 37:383v.–84). Similarly, it was reported in 1865 that Kodiak's cattle were priced at only half their real value (USNA, 65:pt. 1, 113v.).

For the cultivation of grain on Kodiak so much effort has been ex-
erted but unsuccessfully; for almost every kind of grain sprouts but
never ripens, either because no warmth whatsoever occurs or because
sea fogs interfere; and because the Russians, having other more important business in the hunting of sea beasts, have stopped practising
grain cultivation; and the islanders [Konyagas], freely supplying themselves from the sea and not finding great need for grain, do not show
any inclination to it. . . .[106]

Similarly, by the late 1850s even most of the special agricultural class
of colonial citizens had forsaken farming for hunting and fishing; the
latter activities had proved more reliable and, directly and indirectly,
afforded them everything they needed.[107]

By then scattered gardens and straggling herds constituted Alaska's
agriculture. In the words of an official report: "In the colonies there is
some gardening, almost no cattle raising, and no grain cultivation." This
sorry state had, in fact, prevailed almost from the beginning. So it did
not take the company long to realize that perhaps a balmy southern
clime like California or Hawaii would be better suited to its agricultural
efforts.

Readings

Andreyev, A. I., ed., *Russian Discoveries in the Pacific and in North
America in the Eighteenth and Nineteenth Centuries,* trans. by Carl
Ginsburg, Ann Arbor, Mich., 1952.

Mitchell, J. Murray, "The Weather and Climate of Alaska," *Weather-
wise,* October 1958, 151–60.

[Shelikhov, Gregory], "The Voyage of Gregory Shelekhof," trans. by
William Tooke, *Varieties of Literature,* 1795, 1–42.

United States, Congress, Senate, *Russian Administration of Alaska and
the Status of the Alaskan Natives,* 81st Cong., 2d Sess., Senate Document No. 152, Washington, D.C., 1950.

7 FARMING IN NEW ALBION

Although the Russian-American Company's business profited from the great expanse of all the Aleutian Islands and the coastal mainland, for a very long time nowhere could it find a place suitable for grain cultivation. Either the soil or the damp coastal climate thwarts all efforts; and it is quite impossible to do without grain; for grain brought to the colonies from Siberia via Okhotsk is very expensive, and besides it is subject to loss because of frequent shipwrecks, from which the colonies often suffer dire starvation. By unavoidable necessity the company was forced to seek above [sic: below] 55° a place where it would be possible to establish grain cultivation.

Head Office of the Russian-American Company, 1817.

Colonization

Russian exploration and settlement of unoccupied territory south of Alaska was officially sanctioned by the first charter of the Russian-American Company. Article II authorized the company "To make new discoveries not only north of the fifty-fifth degree of north latitude, but farther to the south, and to occupy the new lands discovered, as Russian possessions, according to prescribed rules, if they have not been previously occupied by, or been dependent on, any other nation."[1]* In accordance with this article, the occupation of the Queen Charlotte Is-

---

* The company's second charter (1821), however, stipulated that no settlements were to be founded south of 51° N., but by then Russian California was already in existence.

lands and of Nootka Sound on Vancouver Island (then only recently abandoned by the British) was contemplated by Baranov around 1800. This intention was not implemented, however, probably because of the presence of many unfriendly natives. Then, during his inspection of the starving colonies in 1805–6, Count Rezanov visited San Francisco, where he obtained an emergency supply of provisions. Failing, however, to secure a trade agreement and marveling at Alta California's mild climate and fertile soil, he conceived the idea of founding a colony on the unoccupied coast of New Albion between Cape Drake and Puget Sound, in order "to establish agriculture and supply our population to the north and on the Aleutian Islands with its output."[2] Farming may have been his main motive, but he also wished to establish a base for tapping the almost virgin reserve of sea otters along the New Albion coast. The Gulf of Alaska had been overhunted, and the Northwest Coast bristled with hostile Indians and American traders. In addition Rezanov and Baranov wanted a southern foothold, a point d'appui, for imperial Russia in the scramble for possession of the Pacific coast between New Archangel and San Francisco. Rezanov's proposal was officially approved in 1809, and Governor Baranov dispatched his assistant, Ivan Kuskov, to find a "more suitable and a more advantageous place for a colony, which throughout its region would control hunting and trade with the Indians, open new hunting benefits for the company, and avoid the current difficulties in the delivery to our colonies of vital provisions and heavy ship materials, which the company now gets by virtue of the long, difficult, and often unprofitable route to Okhotsk and which are constantly becoming more expensive to convey."[3] Kuskov made four reconnaissance voyages to the south beginning in 1808. Originally he favored Bodega Bay (which he renamed Port Rumyantsev) as the site of the settlement, but in 1812 with ninety-five Russians and eighty Aleuts he selected instead an old Indian ground eighteen miles farther north. This spot had more timber, as well as arable, pasture, and water. The redwood fort, christened Ross or Slavyansk by Kuskov, was opened in September.* This marked the beginning of Russian California, or Ross Counter, which came to extend eight miles inland between Cape Mendocino and Cape Drake (Map 6).

Fort Ross was situated about 100 feet above the sea atop a marine terrace covering less than a square mile and abutting abruptly on the Pacific on the west and the low but rugged Coast Ranges elsewhere. The

* The establishment was sometimes called Kuskovo by the Californios.

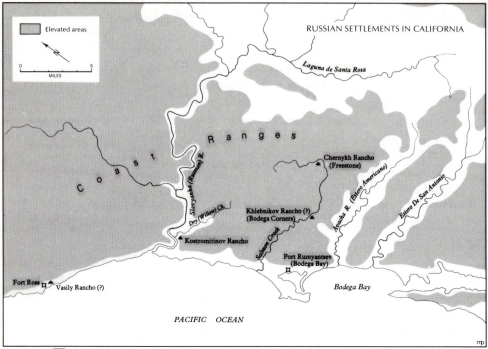

Elevated areas

0   5
MILES

RUSSIAN SETTLEMENTS IN CALIFORNIA

Laguna de Santa Rosa

R   a   n   g   e   s

C   o   a   s   t

Slavyanka (Russian) R.

Dry (Willow) Ck.

▲ Chernykh Rancho
(Freestone)

Salmon Creek

Khlebnikov Rancho (?)
(Bodega Corners) ▲

▲ Kostromitinov Rancho

Atascha R. (Estero Americano)

Estero De San Antonio

Port Rumyantsev
(Bodega Bay)
☐

Fort Ross ⌂ ▲
Vasily Rancho (?)

Bodega Bay

PACIFIC   OCEAN

mp

MAP 6

site was typical of company posts in Russian America, where the hunting of sea otters and the checking of hostile natives were equally urgent. There the Russians faced Europeans as well as indigenous rivals, for the Spaniards of Mexico had long been expecting Russian encroachment. Wrangel inspected Fort Ross in 1833, describing it as follows:

> On flat, clayey ground atop a hill sloping steeply to the sea has been erected a wooden palisade along the edges of a fairly extensive area forming a regular square; at two diagonally opposite corners in connection with the palisade have been erected two watchtowers with cannons defending all sides of this so-called fortress, which in the eyes of the Indians and local Spaniards, however, seems very strong, and perhaps unconquerable. Within this enclosure by the palisade itself stand the Company buildings: the house of the Manager of the Factory, barracks, magazines, a storehouse, and a chapel, all kept in cleanliness and order, conveniently and even prettily situated. However, almost all the buildings and the palisade itself with the watchtowers are so old and dilapidated that they need repairs, or they will have to be replaced by new structures. On this hill, outside the fortress, facing and paralleling its sides, are located two Company cattle barns with pens, spacious and kept in excellent cleanliness, a small building for

Fort Ross, 1840. (*Oregon Historical Society*)

storing milk and making butter, a shed for Indians, a threshing floor, and two rows of small Company and private houses with gardens and orchards, occupied by employees of the Company. On a cleared spot beyond this outskirt stands a windmill. Below the hill by a landing for baidarkas have been built a spacious shed and a cooperage, a blacksmithy, a tannery, and a bathhouse.[4]

Fort Ross Cove was very exposed, so Port Rumyantsev (Bodega Bay), although shallow, became Ross Counter's chief harbor.* It consisted of several houses and some storehouses and corrals which held grain, cattle, and furs bound for New Archangel. Twenty Russians and fifty Aleuts lived there in 1816.[5]

Ross Counter also included the Farallones, a bleak cluster of rocky islets about thirty miles off the Golden Gate. There the company stationed an artel of Aleuts with a Russian foreman for the procurement of sea otter and fur seal pelts, sea lion meat, and sea bird eggs.

The population of Russian California varied from year to year and from season to season but gradually increased, although it rarely included more than 100 Russians or 500 persons altogether.

Trends

Agriculture began at Fort Ross with its founding, seed and stock being obtained from the Californios and the Indians. Initially, however, the

---

* There ships could anchor alongside the beach but at Fort Ross they had to stand offshore and lighter their cargo ashore.

settlement was preoccupied with hunting and shipbuilding. Kuskov, Ross Counter's first manager (1812–21), concentrated on hunting; in 1818 Golovnin noted that "he does not lose sight of his chief business: the dispatch of artels for otter hunting."[6] Already by 1816, however, the counter's annual catch of sea otters had fallen below a hundred. Then, from 1818, in the mistaken belief that California oak was suitable for vessels, attention was focused on shipbuilding. Four ships were built, but they soon rotted, and in 1824 shipbuilding was discontinued. The Russians also undertook some manufacturing, mostly of articles needed by the Californios (implements, utensils, furniture, boats), but this activity declined after the opening in 1821 of Alta California's ports to foreign trading vessels, which brought cheaper goods that undersold those made at Fort Ross.

Agriculture became the colony's dominant activity, with the company even hoping to provision the Kamchatka Peninsula and the Okhotsk Seaboard as well as Alaska from Russian California. By 1817 Kuskov had already begun to pay more attention to farming. That year Baranov had been instructed to leave Ross "in such a condition that the Spaniards have no reason to think that it is anything more than a hunting place only; but meanwhile under this pretense to increase grain cultivation, cattle raising, poultry raising, vegetable and fruit growing, and plantations, augmenting the settlement itself with the necessary buildings."[7] Kuskov's successor, Carl Schmidt (1821–24), greatly expanded agriculture, employing more men in farming and bringing more land under cultivation. He tried to interest not only the Russians and Creoles but also the Aleuts by giving them free seed. Private plowland especially was expanded. In 1823 twice as much wheat as before was planted.[8] Schmidt's efforts were so successful that Fort Ross became self-sufficient, no longer having to use provisions from Alta California bound for Alaska. His successor, Paul Shelikhov (1824–30), was told by Governor Muravyov in 1824 that "as the Kyakhta is the last ship to be built at the settlement of Ross, everybody must now be turned to the repair of buildings, grain cultivation, orcharding, and gardening, as well as cattle raising, which must be increased, not decreased."[9] Shelikhov had every patch of arable land near the fort (some as far as two miles away) cultivated, and from 1826 through 1829 the value of foodstuffs exceeded the value of furs shipped from the settlement to New Archangel.[10] In 1827 the French traveler Duhaut-Cilly observed that "fishing [hunting], which was at first very productive, becomes less plentiful from day to day, and within some years will be entirely null; but the director, counting no more except secondarily upon these products, has been for several years busied chiefly with husbandry."[11]

The concentration on agriculture from the mid-1820s was also closely connected with the opening of Alta California's ports to foreign trading vessels in 1821. Thereafter the market for Russian goods declined, with serious consequences, for the company's procurements of California grain and beef were negotiable in goods or piasters only. (By the early 1830s, however, some California suppliers were accepting bills of exchange redeemable at St. Petersburg.) Nevertheless, Wrangel complained in 1834 that sales of Russian manufactures to the Californios were "rare and negligible because the foreigners controlling trade in California have brought all the possible needs of the inhabitants and supply them at such low prices that it is not possible for us to compete with them."[12] Wrangel's predecessor, Governor Chistyakov, had noted that trade with the Californios was "suffering more and more from visiting foreigners who sell their goods cheaper than ours." "Without piasters," he added, "it will be difficult to get wheat."[13] Chistyakov's fears were not fully realized but at the time the company felt that they would be, and the precaution of expanding agriculture at Fort Ross was taken. With such expansion the company hoped, too, that grain would be cheaper and better, for California grain cost fourteen kopecks per pound and contained sand and pebbles in the proportion of one-tenth.[14] And with the secularization of Alta California's missions in 1833 their agricultural production plummeted. Ross Counter loomed even larger as an alternative source; in fact the same year saw the founding of two new farms. As early as 1825 the head office regarded agricultural expansion at Fort Ross as the best way of solving Russian America's chronic problem of food supply.[15]

Manager Peter Kostromitinov (1830–38) boosted agriculture even more than his predecessors by founding several farms (ranchos) in the interior. In 1831 he explored inland and had grain planted along the Slavyanka (Russian) River and may have undertaken cultivation in the Arroyo de Fumalancia (Tamalancia Valley), some eight miles east of Port Rumyantsev. By 1833, however, the arroyo had been abandoned. In that year Kostromitinov founded a farm on a wooded plain five miles east of the port and two miles north of the Avacha River (Estero Americano). Apparently called Khlebnikov Rancho by the Russians and Three Friends Rancho by the Californios, this farm was probably located near the present town of Bodega Corners. In 1840 it comprised a "sufficient" to a "large" amount of cultivated land.[16]

Kostromitinov also had grain planted on new plowland along the lower course of Dry Creek, which was later renamed the Rotchev River (and is now called Willow Creek). This new farm was called Kostromitinov Rancho, or sometimes Halfway House, since it stood midway on the coastal trail between Fort Ross and Port Rumyantsev. Along the trail were also four hilltop lookouts used by herders from the rancho. Boats were kept at the rancho for crossing the Slavyanka River where it received the Rotchev River. In 1840 the farm, which was quoted as having "superior pasturage," consisted of 98 to 100 acres of cultivated land.[17]

In 1838 Manager Alexander Rotchev (1836–41) founded New Rancho on the Schmidt Plain some fifteen miles northeast of Port Rumyantsev near the present town of Freestone. It was "very suitable" for gardening; mostly peas and beans were sown, as well as corn.[18] In 1839 this establishment was renamed Chernykh or Jorge* Rancho and its locale the Khlebnikov Plain. In 1840 the rancho, which had "remarkable vineyards," extended over about 200 acres of fenced and cultivated land.[19]

At Fort Ross itself, there was an unnamed farm** which in 1840–41 consisted of 70 to 79 acres of mostly fenced and cultivated land.[20] And at Port Rumyantsev, too, there may have been a farm; according to General Mariano Vallejo, Commandant of Alta California's *frontera del norte*, it was called *Fiutuye* or *Fiutinje*.† Forty-three persons lived there in 1833.[21] The Russians may have established more farms; General Vallejo asserted that agriculture was conducted at seven places in Russian California,[22] and General John Sutter, who eventually bought the colony, noted at Fort Ross in 1839 that there were "a great many farms in the vicinity all belonging to the Russians."[23] Suffice to say that by the 1830s Ross Counter's primary function was farming, which was being conducted on an extensive scale. At the beginning of 1839 agricultural assets formed 65 per cent of the value of the counter's total capital assets.[24] Later the same year Sutter noted that the settlement had been established "for seal and sea-otter hunting, but now the agricultural interest was in the ascendant."[25]

---

* Jorge is the Spanish equivalent of Chernykh's first name, George.
** This farm may have been called Vasily Rancho.
† This may have been a Spanish corruption of *vyutyuzhka*, meaning "a flat place."

Chernykh Rancho, 1841. (*Oregon Historical Society*)

Operations and Production

Russian California's seasonal agricultural round followed the example of the Californios. Plowing of grainland (with horses and oxen) occurred right after the first rains in November or December, broadcast seeding in December and January, and reaping (with sickles) in July and August at the height of the dry season (May to November). Threshing was done with horses, who trampled the sheaves on the bare ground or on a wooden platform. Mainly fall wheat and some fall barley were cultivated. Because as much grain as possible was grown, the two-field rather than the three-field system of cultivation prevailed, whereby one field was sown in wheat for three years running and the other field was grazed by cattle.[26] Two crops of vegetables were raised each year; the first crop (hydrophytes) was planted in November and harvested in April and the second crop (xerophytes) was planted in May and harvested in October. Livestock grazed all year; summer was the slaughtering season.

Most of the agricultural work was done by local Indians (Pomos), who initially volunteered but eventually were conscripted. In 1825 the company reported that cultivation was "always done with the help of the neighboring Indians," who were paid in food and clothing.[27] The number of Indian hands increased with the expansion of cultivation—from

100 in 1825 to 150 in 1833 and 200 in 1835.[28] Creoles and Aleuts helped to tend livestock, some of which was privately owned. Plowland, on the other hand, was largely in private hands. The company did not mind private farming so long as it did not interfere with its work, for it served as a means of augmenting production and of collecting debts. In 1826 Governor Chistyakov ordered that one-third of the agricultural produce bought from private individuals at Fort Ross be accepted as payment for debts.[29] Even with a mediocre harvest a farmer could meet his own needs and still have a surplus to sell to the company.

It will be recalled that the company had hoped that agriculture in Russian California would meet the needs not only of Alaska but perhaps of Kamchatka and Okhotsk, too. But production, although not inconsiderable, failed to meet even Alaska's demand. The most important crop was grain, for it was more sorely needed by the company than vegetables, fruit, or beef. Grain yields were higher than the average yield in Russia (3-fold to 4-fold) but still not high enough for the company. Table 8 shows the annual yield of company and (from 1822) private wheat and barley at Fort Ross from 1813, when the first crop was harvested, through 1833, when new farms were established inland.

Yields remained mediocre throughout the twenty-one-year period. On the average company wheat yielded 5½-fold and private wheat 5-fold, and company barley yielded 4½-fold and private barley 7-fold. The best grain yields both achieved by the company, were 14½-fold for wheat and 13-fold for barley. Sowings increased steadily, being negligible under Kuskov, appreciable under Shelikhov, and considerable under Kostromitinov. This progression reflected the decline of hunting during the late 1810s and the decline of manufacturing and cessation of shipbuilding in the mid-1820s as agriculture expanded.

Yields improved somewhat during the first half of the 1830s with the opening of virgin and fog-free plowland in the interior. Wheat acreage doubled between 1828 and 1832. In 1835 the grain crop failed; 420 to 525 bushels of wheat and barley seed yielded 2100 to 2625 bushels (5-fold) instead of 4800 to 6000 bushels (12-fold) as expected.[30] Actually the yield was average. The worst crop failure occurred in 1836, when at Fort Ross itself wheat yielded 7-fold, although Himalayan barley and English oats (both introduced in 1835) yielded 40-fold and 17-fold, respectively.[31]* Another crop failure occurred in 1837. Wheat acreage de-

---

* The crop failure was such that in 1837 it was necessary to ship 331 bushels of Chilean wheat to Fort Ross from New Archangel as seed (USNA, 39: 331v., 374, 406v.).

Table 8. Yields of Wheat and Barley at Fort Ross, 1813–33

Year	Planted (bushels)				Harvested (bushels)			
	Wheat		Barley		Wheat		Barley	
	company	private	company	private	company	private	company	private
1813	1	0	0	0	2	0	0	0
1814	3	0	0	0	13	0	0	0
1815	3	0	0	0	5	0	0	0
1816	9	0	0	0	29	0	0	0
1817	9	0	0	0	5	0	0	0
1818	18	0	7	0	64	0	35	0
1819	19	0	18	0	55	0	48	0
1820	25	0	1	0	104	0	9	0
1821	23	0	9	0	142	0	20	0
1822	33	35	9	6	256	252	26	73
1823	43	69	14	12	441	673	37	69
1824	62	131	0	25	558	722	0	263
1825	122	145	30	49	1093	1102	149	276
1826	258	211	21	68	1240	612	65	459
1827	305	156	32	108	1405	574	106	432
1828	388	133	81	81	2661	364	382	322
1829	516	172	0	0	2077	671	0	0
1830	410	149	40	4	1477	397	32	22
1831	181	99	35	30	2605	475	461	191
1832	—326—		—144—		—3674—		—709—	
1833	—227—		—154—		—2263—		—816—	

Sources: Gibson, "Russia in California," 208; Khlebnikov, "Zapiski," 392–92v.; *Materialy*, III, 151–52; Potekhin, "Selenie Ross," 12; Tikhmenev, *Historical Review*, I, 255, 266.

creased by half between 1832 and 1837. In 1838 up to thirty-two tons of grain were planted—more than ever before—which yielded 10-fold.[32] In the same year a visitor to Fort Ross noted: "Wheat produces here but 10 for 1,"[33] a meager showing, it seemed, in light of the higher yields of Alta California. But it would have satisfied the company had it been the average yield instead of twice the average yield.

Russian California's grain yields were certainly lower than those of the missions of Alta California, where the farmland was fogless, irrigated, and virtually unlimited. In the early 1820s grain yielded on the average 6½-fold at Fort Ross but 40-fold at the missions.[34] Over-all wheat yields averaged 5-fold in Russian California but 12-fold at the northern missions and 20-fold at the southern missions of Alta California.[35] Cyril Khlebnikov, a company employee who frequently visited the missions and ranchos as a commercial agent, contended that during the 1820s wheat at the missions yielded 60-fold to 70-fold in good years, 10-fold to 15-fold in poor years, and 20-fold to 30-fold in average years.[36] Grain yields, it seems, were generally three times as high in Mexican California as in Russian California.

The mediocre yields naturally meant mediocre production. From 1822 through 1836 Ross Counter produced 32,149 bushels of wheat and 325 bushels of barley[37]—an average of 2143 bushels of wheat and 325 bushels of barley annually.* In the eight years from 1826 through 1833 Alaska received only about 4000 bushels of grain from Fort Ross[38]—merely one-twelfth of its needs. Russian California was hardly a company granary.

Vegetable growing was somewhat more successful. Kuskov, who liked gardening, paid special attention to vegetables by raising radishes, beets, turnips, lettuce, cabbage, peas, and beans in abundance; the radishes and the turnips were bland but large. He also raised musk-melons, watermelons, and pumpkins, which yielded abundantly, up to 800 watermelons being grown in good years.[39] Sometimes from 100 to 200 pounds of wild mustard were collected and shipped to New Arch-angel.[40] Potatoes usually yielded from 6-fold to 8-fold but sometimes from 100- to 250-fold.[41]** Most of the vegetables could grow at any time of the year and were double cropped. Their size was remarkable. At Fort Ross in 1817 the American traveler Peter Corney saw radishes weighing "from one pound to 28 pounds, and much thicker than a stout man's thigh, and quite good all through, without being the least spongy,"[42] while inland from Fort Ross in 1824 Otto Von Kotzebue saw cucumbers of "fifty pounds' weight, gourds of sixty-five, and other fruits in proportion."[43] These testimonials are undoubtedly exaggerations; nevertheless, it seems that the vegetables were large. Golovnin described gardening at Fort Ross in 1818:

> Here the land produces many crops in abundance: cabbage, lettuce, pumpkins, horseradishes, carrots, turnips, beets, onions, and potatoes now grow in Kuskov's gardens; watermelons, muskmelons, and grapes, which he has recently cultivated, even ripen in the open air. The garden vegetables are very pleasant in taste and sometimes reach an

* In 1838, 10,320 bushels of wheat were harvested; in 1840, 6450 bushels ([Duflot De Mofras], *Travels*, II, 4; Nunis, *California Diary*, 106).
** According to the company's official historian, however, potatoes never yielded less than 11-fold (Tikhmenev, *Historical Review*, I, 254).

extraordinary size, for example, one horseradish weighed 48 pounds, and 36-pounders are often obtained; here pumpkins are 54 pounds, and one turnip weighed 12 pounds. The potato is especially productive: at Ross one apple [potato] usually yields one hundred, and at Port Count Rumyantsev one apple [potato] sometimes yields 180 or 200, and besides they plant it twice each year; sowings of the first half of February are reaped at the approach of May, and in October ripen those which were planted in June.[44]

The vegetable crop, like the grain crop, probably varied from year to year. For example, it is recorded that very few vegetables and fruits were produced in 1825 but that in 1826 there was a good crop—potatoes, carrots, turnips, beets, cabbage, pumpkins, cucumbers, onions, garlic, and watermelons.[45] Generally, however, more vegetables were produced than could be used locally for food and seed.[46]

It seems that fruit growing was confined to Fort Ross itself (Ross Rancho) and Chernykh Rancho. The first fruit tree, a peach, was brought from San Francisco in 1814; it bore fruit in 1820. More peach trees were brought from Monterey in 1818, and 1820 saw the introduction of 100 apple, pear, cherry, peach, and bergamot seedlings, which bore fruit in 1828. The vine was brought from Lima in 1817; it was picked in 1823. In 1826 it was noted that the orchard at Fort Ross was "well arranged" and contained apples, pears, peaches, and grapes; in 1833 it included 400 trees and 700 vine stalks.[47] By 1840 there were two orchards, situated on the lower slopes of the coastal hills about half a mile behind the fort to avoid the nocturnal settling of cool air. At Chernykh Rancho, there were more vine plants than fruit trees; in 1840 the orchard contained 2000 vine stalks and some trees. Russian California generally produced a surplus of fruit.[48]

The first livestock were probably obtained at the beginning of 1813, when the Spanish officer Moraga brought twenty cattle and three horses to Fort Ross.[49] Subsequently more animals were obtained from Alta California as well as from the neighboring Indians. Between 1823 and 1826 an epidemic decreased the number of livestock, especially sheep. With the opening of new ranchos in the interior from 1833 the number of livestock doubled, and by the late 1830s Ross Counter was by far the foremost stockbreeding district of Russian America.

Nevertheless, because of over-slaughtering, there were probably never more than 5000 head of livestock in Russian California. (By comparison, at Sonoma Mission there were 4000 sheep, 3000 cattle, and 700 horses in 1834 and 10,000 cattle and 4000 to 6000 horses at General Vallejo's Petaluma Rancho in 1838.[50])

The cattle were large, one steer yielding 831 pounds of beef,[51] but the small size of the herd precluded the production of much beef or butter. In 1831 no more than fifty cattle (12,640 pounds of beef) could be killed without depleting the herd and only 2889 pounds of butter (31 to 36 pounds per cow) were made.[52] The number of cows gradually increased—68 in 1825, 147 in 1832, 223 in 1837—but they produced only half of the milk and butter that they should have produced because of the shortage of dairy maids (one cow should have averaged forty-five pounds of butter yearly).[53] Each Russian owned up to three cows, but their wives were "unwilling" to milk them.[54] Butter production did not blossom until the management of Shelikhov, who improved the supervision of cattle.

Pigs ate shellfish, which tainted their meat. Sheep were butchered for mutton, which was used mostly as salary in kind, and sheared for wool, up to 1800 pounds of which was obtained yearly during the 1820s.[55] Chickens, turkeys, ducks, and geese were also kept. Golovnin reported in 1818 that the chickens and geese were numerous and healthy,[56] but Wrangel noted in 1833 that there was an "insignificant" number of poultry at Fort Ross.[57]

Exportation

Owing to the limited acreage and mediocre yield of wheat and barley and the few livestock, small amounts of foodstuffs were shipped from Russian California to Alaska and none whatever to Kamchatka or Okhotsk. The shipments only partially satisfied Alaska's needs. Ross Counter did not begin to export grain until 1826, when New Archangel expected 45 tons from the counter but received only 25 tons.[58] From 1826 through 1833 Fort Ross shipped 108 tons (3600 to 4500 bushels) of wheat and barley to New Archangel,[59] or an average of 13 tons annually, whereas 180 tons were needed annually. From 1833, thanks to the expansion of grain land in Ross Counter, the company had to buy no more than 90 tons of grain yearly, or one-half of its needs, whereas in the late 1820s and early 1830s it had to buy 180 tons yearly.[60] But in 1836, the year of the counter's worst crop failure, no wheat at all was exported to New Archangel.[61] And nothing was exported in the following year, either. In 1833 Wrangel estimated that in order to satisfy all of the beef needs of Ross Counter and half of the beef needs of Alaska (7223 pounds annually) without depleting the counter's herd, at least 1500 to 2000 head would have to be kept,[62] but only during the last five years of its existence were there that many cattle in the counter. And probably only in 1838 did Russian California meet Alaska's total beef needs (14,445 pounds). In order to supplement the counter's inadequate production of meat the Russians hunted mountain goats, mountain sheep, and bison, as well as seals, sea lions, and even murres.[63] Occasionally fish were caught in the Slavyanka River, but the catch was meager; Wrangel reported in 1834 that "in all our Colonies, except the settlement of Ross, the inhabitants feed on fish."[64]

Thus, Russian California failed in its object of meeting the food requirements of Alaska, let alone of Kamchatka and Okhotsk. Inconsiderable amounts of foodstuffs were produced and even lesser amounts were shipped to New Archangel. In 1827 the head office declared that "So far as agriculture is concerned [at Fort Ross] . . . it is unlikely that the results will be satisfactory" and "It is obvious that agriculture at Ross cannot supply the colonies with food, which as before has to be imported from California."[65] In 1828 Governor Chistyakov advised the head office that all hope for grain cultivation at Ross should be abandoned.[66] The head office agreed, adding that it would therefore be "quite useless" to expand agriculture in Russian California.[67] Although expansion was undertaken five years later, it was to little avail.

Problems

Agricultural production was beset by a variety of cultural and physical problems, including the multipurpose nature of the colony. It had been formed for both hunting and farming, and shipbuilding, trade, and manufacturing, were also undertaken. Baranov regarded Fort Ross as mainly a hunting base and a trading depot, and Kuskov considered its hunting function to be primary. Especially during the first decade of the colony's existence was farming overshadowed by hunting, trading, and shipbuilding. Around 1820 the interference of hunting with farming was noted by the promyshlennik Zachary Chechenev:

> The chief manager at Sitka had sent Mr. Khlebnikoff strict orders not to neglect hunting sea-otter and with the Aleuts at the settlement and in many instances either the hunting or the farming had to suffer. Generally the last was the case.[68]

Three years later he noted that shipbuilding, too, was interfering with agriculture:

> In the year 1823 two ship builders were sent down to the settlement [from New Archangel] and nearly all the men were kept busy at getting out timber and building vessels, while scarcely anything was done on the farm.[69]

Various other duties likewise detracted from farming, as Duhaut-Cilly observed in 1827:

> The colonists, at once workmen and soldiers, after being busied all day with the labors of their various occupations, mount guard during the night. Holidays they pass in reviews and in gun and rifle practice.[70]

So agriculture was deprived of undivided attention, and such attention was essential to its success in view of the other problems. These other problems became more critical from the mid-1820s, when farming loomed larger.

There was also conflict between company and private farming operations. Private farming was especially encouraged by Manager Schmidt, who permitted his men to own cattle as well as plowland. Governor Chistyakov expressed the company's attitude in 1826: "The establishment of private plowland would be useful to the company if the men cultivating it—on various pretexts—were not to retard the course of company work."[71] It seems that company work did suffer, for in the same year Cyril Khlebnikov, manager of the New Archangel Counter, complained that the private cultivators tilled their land with much free assistance from the company in the form of implements, horses, seed, and even Indian laborers. Furthermore, a considerable amount of land was already in private hands, and many employees were requesting even more land. Khlebnikov opposed further alienation of company land because the company had little land left suitable for cultivation, and it was already being squeezed for pasture. The company's only consolation was that it still owned the best plowland at Fort Ross. Khlebnikov also suggested that the company should buy back private land when its owners left the counter.[72] This was done, but private farming continued to exist, probably because it was a necessary and productive supplement to company farming.

The multipurpose character of the colony aggravated the chronic shortage of workers, particularly after the founding of new farms during the 1830s. In 1825 the head office blamed the failure of agriculture at Fort Ross on the shortage of hands.[73] The counter's population probably never exceeded 550 Russians, Creoles, Aleuts, and Indians. And of this small number the few Indians did most of the agricultural labor, although Manager Rotchev recalled that every year he had difficulty recruiting enough Indians for harvesting.[74] The Aleuts served mainly as hunters, and the Russians and Creoles acted chiefly as guards, overseers, artisans, cooks, and the like. In 1823 only twelve of the Russian population of fifty were engaged in agriculture.[75] In 1826 Shelikhov requested fifteen men from New Archangel to repair the stockade and buildings but received only six.[76] From 1834 through 1836 a total of fifteen employees left the counter and were not replaced, and at a time when cultivation was being expanded. Governor Kupreyanov reported that Manager Kostromitinov was "now encountering difficulty because of the shortage of men" and that fifteen replacements had to be sent "so as not to forego the commencement there of the extension of cultivation to new places."[77] Thirteen replacements were finally sent in 1837.[78] But the following year half (sixty) of the Aleuts living in the counter were withdrawn to reinforce hunting parties in Alaska which had been decimated by disease.[79]

This shortage of agricultural labor was part, of course, of the larger problem of the shortage of manpower in Russian America, but in Russian California this problem was exacerbated by the loss of men through the capture of poaching company hunters by the Californios and the desertion of disgruntled employees. The Russians were forbidden to hunt in California waters (except by special arrangement), but this stricture did not stop them from taking every opportunity to poach, usually during a trading voyage and often in San Francisco Bay itself, right under the noses of the Californios. Occasionally some hunters, mostly Aleuts, were seized when they went ashore for rest, food, and water and to dry and grease their baidarkas. During his stay at San Francisco in 1816 Von Kotzebue was astonished to hear from the Governor that there were many Russian prisoners in California; Adelbert Von Chamisso, the naturalist on Von Kotzebue's expedition, learned that two Aleut captives and three Russian deserters were imprisoned at Monterey.[80] The more salubrious climate and the more indolent life of Alta California sometimes induced company employees to desert. Father Veniaminov noted this attraction during his 1836 visit to Fort Ross:

It must be confessed that the happy combination of California's air, the clear, blue sky, the location, and the vegetation peculiar to this latitude can at first strike and charm anyone who was born [north of] and had not been south of 52 degrees, especially the inhabitants of Unalaska and Sitka.[81]

Khlebnikov admitted: "From our settlement of Ross at first as well as later several Russians deserted."[82] In 1821 alone six men absconded.[83] "It is bad, very bad, that men are deserting us," Governor Muravyov told Manager Schmidt in 1822.[84]* The desertions were also prompted by the hard work and the stern discipline at Fort Ross. Especially the Indian laborers were abused. Wrangel reported to the head office in 1834:

> At the time when they reap grain Indians from the nearby tundra gather in the settlement for commensurate pay, or by necessity, when there are few hunters, then they forcibly collect as many Indians as possible, sometimes up to 150 persons, who for 1½ months are occupied without rest in Company field work. . . . Not only humanity but also wisdom demand that the Indians be encouraged more: from the bad food and the negligible pay the Indians have stopped coming to the settlement for work, from which the Factory found itself forced to seek them in the tundras, attack by surprise, tie their hands, and drive them to the settlement like cattle to work: such a party of 75 men, wives, and children was brought to the settlement during my presence from a distance of about 65 verstas [43 miles] from here, where they had to leave their belongings without any attention for two months.[85]

Such treatment was hardly conducive to assiduous farmwork. Ironically, the Indians, who at first had welcomed the Russians as their allies against enslavement by the zealous Franciscan missionaries of Alta California, later fled similar enslavement by the Russians, who had become desperate for laborers.

Manpower was further reduced by disease. Within three weeks in April, 1828 at Fort Ross twenty-nine Creoles and Aleuts died of measles.[86] And in the spring of 1833 an infection incapacitated almost the entire payroll and killed many Indians.[87]

The scarcity of farm hands meant that livestock as well as crops were inadequately tended; indeed, the cattle were not tended at all in 1817.[88] During the 1820s two Russians and two natives minded the livestock.[89]

---

* Such desertions may have persuaded Schmidt to permit more private farming.

Because of lax supervision the cattle foraged as far as thirteen miles from the fort from July until December, so that the cows had to be driven long distances for milking and consequently grew tired and gave little milk.*

Russian California's agricultural workers were not only few in number but also short on experience. Not all of the managers themselves were agriculturally competent. Chamisso judged Kuskov a clever, and experienced man,[90] but his main business was hunting, in which he was "very well versed."[91] Although Kotzebue thought that the Spaniards should take a lesson in husbandry from Schmidt, who had brought that science, he noted, "to an admirable degree of perfection,"[92] Governor Muravyov told the head office in 1823 that he was not completely satisfied with Schmidt because "he is foolhardy, and reading and writing are not his forte."[93] And in 1824 Muravyov told Khlebnikov that he had noticed "much thoughtlessness in all his [Schmidt's] activities."[94] The governor was especially dissatisfied with Schmidt's shipbuilding and his promotion of private agriculture.** His successor, Shelikhov, was praised by both Manager Khlebnikov and Governor Chistyakov, who rated the new man as "very good," terming him an expert in agriculture.[95]† Kostromitinov, however, was agriculturally inexperienced, and Rotchev was known as a poor manager.[96] The Russian, Creole, Aleut, and Indian workers displayed ineptness in the growing of crops and the rearing of livestock. Particularly under Kuskov was there a shortage of skilled farm hands. When some Californios from San Francisco brought the counter's first cattle in 1812, they had to show the Russians how to milk the cows.[97] The Russian workers used any pretext to avoid working company land.[98] Such shirking is not surprising, for Kruzenstern noted that "none but vagabonds and criminals enter the company's service as Promuschleniks."[99] Langsdorf agreed, stating that "the greater part of the Promüschleniks and inferior officers of the different settlements are Siberian criminals, malefactors, and adventurers of various kinds."[100] Hagemeister asserted in 1817 that "The promyshlenniks who are sent from Sitka [to Fort Ross] are, with few exceptions, *from the worst of the worst*, and unaccustomed to labor in Russia"; he added that for the Aleuts agricul-

* The cattle foraged far away also because of the paucity of grass during the dry season.
** Schmidt was a navigator by training.
† This is not surprising if one assumes that the company would have naturally chosen such a man to direct the counter at a time when agriculture was being favored.

tural work was "also unusual."[101] And Wrangel declared: "The local farmers scarcely have an understanding of the cultivation of fields; generally like promyshlenniks arriving in America, they consist of all kinds of riff-raff."[102] It is true that some of the promyshlenniks were of peasant stock, but their bucolic experience was usually distant and crude. So in 1826 the head office advised Governor Muravyov to select from new employees those who had been peasants, who had not forgotten their "natural trade," and to send them to Fort Ross for farming.[103] In 1827 five men—"knowledgeable and competent in grain cultivation"—were sent,[104] but so few could not have had much impact.

The Creoles and the Aleuts were even less experienced than the Russians. In 1825 Muravyov asserted that the Creoles were "completely unsuitable" as farmers.[105] So were the Aleuts. A promyshlennik stated that "the Aleuts did not like to watch the cattle, not being used to such large animals, and often the Aleuts, in place of driving in the animals were chased to the fort by wild bulls and steers."[106] Another promyshlennik recorded that the Aleuts knew nothing about raising vegetables; the scarcity of fresh vegetables accounted in part for the prevalence of scurvy at Fort Ross in the summer of 1818 and the winter of 1818–19.[107]

The agricultural ignorance of the Indians was even more critical, since they did most of the farming, at least from the mid-1820s. These Indians were Coast Pomos, who inhabited the coast between the Gualala and Slavyanka rivers and who numbered around 500 when the Russians arrived. They were primarily gatherers, as well as fishermen and hunters. In late autumn they migrated to the interior, and in late spring they returned to the coast, where they harvested wild celery, wild onion, and wild potato on the inner margin of the marine terrace, as well as wild oats, which ripened in late June. In July they were hired by the Russians, mainly for the harvest. But they were unskilled and unreliable. Indian women, for example, milked cows but, according to Khlebnikov, proved "quite inept" and "completely unsuitable" as farm hands.[108] In 1825 the company complained that the Indians, unaccustomed to regular work, quickly became bored and left.[109] If the harvest failed, the Indian laborers were held responsible and made to remain to redeem the lost crop with other work.[110] So they became understandably reluctant to toil for the company. At first they worked voluntarily for the Russians, but eventually they had to be recruited by force. The Indians retaliated; in 1833 Vallejo reported that Manager Kostromitinov was "very disgusted" with the Indians for having stolen standing wheat from the fields.[111] They also rustled cattle; in 1838 they killed up to 100 head.[112]*

Agricultural techniques were as primitive as the agricultural workers. Threshing, for instance, was done with horses in a "very wretched fashion" and was attended with "much loss." The method, employed throughout California, involved a round, wooden threshing floor, 35 or 36 feet in diameter, built inside a wooden or stone wall and completely covered with sheaves of grain to a depth of from two to five feet; thirty or more horses were driven inside this "circus" and whipped around and around, their hoofs threshing the grain, and after about an hour the horses were driven outside, the top layer of trampled straw was removed, and the horses were driven inside again and worked until the remaining sheaves became chaff, which was then winnowed. Although few kernels were left in the ears,** much grain was discarded with the chaff. The animals easily injured themselves while milling around the threshing floor, pregnant mares often miscarrying and sometimes dying.[113] To improve the situation, in 1836 the agronomist George Chernykh built a wooden Scottish threshing machine at Fort Ross. It employed two horses and was capable of threshing 45 to 60 green (undried) sheaves per hour or 700 large sheaves in ten hours, although in the summer of 1836, owing to the obstinacy of the workers and the inexperience of the horses, four or five men and four horses (which were changed every two and a half hours) threshed only 350 to 550 sheaves daily and only up to 10,000 large green sheaves altogether. Formerly the threshing of 1000 sheaves of wheat per day required the services of twenty-five Indians and 120 horses. With Chernykh's machine, however, nearly half of the ears of grain were removed and deposited with the straw or chaff.[114]

The introduction of this threshing machine was part of the company's attempt in the mid-1830s to increase the agricultural productivity of Russian California through modernization. Chernykh, a graduate of the Moscow Agricultural School and a former director of the Kamchatka Agricultural Company who had been hired for "the improvement and the advancement of agriculture," reached Fort Ross in 1836 and immediately proceeded to try to reform farming. He substituted oxen and mules for horses as draft animals and planted a greater variety of crops,

* This rustling prompted the Russians in 1838 to graze the cattle along the left bank of the Slavyanka instead of on the hills around Fort Ross, where they were normally pastured but where they were more accessible to the Indians (USNA, 41: 253).
** The horses threshed more cleanly than flails, for the kernels were very firmly attached to the ears. Besides, as Wrangel said, "On account of the shortage of men, it is not possible to use flails" (Gibson, "Russia in California," 208).

including Siberian rye, English oats, Himalayan barley, and Virginia tobacco. Although the counter had its best harvest ever in 1838, Chernykh's efforts were of little avail. In 1837 Governor Kupreyanov told Manager Rotchev that the "expansion of stock raising, gardening, and orcharding under the supervision of such a manager as Mr. Chernykh should have afforded a commensurate increase in returns, but New Archangel has received very little from them."[115]

The chief physical impediment to agriculture in Russian California was the unsuitable nature and the limited amount of farmland. The colony had been founded amid Russian fears of Spanish and Indian resistance; especially the possibility of Indian hostility must have seemed very likely in the light of previous experience with the Koloshes. So the colony's site was selected with at least one eye to defense. This site, a narrow and sandy-to-stony tableland bounded by a 100-foot precipice on the seaward side and by deeply dissected and thickly wooded hills to landward, was admirably suited to defense but not to agriculture, for the arable land was mediocre in quality and minimal in quantity. The Californio Gervasio Argüello, who visited Fort Ross in October of 1816, stressed the defensibility of the settlement in a report to Governor De Solá of Alta California: "There cannot be observed more than one point of access, since the place is encircled by the mountain range abutting the very shore; therefore access is rather poor on account of the terrain." He added: "The terrain on which this establishment is situated may measure about two miles in length and, on the narrowest point, barely one; all the rest is rugged mountain range and sea. This little area of soil is much broken up and rocky."[116] This impression was echoed one year later by a promyshlennik who wrote: "Our settlement is situated on a rough coast and on land not easily cultivated."[117] In 1833 Wrangel noted that "In the vicinity of the settlement the land is hilly, dissected, cut by deep ravines, and covered with trees; the soil is mostly loam, but there is also chernozem."*[118] According to Khlebnikov, the soil was partly chernozem and partly sandy loam and unequal in fertility.[119] Nowadays generally dark in color, fairly high in organic matter, and usually medium to fine in texture, these natural grassland soils should be grazed rather than tilled; at least they are not well suited to unirrigated field and truck crops such as the Russians planted.[120]

The limited amount of arable land meant that agricultural expansion

* The soil is not, of course, true chernozem, which is confined to the temperate grasslands. Russians tended to classify any dark, tillable soil as chernozem.

was also limited. In 1826 Shelikhov reported that very little land suitable for grain cultivation remained, and even it was needed for pasture.[121] So in 1827 Governor Chistyakov ordered that no more private land be alloted to employees and that no more buildings be erected outside the fort.[122] In 1828 the head office confirmed that all arable land at Fort Ross was under cultivation and that no more arable land was available near the fort; some tracts two miles away were already being cultivated.[123] Hauling sheaves of grain to the threshing floors from these steep-sloped and distant fields was slow, arduous work. Chernykh asserted in 1836 that all land that could be cultivated was then sown.[124] There were probably never more than 250 acres of grainland.

Being tilled every year, the scarce arable land was soon exhausted. In 1833 Wrangel noted that the "necessity of sowing all places suitable for plowland every year without interruption, from which much plowland has now already lost its strength, does not return the seed, and should be abandoned, while they cannot be replaced by other places."[125] Nevertheless, some fields had to be fallowed, and the amount of cropland was reduced even further. For example, exhausted wheat fields that did not return the seed in 1832 were fallowed for several years.[126] Moreover, the fields were not plowed well and were not manured. The livestock supplied ample manure, but it could not be collected because the animals ranged so far. The exhausted land became infested with weeds, especially wild oats, which hampered the growth of wheat, as in 1830, when the fields with the heaviest growths of wild oats were fallowed for a year in order to eliminate them. The weeds could not be exterminated by repeated plowing because of the shortage of hands; it was only with great difficulty that enough hands were recruited for a single plowing, let alone two or three. The grazing of the weedy fields every two or three years became the sole method of weed control in the 1830s; this meant, however, that the precious plowland was periodically unavailable for planting.

Land for pasture as well as for grain was limited by the rugged and wooded locale. (The mild winters, however, permitted year-round grazing, so that no hay had to be made.*) And during the dry season (May-November) grass was so parched that the livestock had to range up to a dozen miles from Fort Ross, making it was impossible to tend them properly. Often the animals strayed off and sometimes perished. Grass

* The little hay that was made was "as coarse as reeds" (Tikhmenev, *Historical Review*, I, 266).

was abundant during the wet season (winter), but by the mid-1820s, owing to the encroachment of cropland, little pasture remained and the stock had to forage afar in this season, too. Pasture grew so scarce that every patch of plowland had to be strongly fenced to exclude hungry livestock.

To overcome the dearth of agricultural land the company made several attempts, mostly halfhearted, to enlarge the area of Russian California. Indeed, the company retained the counter long after it had proved unprofitable partly because its agricultural output was needed to supplement the provisions obtained irregularly by trade with Alta California and partly because its territory might, the company hoped, be expanded inland at an opportune moment. The colony's founders, in fact, never expected that it would be confined to its original site but that it would be enlarged inland with state assistance.[127] The state, however, refused to help directly. Tsars Alexander I (1801–25) and Nicholas I (1825–55), both arch-conservatives, were preoccupied with European affairs. They also feared that bold action in California might cause war with Spain, the United States, or Great Britain. Russian encroachment upon Spanish territory was further complicated by Alexander I's steadfast advocacy of the doctrine of legitimacy and by his treaty of friendship with Spain. Russian expansion in the North Pacific also fell into official disfavor when its most ardent advocates were found to be associated with the abortive Decembrist Revolt of 1825 at the end of Alexander's reign. His successor, reactionary Nicholas I, who was known as the "gendarme of Europe," refused to recognize the revolutionary Republic of Mexico, and this refusal precluded the official negotiations that were necessary to Mexican cession of more land to Russian California. Lacking imperial assistance, the company was not strong enough to enlarge its colony by itself, just as the Californios were never strong enough to dislodge the Russians. Meanwhile, Russian expansion eastward and southward of Fort Ross was being blocked anyway, initially by the founding of new missions (San Rafael in 1817 and Sonoma in 1823) and ultimately by the opening of ranchos by foreign settlers in the last half of the 1830s.*

The climate was characterized by moderate and equable temperatures, ample winter rainfall, and frequent summer fogs; strong northeasterly winds also prevailed. Inland, beyond the coastal mountains,

---

* The breakup of the missions by secularization in the mid-1830s perhaps encouraged the company's main attempt at expansion in 1835.

temperatures were more extreme, rainfall was less plentiful, and dense fogs and high winds were much rarer. Hence the company's desire to expand inland. On the coast the damp fogs, which sometimes blanketed Fort Ross for entire weeks, provided some moisture for crop growth during the dry season; at the same time, however, they kept summer temperatures low, thereby slowing crop growth. Father Veniaminov described the chilling effect of the coastal fogs during his stay at Fort Ross in 1836:

> It is so easy to catch a cold here that the inhabitants of Ross who were born here become ill almost every year on account of the rapid transition from heat to cold; this transition can be from 28 to 8 degrees in no fewer than 2 hours, as if you had been in the mountains in an intolerable heat and then had descended the mountains and suddenly entered a fog and a temperature of 7 degrees [Reaumer].[128]

More important, the fogs were conducive to stem rust, the main cause of wheat failure in the counter. It was described by the agronomist Chernykh:

> It forms under the following conditions: on a foggy summer day (when the wheat is covered with dew), if suddenly at noon, at the hottest [time of the day], the fog clears and the sun shines directly on the wet ears and the entire stems, then a powder just like iron rust forms first on the stem and then on the ear. It is still more explainable by the fact that through the fog at noon a small opening often appears, through which the sun's rays penetrate to the ears, and the spot illuminated by the sun at this time is stricken by rust. It is extremely infectious: beginning from the spot where rust is introduced, the entire area is infected in accordance with the direction of the wind. Californians always mow infected places, but it helps little. Since the causes of rust depend upon the atmosphere, it is hardly possible to find a weapon for wheat against this pernicious disease. If it strikes soon after kernelling, then the grain becomes small and wrinkly, if during blossoming, then the grain will not form at all. It does not affect grain that is fully formed and ripe.[129]*

To avoid the fogs the Russians shifted cultivation from the seashore to the hillsides in 1821. Yields increased, but as Governor Wrangel wrote in 1833:

* Chernykh errs, of course, in ascribing rust to the atmosphere. Rust is a fungus whose spores are spread by the wind, with atmospheric conditions simply retarding or hastening its formation.

The fog bank along the coast of Russian California. (*James R. Gibson*)

Unfortunately, however, such places found here that are not subject to the baneful influence of sea fogs are very few and are small patches on the slopes of high, steep hills accessible only on foot or on horseback, so that, having overcome cultivation of this steeply mountainous plowland with no little labor, after harvesting there remains the extremely difficult and slow work of hauling the sheaves on shoulders to the threshing floor or to such places whence they can be conveyed by horses.[130]

Furthermore, the shortage of plowland forced the Russians to cultivate every available square foot, so that some grainland was still blighted by fog and rust, as in 1826 and 1830.

A dearth of sunshine undoubtedly impeded the ripening of fruit; vegetables certainly suffered, too. And summer drought seared pasture; inland at Khlebnikov and Chernykh ranchos, where summer aridity was aggravated by the higher temperatures and not alleviated by fogs, crops were also desiccated. The high southerly winds of late fall, accompanied by heavy rains, occasionally damaged property. In November 1824, for instance, strong winds killed several cattle and flattened the fort's walls in three places.[131]

It is uncertain whether earthquakes interrupted farming at Fort Ross, which straddled the San Andreas Fault. On this subject the sources are silent. The San Juan Capistrano earthquake of 1812, one of California's four great tremors,* destroyed Capistrano and Santa Ynez missions and killed many residents, and a major earthquake along the San Andreas Fault occurred in 1838. However, even if Ross Counter was affected by these shocks, any agricultural damage was probably minor.

It is certain that diseases and pests hindered agriculture. An epidemic killed 200 sheep in the mid-1820s,[132] and in 1837 up to 70 cattle died from "bloody flux" (scours).[133] Stem rust has already been mentioned as the principal cause of wheat failure; according to Chernykh, the wheat crop was usually ruined by rust.[134] Weeds, especially wild oats and wild mustard, were a problem. So were predators. Occasionally livestock were slain by bears, wolves, and cougars, which were very common. Such losses were inevitable, since the pasture was unfenced and distant and the livestock were unguarded. Some birds were pests; "black sparrows" (blackbirds), for example, ravaged grain. In 1815 the grain harvest was reduced by many birds. So-called "ground hamsters" (field mice, moles, or pocket gophers) greatly hampered gardening, undermining the roots of the plants[135] and devouring potatoes. (Otherwise, it was noted, there would have been enough to meet the needs of the counter.)[136] Even skunks ravaged crops.**

---

* The others were the Fort Tejon quake of 1857, the Owens Valley quake of 1872, and the San Francisco quake of 1906 (which damaged the chapel and displaced the fences at Fort Ross).

** Crops and pasture may have also been damaged by Indian burning, which was practised in order to kill game, especially mice and lizards, and to roast standing wild rye.

LOSSES

In view of the foregoing obstacles it is not surprising that agriculture failed to fulfil the company's high hopes, although production was not negligible. Indeed, considering the formidable array of problems plaguing farming it is a wonder that it produced as much as it did. But the counter was undeniably unprofitable. From 1825 through 1829 upkeep averaged 45,000 rubles annually and income 38,000 rubles (29,000 from hunting and 9000 from farming) for an annual average loss of 7000 rubles.[137]* It is noteworthy that hunting generated more than three times as much income as farming. In 1832 expenses amounted to 55,378 rubles and revenues to 47,779 rubles.[138] The counter went even further into the red with the expansion of farming and the virtual cessation of hunting in the last half of the 1830s; in 1837 upkeep cost 72,000 rubles while farming earned but 8000 and hunting nothing.[139]** From 1838 through 1841 revenues averaged 26,000 rubles and expenses 77,000 rubles yearly, with losses averaging 44,000 rubles per year.[140] The French agent Duflot De Mofras quoted anonymous Russian officers at Fort Ross as saying that the counter was annually losing 10,000 piasters (14,286 rubles) around 1840.[141]

From 1836 hunting was no longer profitable,[142] and by 1840 the company could buy wheat from Mexican California more cheaply than it could grow it in Russian California.[143] In fact the counter was going deeper and deeper into debt to Californios with purchases of grain and beef. These debts totaled 12,000 rubles in September 1838 and 22,676 in May 1839.[144] In the spring of 1838 Governor Kupreyanov told the head office that "the benefit derived from the settlement of Ross for the colonies and for the Russian-American Company is generally quite insignificant and is far from commensurate with the sacrifices that are expended on the upkeep of the settlement."[145] It was agreed that the counter was both economically and politically disadvantageous, and the company decided "to abandon the settlement of Ross, to abolish the counter, to withdraw the garrison, to remove the promyshlenniks, implements, and machinery, and to sell the remainder to residents of San Francisco."[146] In the spring of 1839 the Minister of Finance was informed:

---

* Another source gives the same figure for average upkeep but a lower figure for average income (Tikhmenev, *Historical Review*, I, 421).

** Another source states that income totaled 11,890 rubles (Tikhmenev, *Historical Review*, I, 422).

At first the considerable expenses on the upkeep of the settlement were partly covered by occasional but fairly lucrative catches of sea otters in the vicinity of Ross and along the coast of California. Later, when this hunting had almost ceased, the head office cherished the hope of enlarging its possessions and occupying places suitable for grain cultivation and cattle raising to the extent of being able to supply the other counters with wheat, salted beef, and butter, besides supporting the garrison. Under the present circumstances this hope has been completely dashed, and the head office finds no grounds whatever for, and does not see any good purpose in, further occupation of the settlement of Ross. Even in political terms the possession of Ross is attended with inconveniences. It is not supported by any deed and is not recognized by other powers.[147]

By late April of that year the tsar had approved the company's request to abandon Russian California, and on April 27 the head office issued an order to liquidate the colony. The first to leave were eight families (thirty-three persons), who returned to New Archangel on the *Helena* in September of 1840; the rest, save several dozen, left in September of 1841 on the *Chichagov*.[148]* In the same year the colony was sold to General John Sutter of New Helvetia for 30,000 piasters ($30,000, or 150,-000 rubles), payable within four years in, significantly, California supplies, chiefly wheat.[149]** The sale reduced the company's total losses on Ross Counter to 32,000 rubles.[150] But if the company had been induced to sell in 1839 because the colony was unprofitable, it had been able to sell because of the terms of an agreement signed earlier in the same year with the Hudson's Bay Company. This agreement assured Russian America an adequate supply of provisions for ten years, something that Russian California had not been able to do for even one year.

Readings

Chernykh, E. L., "Agriculture of Upper California," *The Pacific Historian*, Winter 1967, 10–28.

Du Four, Clarence John, Essig, E. O., *et al.*, "The Russians in California," *California Historical Quarterly*, September 1933, 189–276.

Gentilcore, R. Louis, "Missions and Mission Lands of Alta California,"

---

* The abandonment of Ross Counter released sixty-six men for undermanned Alaska (USNA, 46: 223v.).
** Sutter did not pay this debt until 1852, however.

Annals of the Association of American Geographers, March 1961, 46–72.

Gibson, James R., "Russia in California, 1833: Report of Governor Wrangel," *Pacific Northwest Quarterly*, October 1969, 205–15.

———, "Two New Chernykh Letters," *The Pacific Historian*, Summer 1968, 48–56, Fall 1968, 55–60.

Khlebnikov, K. T., "Memoirs of California," trans. by Anatole G. Mazour, *Pacific Historical Review*, September 1940, 307–36.

Kniffen, Fred B., "Pomo Geography," *University of California Publications in American Archaeology and Ethnology*, 1939, 353–400.

Mahr, August C., *The Visit of the "Rurik" to San Francisco in 1816*, Stanford University Publications in History, Economics, and Political Science, II, 1932, 267–460.

Tarakanoff, Vassili Petrovitch, *Statement of My Captivity Among the Californians*, Los Angeles, 1953.

Tchitchinoff, Zakhahar, *Adventures in California*, Los Angeles, 1956.

8 FARMING IN THE SANDWICH ISLANDS

Baranov, retaining in his ripe old age the boldness of his youth, but already less successful in his enterprises, extended his designs right up to the Sandwich Islands and in 1816 tried, through Doctor Schaffer, to occupy that of Atouai [Kauai]. This attempt could form the subject of a ludicrous poem. It had no result other than the cessation of compliments and presents that Baranov and Tameamea [Kamehameha] I sent each other by the masters of American vessels.

Frédéric Lütke

In 1815–17, while the Russian-American Company was trying to strengthen its foothold in New Albion, it was also trying to establish itself in the Sandwich Islands. There, through colonization and trade, the company hoped to procure foodstuffs and other products not only for Alaska but for the Kamchatka Peninsula and the Okhotsk Seaboard as well. This short-lived and somewhat bizarre venture was conducted with much daring and panache by a mercurial German employee of the company who became embroiled in Hawaiian internal politics in a vainglorious attempt to gain the islands for an oblivious tsar. It was the only notable case of bold action by Russia in the international arena of the North Pacific, and even this action was unofficial.

Images

Russian control of the Sandwich Islands was part of Baranov's dream of a Russian commercial empire spanning the North Pacific. The islands were strategically located halfway between Asia and the Americas on the busy trans-Pacific sea lane. In the words of Russian traders, "the highway to Canton leads through the Hawaiian Islands."[1] They were a bountiful victualing station and a salubrious relaxation area, as well as a source of skilled native sailors and valuable sandalwood.*

The question of Russia's presence in the Sandwich Islands first arose in 1804, when the first Russian round-the-world expedition visited the islands. At this time two chieftains, King Tomari (Kaumauli) and King Tomi-Omi or Tomeamea (Kamehameha), were vying for control of the archipelago. Tomari held four islands, while Tomi-Omi possessed seven islands, many sailing vessels, and more than eighty English mercenaries (runaway sailors).[2] Gladdened by the arrival of the Russian ships, the underdog Tomari beseeched the officers of the *Neva* to give him firearms and gunpowder and to assist him against Tomi-Omi, offering in return "to come with his island [Kauai] under Russian domination."[3] The Russians, however, were unable to accept this offer because their plenipotentiary, Count Rezanov, had already left for Kamchatka aboard the *Hope*.

Meanwhile, one of the officers on the *Neva*, Basil Berkh, did not fail to note the possibilities of the islands. Noting that sugarcane, sweet potatoes, yams, taro, bananas, coconuts, and watermelons were the main products of the archipelago, which also abounded in cattle and pigs, Berkh saw it as a promising source of foodstuffs for Kamchatka. He suggested that a Russian navy vessel be sent every fall from Kamchatka to the islands, winter there, and return to the peninsula in May.[4] "These islands, which do not belong to any European power, must belong to Russia," declared Berkh, who envisioned them as a haven for Russian ships as well as a food base for Kamchatka.[5]

In 1809 the *Neva* again visited the islands, this time under Lieutenant Hagemeister. According to a Scottish passenger, "It would appear that the Russians had determined to form a settlement upon these islands; at least preparations were made [on Kodiak] for the purpose. . . . The ship had a house in frame on board, and intimation was given that volunteers would be received."[6] The *Neva* remained for three months, and Tomari again asked for protection against Tomi-Omi. Again the Russians refused his plea. The projected settlement did not materialize, and the

---

* This yellowish, close-grained, fragant wood, whose odor repels insects, was much used in ornamental carving and cabinet-working and was especially suitable for chests and boxes. From it the Chinese extracted an oil for sacramental purposes.

ship returned to Kodiak with a cargo of salted pork and dried taro. Hagemeister reported to the head office that any of the islands could supply all of the wants of every Russian settlement on the Pacific, since sugarcane (for rum and sugar), wheat, and taro (which could be used in place of bread) were grown on the islands in abundance. He added, however, that prospects for Russian trade with the islands were not bright because their commerce was entirely and personally controlled by Tomi-Omi, who demanded high prices; moreover, Hawaiian foodstuffs had become expensive as a result of frequent calls by Yankee ships en route to Canton. Hagemeister felt that such difficulties could be circumvented through the establishment of a Russian settlement on the archipelago. He opined that Molokai, owing to its fertility, would be the most suitable island for Russian occupation, which would require some 40 men (half for defense and half for agriculture).

Colonization

In 1815 Governor Baranov, who since 1806 had periodically exchanged gifts with Tomi-Omi via American vessels, finally launched a scheme for establishing a Russian post on the islands. The pretext for his scheme was not Tomari's plea but the missing cargo (valued at 100,000 rubles) of the company ship *Bering*, which in 1814 had foundered at Atuvai (Kauai) after stopping there for provisions while sailing from Okhotsk to New Archangel. Much of the cargo had been saved, but it was then stolen, and the wreck was looted by the subjects of Tomari, who claimed everything cast ashore on his island. As his agent Baranov chose George Schaffer, a German physician who had arrived in the colonies in 1815 aboard the *Suvorov*.* Schaffer, who spoke English and French, seemed suitable for the venture; besides, Baranov's other qualified lieutenants were then indisposed, Ivan Banner being on Kodiak and Kuskov at Fort Ross. To allay suspicion Baranov instructed Schaffer to sail on the American ship *Isabella* with the alleged intention of investigating the natural history of the islands. Actually, however, he was to win Tomi-Omi's confidence and persuade him to trade with the company, as well as force Tomari to either return the *Bering*'s cargo or compensate the company with sandalwood. The *Discovery* under Lieutenant Jacob Podushkin and

---

* Actually, Lieutenant Michael Lazarev, commander of the *Suvorov*, who quarreled with Baranov, had found Schaffer so contentious and intolerable that he had dismissed him at New Archangel.

the *Kodiak* under Captain George Young (an Englishman in the company's employ) were to follow Schaffer with merchandise for the anticipated trade and with support for Schaffer in case Tomari refused to surrender the stolen cargo. Schaffer and Podushkin were also ordered to seek Tomi-Omi's permission to found a factory on Oahu, to be manned by a dozen Russians. In the words of Baranov's biographer:

> Baranov knew very well that, on account of the proximity of the Sandwich Islands, he should have established a factory there long ago for the receiving and processing of local products, which were needed in the colonies and which cost less than those ordered from foreign ships.[7]

The islands offered rum, tobacco, taro, pork, salt, mulberry oil, rope, fiber suitable for nets, fish, sandalwood, and other products. Baranov especially wanted sandalwood but also pork and beef (there were many tame and feral cattle and pigs on the islands), taro and vegetables, hemp and bark rope, tutui nuts, tobacco, and rum.

Reaching the islands with two Creole boys in late 1815, Schaffer visited Tomi-Omi and soon became his physician, successfully doctoring both the king and his queen. In gratitude Tomi-Omi promised to order Tomari to recompense the company for the *Bering*. More important, he also allowed Schaffer to select "several places in his domain for economic development"; in addition, a lake and several plantations on Rannoa (Lanai) and a lake and some land on Voaga (Oahu) near Honolulu harbor, together with their residents, were granted to Schaffer by the king. Schaffer built a house at Honolulu and planted tobacco, corn, watermelons, muskmelons, pumpkins, and other vegetables on the donated tracts.

Relations between Tomi-Omi and the doctor soon became strained, however, partly because of the latter's arrogant behavior and partly because of rumors circulated by the American Wilson Hunt to the effect that the Russians intended to seize the archipelago. Meanwhile, the *Discovery* arrived in the spring of 1816 with some thirty Aleuts. A month later, seeing that Tomi-Omi was not going to let him build a permanent factory on Voaga, Schaffer (with 100 Russians and Aleuts from the company ship *Ilmen,* which had called at Honolulu for repairs) left Voaga for Atuvai, where he was welcomed by Tomari in the "most friendly fashion." Schaffer had decided to side with Tomari against Tomi-Omi, using the conflict between the two kings as a means of annexing all or part of the "land of eternal spring" to Russia. After winning Tomari's trust by curing him of dropsy and his wife of fever, the doctor proposed that Tomari request Russia's protection, and the latter, without fully understanding the implications of such a request, readily agreed. At an elaborate ceremony staged by Schaffer, Tomari signed a pledge of loyalty to Tsar Alexander I, requesting his protection of the Sandwich Islands, and accepted a naval officer's uniform, which he sometimes wore, and a Russian flag, which he hoisted over his village. Schaffer and Tomari also signed four secret treaties. Tomari agreed to return the salvaged cargo of the *Bering;* moreover, the Russians were granted all of Voaga and parts of other islands and permitted to establish factories and plantations throughout Tomari's kingdom and to monopolize its trade. In October, Schaffer received 400 native families and several tracts of land on Atuvai, where he built a fortified factory and tried to grow cotton, tobacco, sugarcane, fruit, and vegetables on a large scale. Then he built another factory at his plantation near Honolulu. Finally, Tomari also agreed to prepare two shiploads of sandalwood per year for the company and to barter up to 12,000 rubles' worth of foodstuffs (including 15,000 dried taro roots and 100 pigs) per year to the company. In return for these concessions Schaffer promised to help Tomari conquer all of the islands by buying him a warship and taking command of 500 of his troops.

Expectations

To the "Russian doctor" the Sandwich Islands were a paradise awaiting Russian exploitation:

> If the Sandwich Islands could have a monarch like Russia's great Alexander, truly the majority of our brothers could live in a golden age. Here bread grows in trees and on the ground; each can prepare what foods he wishes: pineapples, grapes, bananas, cocoanuts, sugar cane, oranges, lemons, etc . . . , grow here in abundance; wild and domestic livestock abound, domestic cattle can pasture on lush meadows the year round, and the sea teems with tasty fish. Everyone can choose the climate which suits him best; the islands are free of all epidemic ills—even smallpox is unknown here. On all the islands you will meet nothing harmful, not even a poisonous serpent. All human needs and all types of delight can flourish on the Sandwich Islands! With what beautiful garb are their fields covered! What a prospect for maritime manufactures and trade![8]

Schaffer felt that "Cotton should be Russia's main objective in the Sandwich Islands, and yields in a short time more return for a small expenditure and effort than all the fur trade on the Northwest coasts."[9] He figured that 49 square feet could yield 5 pounds of clean cotton fiber twice yearly and that 200,000 piasters' worth of cotton fiber could be harvested annually from up to 3500 acres of poor soil.[10] Taro and corn Schaffer deemed "particularly important for the Russian settlements on the Northwest coast of America and even for Okhotsk and Kamchatka, for these are unrivaled as foodstuffs, and extremely suitable for transport and for prolonged storage."[11] He believed that the company could obtain 200,000 to 300,000 piasters' worth of taro and corn annually from Kauai alone. Schaffer also asserted that he could guarantee to supply tobacco not only to the Northwest Coast of America but even to Kamchatka, Okhotsk, and Japan for an annual return of 100,000 piasters.[12] Regarding Hawaiian salt, Schaffer exclaimed: "What a boon for the Russian holdings on the Northwest coast of America, and Okhotsk and Kamchatka!," where ". . . it could easily yield an annual profit of 100,-000 Spanish piasters, not counting the profit which the company could receive annually through salt herrings, salmon, and other fish."[13] The quixotic doctor also envisioned a return of 200,000 piasters yearly from Russian monopolization of Hawaiian sandalwood and "no small return" from sugarcane which, he noted, was of a height and quality he had never seen anywhere else, from oil nuts, which "could supply not only Russia but all Europe," and from grapes, "which if carefully prepared ought to make wine which should surpass Madeira." The fruits of bread plants, pineapples, coconuts, oranges, lemons, bananas, and melons would also bring high returns.[14] Finally, he foresaw other possibilities:

> Through these holdings Russia can obtain in a short time the most skillful and experienced seafarers. The Chinese will have to permit the Russian flag to wave in Canton. The English and Americans will have their trade cut and limited in Europe as well as in China. . . . Russia is in a position to disrupt the trade of the English in the East Indies, and can be as strong on the sea as she is invincible on the dry land. . . .
>
> The Sandwich Islands must be made a Russian West Indies and likewise a second Gibraltar. Russia must have these islands at any cost!! Not only are these necessary for her trade in the East Indies, but even on the Northwest coast of America and the entire Pacific Ocean.[15]

Operations

Schaffer remained on Atuvai for 14 months, residing with Tomari. There he acquired territory—lands, forests, rivers, and lakes—and workers and established plantations, factories, and three forts (Alexandrovsk and Barclay, earthworks at Hanalei on the northern side of Atuvai, and Elizabetinsk, a stonework at Waimea on the southern side of the island). The port of Hanalei with its thirty native families became Russian property. There Schaffer planted corn, sugarcane, breadfruit, bananas, papayas, and other crops, noting that everything he sowed in the garden grew successfully.[16] Several natural features were renamed; for example, Hanalei Valley became Schaffer Valley and the Hanapepe River was rechristened the Don River. One of the Russians, Basil Tarakanov, recorded in late 1816 that at Waimea, Schaffer had built a large fort from blocks of lava and had planted a large garden with fruit, taro, and sugarcane.[17] On Waimea the doctor also planted 400 grapevines. Altogether, cabbage, potatoes, turnips, carrots, peas, beans, and other vegetables and wheat, corn, pineapples, watermelons, grapes, mustard, cotton, and other crops were planted on the Russian lands. "Everything planted came up well except the wheat."[18] Corn was triple-cropped, yielding 7223 pounds (129 bushels) per acre; cotton was double-cropped, with 490 square feet yielding 181 pounds of pure cotton each time;[*] the vineyard produced grapes nine months after planting.[19] From such fields and orchards Schaffer hoped to provision all of the company's colonies. But agriculture suffered from the inexperience of the Russians, as Tarakanov observed in early 1817:

> We did not know anything about gardening of that [tropical] kind and though Scheffer who was a doctor tried to teach us, he did not know much about it himself and we made poor work of it and then he would abuse us as if it was our fault.[20][**]

Besides foodstuffs the Russians procured large quantities of sandalwood on Atuvai. Tarakanov recalled that "For many weeks we were employed in carrying logs from Tomari's plantation to our settlement and piling them up ready for shipment."[21] At Hanalei 2400 logs were cut for the Russians, and at least 24,000 logs were readied for shipment altogether.[22] In early 1817, 24 Russians and Creoles and 40 Aleuts lived in the Sandwich Islands.[23]

---

[*] Schaffer figured that one acre of cotton could annually yield 370 pounds of fiber worth fifty-nine piasters in Canton (USNA, 1:251).

[**] In this vein Tarakanov added that Schaffer was a "bad man who treated us all like slaves. . . ." (Tarakanoff, *Statement*, 33).

Expulsion

Schaffer's bold actions soon alarmed the Americans and the Englishmen on the islands, some of whom had bought land and timber on Atuvai from Tomari in 1816 but were thereafter out-maneuvered by Schaffer. They convinced Tomi-Omi that the Russians had erected a fortress on Atuvai and had subverted Tomari's allegiance. A longtime English resident, John Young, who considerably influenced Tomi-Omi, especially intrigued against Schaffer. Some of the American agitators were naval employees of the Russian-American Company.* An ultimatum from Tomi-Omi, who was supported by most of the archipelago's natives and by all of the foreigners, soon forced Schaffer to abandon Voaga for Atuvai, where he did build a fortress. His post on Voaga was destroyed by Young. Becoming openly hostile to the Russians because of pressure from Tomi-Omi, Tomari then evicted them from Atuvai and seized their holdings. They tried to regain their property but were outnumbered and retreated to Voaga; three Russians and several Hawaiians were killed during the fighting. At Honolulu Schaffer was forced in July to board an American ship bound for Canton, leaving behind sixty-five men under Tarakanov, who "was left in charge of the settlement and the company's property . . . until a vessel was sent out expressly from Novo Arkhangelsk to remove us back to the Colonies."[24] In 1818 Tarakanov's party left for Russian California on an American ship.

Thus ended Russian Hawaii but not the Schaffer affair. In 1819 the head office still regarded the Sandwich Islands as a desirable possession:

> It would be very useful to Russia to have these islands, especially to our colonies, Kamchatka, and Okhotsk, as attested by Schaffer's experiments with the planting of fruit, grain, cotton, sugarcane, etc. . . . and it would be possible to acquire a paradisiacal refuge for Russian ships going around the world and to augment our commerce with many articles of trade.[25]

This sentiment was expressed to Hagemeister, who pinpointed the reasons for Schaffer's failure when he reported to the head office in 1818 that Schaffer had exceeded both his authority and his resources.[26] His abortive venture cost the Company 200,000 to 300,000 rubles.[27]

---

* The American seamen opposed Russian trade with the islands so that the company would still have to trade with American ships at New Archangel.

This loss did not deter Schaffer, however, for upon reaching St. Petersburg in November, 1818 he submitted to the Minister of the Interior a project for Russian occupation of one of the islands and the establishment there of a permanent settlement. The Minister of the Interior requested the opinion of the company, which replied in support of Schaffer's plan. The head office believed that the islands would be invaluable as a food base for the Russian Far East and Russian America* and as a refreshment and relaxation station for Russian ships.[28] However, the tsar ruled that the company must confine itself to friendly trade relations with the Sandwich Islands, hoping that "with careful management and careful choice of executives of its instructions, the company would acquire the same advantages from trade as it would if it had settlements on the islands."[29] This alternative of trade had, in fact, already been tried by the company as a means of satisfying the food needs of its colonies. The chief trading partners were not, however, the Sandwich Islanders but the company's three main rivals—the Americans, the Mexicans, and the British. Ironically, they were to prove the best sources of provisions for Russian America.

Readings

Golder, Frank A., "Proposals for Russian Occupation of the Hawaiian Islands," in Albert P. Taylor and Ralph S. Kuykendall, eds., *Hawaii: Early Relations with England-Russia-France*, Honolulu, 1930, 39–49.

Mazour, Anatole G., "Doctor Yegor Scheffer: Dreamer of a Russian Empire in the Pacific," *Pacific Historical Review*, February 1937, 15–20.

Pierce, Richard A., *Russia's Hawaiian Adventure, 1815–1817*, Berkeley, Calif., 1965.

Tarakanoff, Vassili Petrovitch, *Statement of My Captivity Among the Californians*, Los Angeles, 1953.

* This was especially so because Russian California was not yet concentrating on farming, and trade with Alta California was not yet regular.

PART IV FOREIGN TRADE

9 TRADE WITH BOSTON MEN

The settlement of New Archangel will always be a place of resort for ships trading on the coast; as the Russian company are ready to purchase flour, brandy, woollen cloth, and every necessary, at a profit of at least fifty per cent to the trader; which is more than he would obtain at Canton, besides the chance of his being obliged to sell there at a loss.

Yury Lisyansky

The clash of Russian, British, American, and Spanish interests on the Northwest Coast provided an opportunity for trade as well as for trouble. Indeed, in the nineteenth century relations among these competing powers on the Pacific slope were characterized more by amicable compromise than by acrimonious conflict. Probably the stakes were not high enough to warrant bloodshed. And perhaps white solidarity in the face of hostility from the native inhabitants unconsciously promoted cooperation. That as well as the need for vital necessities and the greed for high profits.

Article 5 of the Russian-American Company's first charter (1799) authorized it "To extend their [company's ships'] navigation to all adjoining nations and hold business intercourse with all surrounding powers, upon obtaining their free consent for the purpose."[1] The "adjoining nations" and "surrounding powers" were specified by Count Rezanov, who during his inspection of Russian America in 1805–6 concluded that foreign trade was essential to the well-being of the colonies. In 1806 he issued a directive to Governor Baranov that amounted to a blueprint for company commerce:

> The shortage of foodstuffs causes diseases, starvation and death among the people. Okhotsk is not able to supply America with the necessary quantity of foodstuffs; consequently, it is necessary to extend our commercial operations to find new sources of supply.
>
> My experiment in California and agreement with the people there already has provided a dependable and inexhaustible source, which upon my return I shall endeavor to make effective by presenting its advantages to the Government. I hope to find a second source in Japan, where I intend to proceed now. If God will crown my efforts with success, I hope to force this nation to trade with us. Then, the rice alone which abounds in Japan will provide ample food for this region. Meanwhile, I hope to make the necessary arrangements for the emigration of Japanese to America. . . . A third source are the Philippine Islands with their free port of Manila. I am positive that even at the first attempt it will be possible to bring an abundant supply of grain from there. The fourth and the most reliable source are the coasts of New Albion, to which I shall endeavor to attract the attention of the Government to the end that through the establishment of our settlement there, by sending Jesuits and missions, we could utilize the innumerable Indian aborigines for the establishment of agriculture which, because of the fertility of the land, will prove as successful as in California. If these sources proved unfeasible, there is a fifth source—Boston. The grain shipped from there will cost at all times less than twice [*sic:* half] as much as the grain from Okhotsk. In addition to this I point out a sixth source, export from Canton by the ships sailing from here to China and back to the coasts of America. If the Government will grant the needed assistance, I have no doubt that, even with one of these several sources successfully tapped, America will have no want of anything.[2]

The Japanese and Chinese sources proved illusory, thanks to the self-imposed isolationism of the Tokugawa Shogunate and the Manchu Dynasty. The Philippines had little to offer, and the New Albion settlement did not prosper. The Bostonians and the Californios, however, did become important suppliers of foodstuffs. By 1825 provisions constituted the foremost item in the trade of the Russian-American Company.[3]

The Northwest Trade

Owing to the sorry state of company shipping, the Russians could not at first reach these sources of provisions; rather, the provisions had to be brought to New Archangel in foreign bottoms. But foreign traders needed more than the opportunity to help fill Russian bellies to draw them to the remote and foggy shores of the far North Pacific. The magnet was afforded, of course, by sea otters and fur seals (and later by whales). The peltry was first brought to the attention of the European and American public in the journal of Captain Cook's last voyage, published in 1784. In 1779 the expedition's cargo of tattered furs (which represented only one-third of the number obtained, the rest having been bartered or spoiled) brought about 2000 pounds sterling at Canton, with some of the prime sea otter pelts fetching $120 each. The eagerness of the crew to return to the Northwest Coast to procure more furs was, in the words of Cook's second lieutenant, James King, "not far short of mutiny." He added that "the advantages that might be derived from a voyage to that part of the American coast, undertaken with commercial views, appear to me of a degree of importance sufficient to call for the attention of the Public."[4] A few enterprising Englishmen promptly heeded King's understated counsel, the first being James Hanna in 1785 in a British vessel fittingly named *Sea Otter*. Americans entered the "Northwest trade" in 1788, and by the end of the century the shrewd Yankee bargainers predominated. The number of British and American vessels trading on the Northwest Coast totaled, respectively, 35 and 15 from 1785 through 1794, 9 and 50 from 1795 through 1804, and 3 and 40 from 1805 through 1814.[5] Englishmen had to buy licenses from the South Sea Company, which monopolized British hunting on the Pacific Coast, and from the East India Company, which monopolized British trading in the Orient; moreover, the licenses permitted only the selling of furs in China, not the buying of Chinese goods for importation into England. This privilege was so jealously guarded by the East India Company that even the powerful and influential Hudson's Bay Company failed to obtain it. And Russian vessels—what few there were—were not admitted to Chinese ports. American traders were not hampered by such restrictions; indeed, they were so successful that sometimes their rivals shipped pelts to Canton on vessels chartered from Yankees and flying American colors. Most of the ships were from Boston; in fact, of the seventy-two American voyages to the Northwest Coast between 1787 and 1806, sixty-one sailed from Boston.[6]*

---

* The Northwest Coast Indians called the Americans "Boston men" or "Bostonians," just as they called the Englishmen "King George's men," the Spaniards "Espagnols," and the Sandwich Islanders "Kanakas."

These American argonauts reaped a harvest that was truly bountiful. According to the Russian-American Company, around the turn of the century the Americans obtained 10,000 to 15,000 sea otter pelts annually, which they traded at Canton at lower prices than those traded by the Russians at Kyakhta.[7] In 1799, when one vessel could get 800 skins in four days or 1000 to 1200 skins in one season, seven American ships obtained 11,000 sea otter pelts, which fetched $25 each at Canton.[8] And in 1800 the Americans procured 18,000 sea otters, of which 15,000 were obtained by Boston ships.[9] Sometimes an investment of $40,000 returned a profit of more than $150,000.[10]

Furs were a means to the American Nor'westmen, not an end, as they were to the British. Pelts were used in lieu of specie at Canton, where they were exchanged for Chinese teas, textiles, and curios. These goods were brought back to the United States via the Cape for ready and lucrative sale (just as Russian furs were bartered at Kyakhta for Chinese goods sold in Russia). To obtain pelts from the Northwest Coast Indians the Yankee China trader around 1800 needed a cargo worth about $17,000, comprising mostly tin and iron hollow-ware, brass kettles, wire, beads, lead, knives, nails, small looking-glasses, bar iron, hatchets, firearms, powder, flints, rum, and molasses.[11] From 1800, bread, rice, and molasses were also traded in response to both native preference and Russian demand. The Russians were a source of additional furs, for they commonly exchanged pelts for the American foodstuffs. Thus, along with the sandalwood trade of the South Sea islands (especially the Sandwich Islands) and the contraband trade of New Spain (and the hide and tallow trade from 1822), the alimentary needs of Russian Alaska came to be another profitable adjunct to the China trade of New England. This diversification, in fact, helps to explain the great success of the Bostonians in the face of the powerful Russian and British monopolies, who had the advantage of permanent posts alongside the hunting grounds.

The Boston Trade

Again it was the ambitious and provident Gregory Shelikhov who first attempted foreign trade as a source of provisions. As early as 1786 the Golikov-Shelikhov Company tried to arrange for the regular acquisition of goods, including foodstuffs, from British vessels at Petropavlovsk through purchase and barter, but the British would not agree to the company's conditions.* In the late 1780s Spanish ships in the Gulf of Alaska occasionally bartered provisions to the Russians. Then, at the turn of the century, despite Governor-General Pil's warning to the company in 1794 to avoid dealings with foreign vessels,[12] a drastic shortage of supplies compelled Baranov to exchange furs and piasters with American skippers for not only "everything necessary for the provisionment of the colonies, but even their ships themselves, so superior in everything to our own vessels of local construction."[13] The selling of Russian-American Company furs was against regulations, since until the abandonment of the share system in 1818 all furs were supposed to be divided between the company and the promyshlenniks, but the colonies were so desperately short of provisions between 1799 and 1803 that, according to Klebnikov, "Necessity changed the rules."[14] Disaster was avoided only by the chance arrival at New Archangel of a British vessel in 1801 and an American vessel in 1802. And in 1805 Baranov's purchase of the Yankee ship *Juno* and its cargo from Captain John D'Wolf saved the colonial capital from starvation; the cargo included beef, pork, flour, bread, rice, sugar, molasses, and rum.[15]

Foreign trading vessels began to call regularly at Russian America's ports at the turn of the century. In 1799–1800, eight American and British ships dropped anchor at New Archangel,[16] but apparently no trade occurred. From 1805 foreign ships began to visit New Archangel very often; during the first decade of the century 6 to 10 American and British ships put in at New Archangel each year.[17] The first American vessel to trade was the *Enterprise* of New York under Captain James Scott in 1801 at Kodiak. By then Baranov was in dire need of supplies, and the articles brought by American ships were cheaper than those delivered by the irregular Okhotsk ship or the occasional Cronstadt ship. Finally, in 1803 Baranov and several Yankee shipmasters concluded a loose agreement that formally inaugurated permanent trade for the next four decades, as well as joint hunting along the coast of California, with the Russians providing Aleuts, baidarkas, and trade goods and the Americans furnishing ships and crews. This accord underlined both the failure of the Siberian supply line and local Alaskan agriculture and the inadequacy of company shipping. For some time the company was forced to hire American shipwrights and skippers, buy American vessels, and char-

* Shelikhov did reach a commercial agreement with Captain Peters of the British East India Company at Petropavlovsk in 1786, but this arrangement was apparently nullified by the loss of Peters and his vessel on the Commander Islands.

ter American ships to deliver furs to Okhotsk and Canton. Paradoxically, the exigencies of the maritime fur trade forced the two keen rivals to cooperate for their mutual benefit. This cooperation saved the colonies. As Governor Muravyov recalled in 1822: "the shortage of grain at Sitka under Alex. Andreyevich [Baranov] did not last more than three years, and then with the help of American traders he never felt any lack. . . ."[18] Baranov's transactions were advantageous. In the words of his superiors:

> This trade with foreigners was a most beneficial event for the company, and it was essential to its rapid recovery. On the one hand it spared the company the necessity of sending all essentials to the colonies at great expense and difficulty via Okhotsk and around the world; and on the other hand it facilitated the local sale of those surplus furs that could not be marketed in Russia and which would rot or burn from long storage, as formerly often happened to fur seal pelts. Baranov bought from the foreigners not only everything necessary for provisionment of the colonies but even their ships, which were superior to all of his own ships of local construction.[19]

By 1811, thanks mainly to the Bostonians, Baranov had enough provisions to last three or four years.

Problems

The American presence, however, was a mixed blessing. Both the Yankees and the Limeys offered ruthless competition. They traded wantonly and rapaciously, and often on what the company regarded as its territory. Moreover, the foreigners (who only traded for furs, whereas the Russians both hunted and traded) offered the Indians more and better goods for pelts than did the Russians, including liquor, knives, guns, and ammunition, even demonstrating how to use the firearms against the promyshlenniks. In the spring of 1808 Directors Michael Buldakov and Benedict Kramer of the head office noted:

> . . . beginning in 1792 from 10 to 15 seagoing trading vessels of citizens of the North American United States have been coming there each year to bypass the company and trade with the American savages living in various places on the islands and the mainland, exchanging goods that they bring—especially weapons, such as cannons, falconettes, rifles, pistols, sabers, and other destructive things and gunpowder, which they even teach the savages to use—for up to 15,000 sea otters and up to 5000 river otters alone every year, besides other pelts, which they sell at Canton.[20]

Once-friendly Indians in the straits now fired on Russian promyshlen-niks instead of trading with them. Armed and riled by Americans, the Koloshes destroyed New Archangel once and Yakutat twice, killing 200 Aleuts and more than 100 Russians altogether.[21] Baranov warned the Bostonians not to trade with the Koloshes but, in Khlebnikov's words, "they answered him with laughter, saying that they had heard nothing about it from their Government."[22] The aging governor was powerless to prevent American poaching and smuggling because of his shortage of ships and men (for example, he had only about 400 promyshlenniks in 1817[23]). So he wisely joined the Yankees instead, making deals for the delivery of furs to Okhotsk and Canton and joint hunting on halves along the California coast. There was little else Baranov could do, for he could not expect much help from St. Petersburg. The motherland could not readily or easily assist the faraway colonies; for example, it was not uncommon that goods needed by the colonies arrived from Russia two and three years after they were requested.*

The company still tried to stop American smuggling and poaching by official representations. In 1808 the Minister of Commerce and Foreign Affairs, Count Nicholas Rumyantsev, lodged a written protest on the company's behalf with the American Consul-General in St. Petersburg, stating that "the ships of the United States, instead of trading with the Russian possessions in America, have there carried on a clandestine trade with the savages, to whom, in exchange for otter skins, they furnish fire-arms and powder, the use of which, till then unknown to these islanders, has been in their hands very prejudicial to the subjects of his Imperial Majesty."[24] In Philadelphia the Russian Consul-General, Andrew Dash-kov, was instructed by Rumyantsev to pursue the matter, but to no avail. At the end of 1809 the Russian government advised the company that representations would be made through ambassadors Theodore Von Pahlen and John Adams to try to stop the arms trade on the Northwest Coast. But these diplomatic efforts were also in vain. The American government argued that its citizens had the right to trade wherever and however they wished. In 1810 Von Pahlen told the company that "the Government of the United States has neither the desire nor the power to stop this illicit trade. Many individuals who have influence in the East of this nation and who greatly dislike the present adminis-tration share in the profits of this trade, and the Government is afraid

* By comparison, it took Yankee ships 140 to 160 days to sail from Boston directly to New Archangel via the Horn (*Materialy*, III, 128).

of annoying those who act against its interests."[25] The United States, then, bowed to pressure from Yankee members of Congress who had a stake in the Northwest trade, and, in order to absolve itself of any responsibility for an unseemly commerce, invoked the principle of laissez faire as an alibi.

Meanwhile, the nefarious activities of the Boston men continued. In 1812 the head office informed its stockholders:

> Baranov complains loudly about the presence of more and more seafarers, citizens of the North American United States, who bring other colonial goods and exchange them with the Indians for furs, which they take to Canton for sale. If these seafarers did not go there, all Indian furs—near and far—would be in the hands of our company. Most of all he complains that these seafarers trade firearms and other ordnance, gunpowder, shot, and lead, and that the Indians, having learned how to use these weapons, impede, as it were, easy and safe hunting by our Russian promyshlenniks, since in trading with them various devices must be used to procure furs, such as: either going to much more distant places than before, with more men and expense, and always taking military precautions or having mutual relations with the seafarers themselves, with whom Baranov makes contracts almost every year, providing them with promyshlenniks, baidarkas, and gear, which are sent with them to various hunting grounds, even faraway ones, to hunt on halves.[26]

ASTOR'S OVERTURE

It was at this juncture that John Jacob Astor, the leading American trader with interests on the Northwest Coast, came forward with a proposal that would resolve the dispute and further his aim of undermining the British fur trade on the Northwest Coast. In 1809 Consul-General Dashkov had also been instructed to seek a means of establishing regular trade with the United States "to provide our settlements with necessities in the most profitable way and to avoid the harm done locally to hunting and trading by republicans through improper commerce with the savages on the northwestern shores and islands of America."[27] Dashkov then contacted Astor, who agreed to send two or three ships annually (for at least three years) to New Archangel with supplies and to take company furs to Canton, where he would act as the company's sole agent.[28] Astor hoped that the resultant expansion of his Pacific Fur Company northward from Astoria (at the mouth of the Columbia River) and the expansion of the Russian-American Company southward from New Archangel would thwart the British. In May 1812 the Russian-American Company and Astor's American Fur Company signed an agreement whereby they promised to respect each other's hunting grounds above and below 55° N latitude and not to trade weapons or ammunition to the Indians; also, the American Fur Company agreed to deliver supplies to New Archangel from Astoria for pelts or bills of exchange at fixed prices and to ship Russian furs to Canton and Chinese goods back to New Archangel on a commission basis. The Russian-American Company agreed to buy supplies from nobody else, although Astor was not allowed to import certain furs into Russia duty free as he had hoped. The main advantage of the agreement for the Russians was that their settlements could buy better provisions at cheaper prices and much more regularly.[29] Washington Irving, propagandizer of the "lords of the Pacific," noted: "This agreement was to continue in operation four years, and to be renewable for a similar term, unless some unforeseen contingency should render a modification necessary."[30] An unforeseen contingency soon arose—the War of 1812. In 1813 Astoria was hurriedly sold to the North West Company (and renamed Fort George) before it could be captured by the British Navy. The agreement perforce lapsed. But Russian disappointment was not abject, for the supplies that Astor had been able to deliver on two ships had proved either insufficient, unwanted, or overpriced.[31] With the return of unregulated trade the old evils reappeared. In 1823, for example, Governor Muravyov complained that the Bostonians were trading guns and ammunition to the Koloshes and inciting them against the Russians; "many Kolosh chiefs" even had cannons, he added.[32] He further noted that some "sensible" Boston men desisted, however, since New Archangel afforded them security and assistance in "unhappy" circumstances; that is, in times of distress. These sensible traders also felt that the Russians were a negligible threat to their trade and even regretted the clandestine activities of their compatriots.[33]

Dimunition

The Boston trade remained very active until 1814, when the head office, frustrated by the failure of the agreement with Astor and alarmed by the number of pelts traded to the Americans and by the number of American firearms acquired by the Koloshes, ordered Baranov to halt his trade with the Bostonians.* Also, by now the company's need for

* By the end of 1814 Baranov had bartered to foreign vessels 529,731 pelts and tails (including 495,791 fur seals), 1476 pounds of walrus teeth, and 16 pounds of castoreum valued at 1,257,841 rubles (AVPR, f. RAK, d. 183, 1–1v., d. 192, 1).

American provisions was less urgent because some foodstuffs were being obtained from Alta California via Fort Ross, where incipient farming was expected to produce surpluses. In 1816 one of Astor's ship captains wrote: "I sincerely hope, that you have not embark'd in any more shipments to Shitka; the Company have taken *new grounds,* no more skins are to be sold to foreigners. California supplies them with provisions."[34] Furthermore, during the War of 1812 the might of the British navy discouraged American ships from plying the Northwest trade. Many American skippers in the Pacific repaired to New Archangel and offered to sell their ships and cargoes at bargain prices.

The transactions continued, although on a reduced scale. In the mid-1810s 250 American ships still visited the Pacific coast of New Spain annually; half of them engaged in smuggling and made, according to the artist Louis Choris, "enormous profits," for they outsailed Spanish warships and were rarely caught.[35] Many of the other half pursued the sandalwood trade, now at its peak, and the fur trade, although the animals were less numerous and the Indians were more dangerous than during the boom years at the beginning of the century. In the early 1820s Boston ships procured 3000 to 4000 sea otter pelts annually[36] (only about a quarter of the catch during the early years). The Boston men bartered mainly blankets and flannelette, but they acquired at least a third of their pelts in exchange for rifles.[37] Often their ships were attacked with the very arms that they themselves had traded, and even on the day of the trade, but most of them were securely defended with cannons (8 to 14 in number).[38] Sometimes these attacks were actually beneficial, in that Indian chiefs captured during the fighting could be handsomely ransomed.

PROHIBITION

In 1818, when Baranov, the old trading partner of the Bostonians, was unceremoniously replaced, the head office expressly forbade the sale of colonial furs to foreign vessels.[39] In the light of critical reports by Lazarev, Golovnin, and Hagemeister the colonies were reorganized. The new order included a firm stand against American competitors; connivance was no longer disapproved but strictly prohibited. Upon his return to St. Petersburg in 1819 Hagemeister, Baranov's successor, reported that company trade with the Americans was harmful,[40]* and in 1820 the

* From 1805 through 1817 Baranov exchanged 189,175 rubles (94,587½ piasters) in money and 980,825 rubles in furs (362,730 fur seals, 9694 beavers, 8729 sea otters,

head office reiterated its prohibition of such trade. Finally, in September, 1821 the Russian government issued a decree entitled "Rules Established for the Limits of Navigation and Order of Communication Along the Coast of Eastern Siberia, the Northwest Coast of America, and the Aleutian, Kurile, and Other Islands," whereby all foreign vessels were prohibited from approaching within 115¼ miles of the Northwest Coast north of 51° N latitude and the eastern coast of Siberia north of 45° 50' N latitude, as well as the Aleutian and Kurile islands, unless in genuine need of repairs or provisions.[41] Ironically, this decree was linked with another of the same year that did just the opposite—the edict of 1821 opening Alta California to foreign traders. This opening meant that the company could regularly obtain California provisions, so that it would no longer have to depend upon Bostonian suppliers. At the same time the company announced that henceforth supplies would also be sent from Russia on an annual ship, whose cargo would both supplement and complement supplies from California and so even further decrease dependence upon the Bostonians. And the Russian ships, bringing force of arms as well as supplies, would perhaps deter American traders in the Gulf of Alaska and American whalers in the Okhotsk and Bering seas.

The new system failed dismally, however. Under the old system the colonies could obtain exactly what they needed from foreign vessels, but under the new system they had to be content with whatever was shipped from Cronstadt. Either too much, too little, or none at all of some items was sent, and many other items such as rope, mooring chains, glass, and shoes, rotted, rusted, or broke. Expenditures, it was noted, were in vain.[42] Also, formerly all of the colonies' needs had been procured in exchange for pelts, but now these pelts were marketed elsewhere, which took at least three years during which time furs spoiled and supplies were lost.[43] And large numbers of fur seals formerly traded to the Americans (because not all the pelts could be sold in Russia) were now sent to Russia, where they lay rotting in warehouses.[44] Furthermore, colonial supply, formerly certain because there were always a few American ships docking at New Archangel for firewood, water, and repairs, was now dependent upon the safety of navigation and the political relationships of the great powers.[45] Finally, the supplies sent from Cronstadt generally cost

864 river otters, and 235 foxes) for 1,170,000 rubles worth of goods and five ships. The company suffered considerable losses when the ruble/piaster rate of exchange increased from 2 : 1 to 5 : 1 between the time Baranov issued bills of exchange and the time they were cashed in St. Petersburg (Khlebnikov, "Zapiski," 16v.–17).

the company twice as much as those obtained from the Americans.[46] To crown everything, agriculture in Russian California remained unproductive and, because of occasional crop failures and high export charges, Alta California proved unsatisfactory as a source of provisions.

The voyages of supply from Cronstadt during the first half of the 1820s were disastrous. In 1820 it cost the company 700,000 rubles to send a cargo worth 200,000 rubles on the *Kutuzov*.[47] In 1821 the *Elizabeth*, which had cost 30,000 rubles to buy and 70,000 rubles to outfit, got no farther than the Cape of Good Hope because of disrepair, and 20,000 rubles' worth of rye on board spoiled even before the ship reached the Cape.[48] "It is clear that this expedition was dispatched more for show than for vital necessity; nevertheless, about 435,000 rubles were spent on it," recalled the head office in 1824.[49] Just before this debacle the Ministry of Finance, in response to a complaint from the Siberian administration about the impoverishment of the Yakuts who transported freight from Yakutsk to Okhotsk, asked the company to transport grain from Cronstadt to Okhotsk and Petropavlovsk on its own ships in order to lessen dependence upon the "harmful visits of foreigners."[50] Instead of refusing this new responsibility, which exceeded its resources, the company agreed, so that much of the rye aboard the *Elizabeth* was intended for the Okhotsk Seaboard and the Kamchatka Peninsula.[51] Owing to the resultant depletion of capital, the company decided against sending a ship from Cronstadt in 1822.[52] Meanwhile, transport via Okhotsk almost stopped; nevertheless, virtually empty company ships continued to sail from New Archangel to Okhotsk, and new construction was continued at the Okhotsk factory. More than 100 men were even being transferred from undermanned Alaska for this work.[53] Consequently, the company's books showed a profit of only 8 per cent in 1820 and in 1821 as against 15 per cent in 1819.[54] Although it was clear by the beginning of 1823 that the continuation of the new system of supply would quickly lead the company to ruin, it was decided to dispatch a ship from Cronstadt in 1823 with 361 tons of state (non-company) rye for Okhotsk and Petropavlovsk.[55] The *Helena* was sent, although with only half that tonnage of rye and even though experience had already shown that whole grain could not be shipped through the tropics without damage.[56] The voyage cost the company 500,000 rubles, most of which had to be borrowed.[57] Governor Muravyov declared the expedition useless, for it had not brought the needed supplies; he added that he had not so much to hunt furs as to defend the colonies from hostile natives incited by American traders.[58] The expense, evidently, was the last straw. In 1824 the company decided to send supplies to New Archangel via Okhotsk rather than from Cronstadt, and in the same year the government freed the company from its obligation to provision Okhotsk and Petropavlovsk. Also in 1824 Russia and the United States signed a convention that readmitted American ships to New Archangel, and Muravyov received permission from the head office to trade with foreign ships, provided that such trade was necessary and profitable.[59] The *Helena* was sent from Cronstadt to New Archangel in 1824 in order to meet the colonies' needs until the Boston trade could be resumed.*

RESUMPTION

Thus, the cooperation between Muscovite and Yankee on the Northwest Coast was recommenced after a hiatus of three years. At first, as in the 1810s, the Russians exchanged almost solely fur seal pelts for supplies, for by now sea otters were too scarce.** For example, in the mid-1820s three or four American ships traded annually with the Koloshes in the straits, and each managed to procure no more than 500 sea otter skins.[60] And in 1827 the *Louisa* under William McNeill, who was considered the best American fur trader in the straits, obtained only 160 sea otters and 1000 beavers.[61] In the last half of the 1820s some 60,000 rubles' worth of fur seals were bartered yearly to American traders.[62] From 1826 through 1830, 87,740 fur seals—probably 60 per cent of the colonial catch—were exchanged for American supplies.[63] Before long the company became alarmed by the lopsided exchange; it not only stood to lose 25 per cent of its income, but there were no longer enough fur seals for both itself and the Americans.[64] The skins were bartered to the Americans at a value of 8¾ rubles each, which was slightly lower than their selling price at Canton (10 rubles) and considerably lower than in Russia (20 rubles).[65] The head office complained to Governor Chistyakov, who replied in 1830:

> Referring in it [an earlier dispatch] to all the reasons that compel us to enter into transactions with foreigners for fur seals, I clearly demonstrated with extensive arguments that trade with them is conducted

* In fact, this trade had never really ceased, for the failure of oceanic supply had forced the colonial administration to overlook the ban on trade with foreigners. Even before the ban was officially rescinded the company had requested exemption.
** The Americans flooded the European market with sealskin hats made from fur seals.

only as a last resort, for many foreign ships that visit Port New Archangel leave without having made any transactions. The head office
knows that throughout my governorship of the Russian colonies in
America many of the most important items for the colonies—such as
sugar, rum, tea, and the like—that have been sent annually via Okhotsk
and even [around the world] on the *Helena* have, despite the promises
of the head office, either been missing or, as in the case of sugar, been
sent in negligible quantity by comparison with the considerable supply
that is needed for the subsistence and necessary provisionment of all
districts of the colonies, so that I to my great distress have been forced
—and shall now again be forced—to resort to buying these articles from
foreigners. With the adoption of a definite resolution—as is now
promised by the head office—to supply the colonies independently of
foreigners with all possible needs via Okhotsk, the number of fur seals
exported to Russia will, of course, be more considerable than formerly;
this could have been so already if the company had adopted these useful measures several years ago. The insignificant purchase of goods
from foreigners in 1829, which . . . reached only 5316 fur seals,
serves as clear, incontestable proof of this![66]

But the head office was not convinced.* It believed that cessation of the
trade with the Americans would save 10,000 fur seals annually (and that
another 30,000 could be bagged by renewing hunting on Atka and St.
George islands).[67] In 1830 the company informed Governor Wrangel
that fur seals should be traded to the Americans in emergencies only because it could not satisfy the growing demand for skins in Russia and
because they brought low prices when traded for American goods.[68]
Generally the Bostonians made a profit of at least 50 per cent on their
transactions at New Archangel, thanks to their lower freight and in-
surance costs, according to the estimate of the head office in 1833.[69]

DEMISE

In order to conserve fur seals the company from 1831 paid the American
traders in letters of credit or bills of exchange (redeemable at St. Petersburg) instead of pelts. This measure, it was found, also reduced the
cost of American supplies by 50 per cent,[70] although sometimes the bills
of exchange were cashed when company funds were low. Nevertheless,
trade at New Archangel proved less remunerative. The company's average annual profit from the Boston trade fell from 181,000 rubles in 1826–

* Under Governor Chistyakov 942,305 rubles' worth of goods and one ship were
bartered from 18 foreign vessels for 97,378 fur seals and 55,000 rubles' worth of
various goods and materials ([Khlebnikov], "Zapiski," 101).

30 to 102,000 rubles in 1831–33.[71] At the same time, however, New Archangel was able to ship annually 21,600 fur seals to Russia in 1831–33 as
against 17,105 in 1826–30.[72]* The decrease in profits stemmed from the
fact that fewer and fewer American ships visited the Northwest Coast
during the 1830s in the face of depletion of the fur seal herds of the
Bering Sea from the late 1820s. Increasing competition from the Hudson's Bay Company, starting in the early 1830s, and more direct Russian
trade in the straits from about 1835 further discouraged the Bostonians.
Between 1821 and 1830 the number of foreign vessels plying the Northwest trade dropped from 13 to 2, and during the late 1820s only 2 to 4
foreign vessels called at New Archangel each year.[73] Even during the
ten-year period of unrestricted navigation allowed by the Conventions of
1824 and 1825 only 4 to 6 American and English ships annually traded
on the Northwest Coast.[74] During the 1830s the Americans were gradually ousted from the coastal trade, as planned, by Governor Simpson's
policy of the use of both vessels and posts to trade superior goods. The
coup de grace was the Russian-American Company's use of its enlarged
and improved fleet to trade directly with the Indians of the straits. Already in 1830 Chistyakov reported that American vessels visited New
Archangel very rarely.[75] And by the end of the decade so few Boston
ships were calling at New Archangel that the company tried to regular-
ize transactions by making contracts with such reputable Boston firms as
Boardman, Farnham, French, and Thompson. The 1839 agreement with
the Hudson's Bay Company completely freed Alaska from any dependence upon American supplies. In 1840 Governor Etholen reported: "I
have fully noted the will of the Head Office—'not to place any orders or
to make purchases from foreigners other than the agent of the Hudson's
Bay Company'—which will be faithfully observed during my administration, and the New Archangel Counter will order its strict implementa-
tion. . . ."[76] Later the same year Etholen reiterated that "In the future
during my five-year term absolutely no goods whatever will be bought
here from foreigners, except those which will be delivered here by the
Hudson's Bay Company on contracted terms."[77] But the American traders probably did not fret very much, for by then the Northwest trade,
Boston's "high school of commerce," had ended. The sea otters and the
fur seals had all but disappeared, and American shipmasters were turn-
ing to whaling in other waters. Undoubtedly the Russians did not regret
the passing of the trade either, for it had always been an informal and

* At this time the company needed 30,000 fur seals annually (USNA, 36:51).

irregular source of provisions whose steady supply had depended upon an abundant population of fur bearers and the maintenance of friendly relations between Russia and both the United States and Great Britain.*

Trends

The vicissitudes of the Boston trade are illustrated by Table 9, which also clearly distinguishes the three phases of the Boston trade. During the first phase (1801–14), when it was the colonies' chief source of provisions, more than two ships per year sold about 83,000 rubles' worth of goods. During the second phase (1815–24), when the colonies began to acquire provisions in Alta California and Russian California, and the Boston trade was banned, two ships a year sold only about 63,000 rubles' worth of goods. And during the third phase (1825–41), when a series of crop failures in the last half of the 1820s and secularization in the mid-1830s devastated Alta California's agriculture, about three ships per year sold about 168,000 rubles' worth of goods. Of the approximately 120 trading vessels, only nine were not American.

Commodities

The supplies traded by the American vessels at New Archangel consisted mostly of provisions from New England (flour, groats, butter, lard, gin, vinegar, tobacco) and the West Indies and Brazil (rice, sugar, molasses, coffee, rum), plus some American manufactures (utensils, textiles, soap, guns, gunpowder).** Between 1805 and 1811 the Russians bought mainly flour, millet, salted beef, sugar, salt, molasses, vinegar, rum, brandy, wine, tobacco, soap, plates, guns, cloth, and blankets.[78] With the resurgence of trade in 1825 fewer foodstuffs were purchased because some were being obtained from both Mexican and Russian California. Particularly less grain and beef were bought. During the last half of the 1820s the Americans bartered principally such "colonial" provisions as millet, tapioca, sugar, salt, molasses, vinegar, tea, rum, wine, gin, and tobacco; a lot of tea; and such manufactures as woolen blankets,

* The head office admitted that supply by Yankee skippers was not very reliable because they did not always keep their word and sometimes failed to appear, leaving New Archangel to rely upon chance visits (USNA, 13:104v.).
** Almost no figures are available on the amount of provisions obtained from the Bostonians at New Archangel. It is known that in 1818 the company bought 49 tons of "Boston flour" (*Materialy*, III, 24).

Table 9. Company Trade with Foreign Ships at New Archangel, 1801–41

Year	Ship*	Captain	Sale (rubles)
1801	Enterprise	Scott	12,000
1802	Unicorn (Eng.)	Barber	27,000
1802	Alert	Ebbets	43,000
1803	"various"**	?	37,000
1804	?	?	?
1805	Juno	D'Wolf	12,320
1805	Mary	Trescott	9,041
1805	Juno	D'Wolf	136,000***
1806	O'Cain	J. Winship	9,768
1806	Vancouver	Brown	3,530
1806	Peacock	Kimball	345
1806	Eclipse	O'Cain	9,690
1807	Myrtle (Eng.)	Barber	84,000***
1807	Peacock	Kimball	7,921
1807	O'Cain	J. Winship	4,049
1807	Derby	Swift	18,036
1807	Mercury	Ayres	4,710
1808	Derby	Swift	34,516
1809	Mercury	Ayres	1,210
1809	O'Cain	J. Winship	40,427
1810	Mercury	Ayres	7,726
1810	Enterprise	Ebbets	53,731
1810	Isabella	Davis	24,750
1811	Mercury	Ayres	25,400
1811	O'Cain	J. Winship	16,702
1811	Katherine	Blanchard	22,050
1811	Enterprise	Ebbets	94,843
1811	Isabella	Davis	19,693
1812	Mercury	Ayres	12,425
1812	Charon	Whittemore	22,617
1812	Beaver	Hunt	124,057
1812	Amethyst	T. Meek	35,477***
1813	Charon	Whittemore	6,065
1813	Atahualpa	Suter	27,753***
1813	Lydia	Bennett	95,512***
1813	Pedlar	Clark	22,378
1813	Isabella	Davis	2,432
1814	Pedlar	Pigot	99,982
1815	Brutus	T. Meek	43,288
1817	Lydia	Gyzelaar	33,204
1818	Le Bordelais (Fr.)	De Roquefeuil	27,570
1818	Brutus	Nye	?
1818	Columbia (Eng.)	Robson	?
1818	Mentor	Suter	?
1818	Volunteer	Bennett	?

Year	Ship*	Captain	Sale (rubles)
1818	*Eagle*	T. Meek	11,730
1819	*Brutus*	Nye	13,539
1819	*Eagle*	T. Meek	8,950
1819	*Clarion*	Gyzelaar	20,746
1819	*Volunteer*	Bennett	4,650
1820	*Thaddeus*	Blanchard	58,005
1820	*Pedlar*	Pigot	20,675
1821	*Arab*	T. Meek	64,697
1822	*Sultan*	Clark	4,469
1822	*Pedlar*	J. Meek	38,880
1822	*Arab*	T. Meek	105,889
1823	*Pearl*	Stevens	3,404
1823	*Arab*	T. Meek	171,015***
1824	*Tamaahmaah*	J. Meek	?
1825	*Lapwing*	Blanchard	213,275***
1825	*Paragon*	Wildes	6,060
1826	*Sultan*	Allen	87,753
1826	*Chinchilla*	T. Meek	95,462
1826	*Tally Ho*	McNeill	14,367
1827	*Active*	Cotting	41,268
1827	*Tally Ho*	McNeill	111,688***
1827	*Triton*	Bryant	20,959
1827	*Diana*	Blanchard	140,543
1827	*Louisa*	McNeill	?
1827	*Chinchilla*	T. Meek	116,137
1828	*Active*	Cotting	?
1828	*Sultan*	Allen	47,306
1828	*Washington*	Carter	28,254
1828	*Paragon*	Blinn	?
1828	*Chinchilla*	T. Meek	} 84,304
1828	*Tamerani* (Hawaiian)	Marina	
1828	*Volunteer*	Barker	?
1828	*Griffon*	Pierce	?
1829	*Herald*	Hammet	11,361
1829	*Volunteer*	Taylor	1,483
1829	*Plant*	Rutter	35,158
1829	*Alabama*	De Brot	4,527
1829	*Cadboro* (Eng.)	Simpson	?
1830	*Sultan*	Heintzman	54,749
1830	*Convoy*	Thompson	?
1830	*Sultan*	Heintzman	24,980
1831	*Little* (Eng.)	Carter	4,538
1831	*Louisa*	Johns	63,090
1831	*Lama*	McNeill	?
1831	*Crusader*	J. Meek	10,615

Year	Ship*	Captain	Sale (rubles)
1832	Smyrna	Barker	73,287
1832	Lama	McNeill	20,451
1832	Bolivar	Underwood	27,920
1832	Crusader	Pitcher	64,441
1832	Cadboro (Eng.)	Ogden	?
1832	Diana	Little	70,000
1832	Caernarvon (Eng.)	Aldred	?
1833	Diana	Carter	74,661
1834	La Grange	Snow	112,009
1834	Europa	Allen	8,769
1834	Bolivar Liberator	Dominis	52,036
1834	Diana	Carter	112,231
1834	La Grange	Snow	1,792
1834	Bolivar Liberator	Dominis	50,248
1834	Diana	Carter	40,000
1835	Diana	Harth	60,369
1836	Joseph Peabody	Moore	33,844
1836	La Grange	Snow	49,623
1836	Europa	Benton	} 114,485
1836	Diana	Carter	
1836	La Grange	Snow	12,500
1837	Hamilton	Barker	189,348
1837	Jones	Dominis	4,510
1838	Suffolk	Allen	156,835
1839	Clementine	?	61,102
1839	Thomas Perkins	Harney	85,535
1839	Joseph Peabody	Dominis	19,000
1840	Alciope	Clapp	41,750
1840	Joseph Peabody	Dominis	44,540
1841	Morea	Snow	70,495

* Ships are of American registration unless noted otherwise.
** Includes a purchase of 10,000 to 12,000 rubles from the American ship *O'Cain* under Captain O'Cain (Khlebnikov, *Baranov*, 41; Khlebnikov "Zapiski," 11).
*** Includes the ship as well as its cargo.

Sources: Gibson, "Russian America," 12; Khlebnikov, "Zapiski," 9v., 11, 14–16v., 56–58v.; Tikhmenev, *Historical Review*, I, 108, 112, 117; USNA, 36: 33, 221v., 222v., 37: 124v.–25v., 236v., 438v.–39, 444, 38: 64, 106v.–07v., 169, 284v.–85v., 39: 19, 20–20v., 130v., 131v., 360v.–63, 449, 40: 181v., 41: 113–13v., 42: 313v.–14, 400v., 439v., 442, 443–43v., 43: 116–17, 44: 124v.–25, 45: 92–92v., 184v.–85.

flannelette, broadcloth, cottons, silks, and soap.[79] From 50 to 100 tons of these commodities were procured annually.[80] More grain was included in the last half of the 1830s in the wake of the decline of mission agriculture in Alta California.

The foodstuffs brought by the Boston men were used by company employees; the manufactures were mostly traded to the natives. The more luxurious items—millet, ham, rum, wine, cheese, jam, chocolate, cigars—went to the colonial officials and officers. This helps to explain the maintenance of the trade by the colonial administration in spite of the head office's disapproval. In 1829 Chistyakov stated that colonial officials spent 90 per cent of their living expenses on American imports and the rest on Russian imports; colonial laborers spent one-third of their salaries on Russian goods (clothing) and the rest on American goods (provisions).[81] Every month a laborer bought over 4 pounds of rice, 3 pounds of sugar, 2 pounds of tobacco, and one pound of tea, and on holidays he also bought 2 to 4 pounds of fine flour and one or two glasses of rum.[82]

Thus, Boston supplies were vital to the feeding of company employees—high and low—and to the prosecution of the Indian trade. Indeed, during Baranov's governorship they were the mainstay of colonial supply.[83] So important were American supplies that the governors of Russian America persisted in acquiring them despite company discouragement and even prohibition. Not even the Regulations of 1821 were able to stop this traffic, for it was "often the only source from which the colony could draw indispensable merchandise and even provisions."[84] This source was not repudiated until Governor Simpson and the Hudson's Bay Company managed to achieve what the Astorians and Nor'Westers (North West Company men) had failed to do 25 years earlier—gain control of the coastal trade. In so doing the weighty and efficient Hudson's Bay Company also secured half of the Northwest Coast for the British flag, just as they were to preserve half of the continent for the crown. Twenty years before this happened, however, the American source of provisions was challenged from a quite different quarter—Alta California.

Readings

Bradley, Harold Whitman, "The Hawaiian Islands and the Pacific Fur Trade, 1785–1813," *Pacific Northwest Quarterly*, July 1939, 275–99.

Cowdin, Elliot C., "The Northwest Fur Trade," *Hunt's Merchants' Magazine*, June 1846, 532–39 (reprinted in *British Columbia Historical Quarterly*, January 1944, 14–25).

D'Wolf, Captain John, *A Voyage to the North Pacific and A Journey through Siberia*, Cambridge, Mass., 1861.

Howay, F. W., *A List of Trading Vessels in the Maritime Fur Trade, 1785–1825*, ed. by Richard A. Pierce, Kingston, Ontario, 1973.

———, "An Outline Sketch of the Maritime Fur Trade," *Annual Report of the Canadian Historical Association*, 1932, 5–14.

Irving, Washington, *Astoria*, Clatsop Edition, Portland, Oreg., n.d.

Kushner, Howard I., " 'Hellships': Yankee Whaling Along the Coasts of Russian-America, 1835–1852," *New England Quarterly*, March 1972, 81–95.

Mazour, Anatole G., "The Russian-American and Anglo-Russian Conventions, 1824–1825: An Interpretation," *Pacific Historical Review*, August 1945, 303–10.

Morison, Samuel Eliot, "Boston Traders in Hawaiian Islands, 1789–1823," *Proceedings of the Massachusetts Historical Society*, 1920–21, 9–47.

———, *The Maritime History of Massachusetts 1783–1860*, Sentry Edition, Cambridge, Mass., 1961.

Ogden, Adele, "New England Traders in Spanish and Mexican California," in *Greater America: Essays in Honor of Herbert Eugene Bolton*, Berkeley, Calif., 1945, 395–413.

Wheeler, Mary E., "Empires in Conflict and Cooperation: The 'Bostonians' and the Russian-American Company," *Pacific Historical Review*, November 1971, 419–41.

10 TRADE WITH ESPAGNOLS

The principal object which we Russians had in view in this trade with California, was the insuring to the Russian possessions in North America and the Aleutian islands, quite to Kamchatka and Ochotsk, a regular supply of corn and flour from New California.

G. H. Von Langsdorff

The Economy of Alta California

Along with the Bostonians, the Espagnols or Californios of Alta California provided most of Russian America's provisions during the first third of the nineteenth century. Although New Spain had been conquered for God, gold, and glory, the foremost activities by 1800 were cattle ranching and grain farming. Farming was especially dominant in Alta California, where mining was virtually nonexistent. There, agriculture was based upon a chain of Franciscan missions begun by Father Junípero Serra on the coast between San Diego and San Francisco, most of them situated one day's march apart on the Camino Real. Cattle herding was the chief agricultural activity; in 1818, 351,130 head of livestock, including 142,607 cattle, were kept on mission lands,[1] and by the 1820s many missions owned 20,000 to 30,000 head.[2] The ranchos also had large herds; for example, on one near San Pedro Bay there were 13,000 head.[3] Valued mainly for their hide and tallow, cattle were the basis of trade. Wheat was the principal crop at all the missions (especially the northern ones), with yields in the 1820s averaging from 20-fold to 30-fold.[4]

In 1818 the 20 missions produced about 180,000 bushels of wheat, barley, corn, and oats and nearly 7400 bushels of beans and peas,[5] and the French navigator De Roquefeuil estimated that Alta California was capable of exporting 2000 tons of grain or vegetables and 150 to 200 tons of dried or salted beef per year.[6] The province was understandably renowned for its agricultural productivity and climatic salubrity (despite the equally renowned indolence of its *razones,* or Spanish inhabitants). "The fertile soil and healthful climate of Upper California is so famous as to be almost proverbial," declared Governor Wrangel in 1835.[7]

Trade was an important activity in Alta California, although until 1816 Spanish colonial policy forbade commerce with foreign vessels. Nevertheless, much contraband trade was conducted along the western coast of New Spain by well-manned, well-rigged, and well-armed American ships, which outmaneuvered and outsailed the few Spanish warships. Manufactures were in great demand and neither officials nor missionaries, especially the latter, were above smuggling. Thus, lying close to Alaska, abounding in foodstuffs, and susceptible to trade, this Elysian province was an attractive source of provisions for the Russian-American Company.

THE REZANOV VISIT

The decision to tap the cornucopia was precipitated by a food crisis in the winter of 1805–6 at New Archangel. For several years no supply ship had arrived from Okhotsk, and the Bostonians provided only irregular and temporary relief. By 1805 each of the colonial capital's 200 residents was receiving no more than one pound of bread daily, and after October 1 they lived on dried fish and sea lion and seal meat, finally resorting to cuttlefish, crows, and eagles. Only the sick were fed wheat with molasses and beer brewed from fir cones.[8] The situation was only momentarily relieved by the purchase of the American vessel *Juno* with its cargo in the fall. Von Langsdorff, arriving with Rezanov at New Archangel late in August, found the settlement "in want of almost all the necessaries of life,"[9] the workers so debilitated that "all work was in danger of being stopped."[10]

Rezanov was appalled by what he termed the "extremely calamitous situation."[11] By the end of February 1806, malnutrition had killed at least eight and disabled about sixty of the 192 Russians at New Archangel; by winter's end seventeen Russians and many natives had died.[12] According to Von Langsdorff, the situation "became every day more and more critical; almost all the works were at a stand, and scarcely any of the Promüschleniks could be said to be free from disease; it became then absolutely necessary that some measures should be taken, if possible, to stop the progress of scurvy."[13] In late February, Rezanov reported to the head office that he would have to sail to California to obtain supplies.[14] According to Khlebnikov, the colonies' grain supply was the chief concern of Rezanov,[15] who had resolved to get flour and possibly furs either publicly from the authorities or privately from the missions. Rezanov knew that Alta California was short of certain goods and that the ban on trade with foreigners had led to contraband trade, in which the missionaries were known to be instrumental. Certainly the head office knew that, despite the prohibition, American navigators secretly bought from the Californios anything they needed.[16] Baranov learned from the same clandestine traders of Alta California's scarcity of manufactures and collusion in smuggling.

Early in March, Rezanov left New Archangel aboard the *Juno*. The wretched condition of the scorbutic crew prompted him to try to ascend the Columbia River for fresh provisions, but contrary winds and currents prevented the ship from entering the river. By April he had reached San Francisco, where the padres of San Francisco Mission invited him to dinner and told him of their strong desire to trade, offering to sell a cargo of breadstuffs. With the arrival of Governor Arrillaga from Monterey, Rezanov declared, "I frankly tell you we need breadstuffs,"[17] adding:

> I want to purchase the breadstuffs in order to learn, upon their distribution in the possessions of Russia in America and in Kamchatka, if the purchase price would be suitable, and to determine the needs of each place, and in the general plan the total quantity required, as we now know in detail what Nueva California can supply, and the amount.[18]

Although the officials and missionaries were eager to establish regular trade, they could not do so without Madrid's consent. "If the court of Madrid knew the needs of this province," Arrillaga stated, "it would surely commence reciprocal trade relations with Russia, from which common benefit would result, and then the Bostonians would not corrupt the savages."[19] Rezanov then moved to allay the suspicion long entertained by the Spanish that the Russians wanted to occupy their territory[20] (Yankee rumor contended that the company was eyeing Alta California and that its colonies were poor), presenting expensive gifts to the presidio's authorities. He made a favorable impression and obtained a promise of provisions, but was only permitted to buy, not barter, one cargo of grain. Arrillaga refused to consent to general trade because he lacked authority to do so.

Meanwhile, Rezanov's efforts were hampered by news of animosity between Russian and Spanish allies and by rumors of war between Russia and Spain. These tidings, as well as the mutinous intentions of several foreigners in the *Juno*'s crew, prompted him to cultivate the affection of Concepción Argüello (daughter of the commandant of San Francisco Presidio) in order to improve the chances of securing trade. Reputed to be the most beautiful girl in Alta California, the 15-year-old maiden was soon betrothed to the 42-year-old widower.

Because he was then able to barter for foodstuffs, Rezanov obtained more provisions in place of the Russian goods. The cargo included some 2000 bushels of grain and five tons of flour,[21] and in exchange the Californios received 11,174 rubles' (5587 piasters') worth of Russian goods.[22]* Von Langsdorff was somewhat surprised: "instead of so very large a proportion of corn, he [Rezanov] did not rather take more salted meat, as it was of an excellent quality, and much cheaper. It is however a certain fact, that a Russian always prefers a piece of bread to a proportionate quantity of meat, and M. Von Resanoff probably thought that in procuring the means of having plenty of bread he had superseded all other wants."[23] Significantly, most of the grain was furnished by Concepción's brothers and the rest by the missionaries. The *Juno* left San Francisco in mid-May and reached New Archangel a month later, where the provisions were sold at low prices in order to alert the residents to the advantages of trade and to encourage them to undertake voyages for this purpose.[24] Before leaving San Francisco Rezanov left the following letter with Arrillaga for delivery to the viceroy of New Spain:

> Dear Sir. The complete agreement existing between our governments, the proximity of their settlements in the New World, and the mutual advantages that can spring from trade—all this induced me to come to New California in order to discuss with the Governor how many beneficial results there can be for a region found so far from its motherland. Here, my dear sir, is my sole purpose, following which I have the pleasure to sojourn in so happy a country. . . .
>
> New California, abounding in grain and cattle products, can market

* Von Langsdorff, however, states that 24,000 piasters' (48,000 rubles') worth of Russian goods were bartered (Von Langsdorff, *Voyages and Travels,* II, 215).

its output only in our settlements, and it can most quickly receive assistance [by] getting every necessity by means of trade with our territories; the best means for securing the well-being of the missions and for leading the country to prosperity is the exchange of its surplus products for merchandise, for which it is not necessary to pay cash and the importation of which is not connected with any difficulties, with a view to obtaining at any time all products, the shortage of which now retards the development of crafts and industry. To the same extent the nearness of transport will facilitate the maintenance of our settlements in the North, which are now supplied from afar with everything that the severity of the climate denies. Such ties, my dear sir, are predestined by Nature herself to make the subjects of both countries as happy as possible and also to preserve forever friendship between both powers possessing such extensive territories.[25]

Rezanov had managed to barter provisions in Alta California but he had not succeeded in negotiating a trade agreement. Nevertheless, contraband trade had been initiated, and the question of regular trade was to be considered by Madrid. Rezanov rejoiced: "Our American possessions will not be in want. Kamchatka and Okhotsk can be supplied with grain and other food supplies."[26] He hoped to ship grain from San Francisco to Petropavlovsk and Okhotsk for sale there at prices 50 per cent lower than local prices.[27] This hope was part of his plan to trade Siberian cloth and hardware in Alta California, Chile, and the Philippines for foodstuffs for Russian America and the Russian Far East.

Official Efforts

Rezanov's optimism, however, was premature. Rezanov himself died in Siberia in 1807 on his way to St. Petersburg.* In early 1808 the Russian-American Company, following his suggestions (and perhaps encouraged by the alliance formed between Russia and Spain in 1807), asked the tsar to solicit Madrid's permission for the sending of one or two company vessels each year to San Francisco, Monterey, and San Diego to exchange manufactures for provisions. The company's director, Michael Buldakov, wrote Alexander I:

California abounds in grain, and there being nowhere to market it more than 5417 tons are left to rot each year; by contrast, our Ameri-

* His California fiancée supposedly waited faithfully until hearing of his death in 1841, whereupon she became a nun. This romance has been popularized in a novel by Gertrude Atherton and a poem by Bret Harte.

can settlements have to obtain grain which is transported more than 2000 miles overland across Siberia and which costs the company about 41½ kopecks per pound. The same transport to Kamchatka for the troops there costs the state more than 27½ kopecks per pound, not including the salary of agents and the annual loss of horses by the Yakut packers, who sometimes will not haul.

California abounds in cattle and horses, which roam unattended in the woods and extend in large herds even as far as the Columbia River. The Spanish Government, in order to prevent the cattle from damaging the cornfields, has from 10 to 30 thousand of them slaughtered yearly; by contrast, Okhotsk-Kamchatka Kray, which very often suffers from general starvation, is in great need of such cattle. During Rezanov's stay in California several hundred cattle were purposely killed just for their hides for holding the grain that he had bought from the Spaniards, and their flesh was discarded.

California has the greatest lack of all kinds of linen and iron. In place of the latter there as fasteners to strengthen house construction they use hide straps, which even support roofs and other heavy suspensions. Russia has not only this metal but linen in abundance and could supply other countries with them without impoverishing itself.[28]

Buldakov added that Arrillaga had admitted to Rezanov that the Californios could not manage without trade with the Russians.[29] Accordingly, the Russian government instructed its ambassador to Spain, Baron Strogonov, to seek permission for trade with Alta California. Revolts in Spain and the Napoleonic wars, however, nullified Strogonov's efforts, and the company was advised to seek permission on its own accord until peace was restored in Europe.[30] In 1810 the head office lamented: "the company still has not established the ties with California that are extremely necessary for the acquisition of provisions, which the company's business urgently needs because everything sent there [New Archangel] via Okhotsk is expensive, not always fresh, and not in the proportion that is needed there."[31] Clearly Alta California was seen as an alternative to Siberian supply and Alaskan agriculture.

The reason for desiring this trade is the usual dearth in the company's colonies of the primary necessities of life, with which California, a close neighbor, overabounds. That in the colonies there have been undertaken long and diligent attempts to establish agriculture, which the damp climate does not favor at all; cattlebreeding, although successfully propagated, is still found in such a condition that it is impossible, barring a great increase, to utilize it for sustenance, except in emergencies; and that is why all provisions, as well as rigging and sailcloth, are imported there by the company from Russia and Siberia over a long route at high cost for transport; sea accidents sometimes occur, depriving the colonies of such imports.[32]

From Alta California the company figured that it could obtain "various grains, which are grown in abundance among them [the Californios], live and butchered cattle, countless of which even run wild in the woods, their fat, silken and manufactured articles, and other necessities . . . ," for the province had "no iron at all (in place of which ox hide and sinew are used in all fastenings), manufactured linen and flaxen articles, glass, and many other things. . . ."[33]

Now the company dealt directly with the commandants and padres in the hope that the Mexican uprising of 1810 had made them more receptive to foreign trade.* A "proclamation" was sent in 1810 via an American ship to the commandant of San Francisco. Addressed to "noble persons living in California," it urged reciprocal trade, stating that the company's "sincere desire is to supply you in the future with everything that your country needs" and "to receive grain, cattle fat, live cattle, etc., which you have in abundance."[34] The Espagnols replied that they would like to trade but that not even the governor of Alta California or the viceroy of Mexico could infringe Madrid's ban. The company was well aware of this ban, of course, but it also knew that American shipmasters clandestinely bought everything they wanted from the Californios.[35] So Baranov sent additional requests to the missionaries and commandants at every opportunity. His requests were in vain, but in 1813 José Manuel Ruiz, one of the most influential California missionaries, promised to supply the colonies with various needs "without publicity."[36] The civil authorities advised the company to again petition the Spanish through Russia's Minister of Foreign Affairs. Nothing resulted, even though the Spanish consul at St. Petersburg reported to Madrid on the mutual advantages of trade between Russian Alaska and Spanish California.

Unofficial Trade

Meanwhile, contraband was resumed with the joint Russian-Yankee hunting ventures along Alta California's coast from 1809 to 1813, when the American skippers sometimes procured wheat, barley, beans, salted

* The Mexican Revolution, however, was weakly felt in remote Alta California, whose *peninsular* missionaries in particular remained partial to Spain and hence unsympathetic to revolution.

beef, lard, and salt for New Archangel. In 1812 the necessity of joint hunting was obviated when the company established Fort Ross, which soon became a station for contraband trade as well as for hunting. About a month after its dedication (September 1812) Fort Ross was visited by eight Spanish soldiers officered by one Moraga, who said that all Californios would be glad to be able to acquire much-needed goods and who promised to ask the governor at Monterey to allow trade between the Russians and the Californios. Moraga returned to Fort Ross in January 1813 with Arrillaga's permission for mutual trade and joint hunting, subject to the condition that until formal permission was received from Madrid, company trading vessels were to anchor offshore, and all trade goods were to be transported between the mainland and the ships by rowboats.[37] Manager Kuskov readily accepted this arrangement, immediately sending a clerk with various goods to San Francisco, where they brought 1400 piasters (2800 rubles), part of which was paid in grain.[38] The company also sent commercial agents to Alta California as supercargos on Boston ships.

The Californios badly needed the contraband merchandise because both Old and New Spain tended to neglect their needs. In 1816, when Von Kotzebue's first expedition visited San Francisco, the local military authorities bemoaned the "misery in which they languished, forgotten and deserted for six or seven years by Mexico, their mother-land."[39] The expedition's botanist, Von Chamisso, stated: "Discontents arose, also, because the new Governor of Monterey, Don Pablo Vincente de Solá [1815–22], had, since his entry upon the duties of his office, set himself in opposition to smuggling, which alone had provided them with the most indispensable necessaries."[40] With the death in 1814 of Arrillaga, who had favored the Russians, relations worsened and trade declined, especially with the arrival in 1815 of De Solá, the new governor, who resented the presence of Fort Ross on what he regarded as Spanish territory.* De Solá halted all relations with the Russians, including clandestine trade and joint hunting, and began stricter surveillance of Russian activities, with the result that several company clerks and hunters were arrested and sentenced to forced labor. But the pressing needs

---

* The company usually responded to protests from the Californios by saying that Fort Ross had been founded on unoccupied territory with the approval of the tsar, while the Russian Government usually responded to Spanish objections by simply ignoring the existence of the settlement. Fort Ross was regarded as a beachhead by Californios, who from their own weakness feared the Russians.

of the Californios, particularly his soldiers, soon obliged De Solá to renew trade. The revolutionary war in Mexico was causing shortages, and
New Spain was no longer being subsidized by Old Spain. In the summer of 1815 De Solá complained that no supply ship had reached Alta
California from Mexico for five years.[41] In the same year the last Manila
galleon ended Mexico's Philippine source of consumer goods. Perhaps
for this reason the ban on colonial trade with foreigners was lifted in
1816, although high tariffs and duties were imposed. In Alta California
both soldiers and padres were running short of supplies. The *frontera
del norte* obviously required loyal and ready troops. And the missions,
the keystone of the province's economy, surely needed goods. The missionaries were friendly and helpful to Kuskov, just as they had been to
Rezanov, and were inclined to ignore any objections to smuggling by
the military authorities, particularly as there was not a little antagonism
between the two groups anyway. Perhaps, too, the self-righteous fathers
automatically rejected any secular objections to transactions that satisfied clerical needs. Besides, the missionaries needed the Russians as a
market for surplus wheat. As a Russian naval officer noted in 1820: "the
missionaries . . . are always glad at the arrival of any vessel, for they
will accept anything because of their poverty. . . ."[42] Furthermore, the
Californios were probably placated somewhat by gifts, such as two
dozen knives and a carriage, presented to De Solá in 1817–1818.[43]

Official Trade

Meanwhile, deeming it necessary to resolve the hunting and trading
difficulties of Russian California, Hagemeister, en route to New Archangel to inspect the colonies and replace Baranov, stopped at Fort Ross
in September 1817. At Kuskov's suggestion he visited San Francisco on
the two-fold pretense of collecting some money due on goods sold and
obtaining the release of some Aleut prisoners, but he actually hoped to
negotiate a trading and hunting agreement with the authorities. Despite
De Solá's absence, Hagemeister secured the release of twelve Russians
and two Aleuts and permission to barter for provisions (but not to hunt),
for the province's soldiers had received nothing but food for the previous
seven years.[44] In 1818 he returned to Alta California (this time as governor of Russian America) and obtained permission to trade from De Solá.
The effort cost Hagemeister "much labor" and "no little expense," for he
had to make 500 piasters' (1000 rubles') worth of gifts to officials and

to pay a delivery tax, which, according to De Solá, were necessary in view of the lack of subsidies from Spain. De Solá also said that he had allowed Hagemeister to trade as a personal favor and that he hoped that no more Russian ships would come to trade. One of the Russian officers, however, felt that with "skill and prudence" more deals could be made because the Espagnols would reap personal profits and needed goods for the neglected province.[45] The officer was right. Thereafter, with special permission from Monterey, two or three company ships traded annually at Alta California's ports, procuring from 3388 to 6775 bushels of wheat each year.[46] The ships traded at San Francisco and Monterey (and sometimes at San Quintín, Santa Cruz, San Pedro, and San Diego), leaving New Archangel in the fall, after hunting in Alaska and harvesting in California were completed, and returning in the spring.* Cyril Khlebnikov, the *Kutuzov's* supercargo, noted: "We began to have regular [trade] relations with California from 1817, for the purchase of provisions, and always with the special permission of the Governor. . . ."[47] Finally, in 1821, when Mexico became independent, Alta California's ports were opened to unrestricted foreign trade. In the following year the head office ordered Governor Muravyov "to direct every effort to the expansion of trade connections with California, especially now that Spanish dominion in America on both sides of the equator has ended, so that the law closing the ports of that region to foreigners has lost its force."[48] In 1826 the company received permission from the governor of Alta California to establish a permanent commercial agent at Monterey, filling the post with Khlebnikov, who had held it de facto since the early 1820s.** Captain Aemelius Simpson of the Hudson's Bay Company noted in late 1827 that the Russian-American Company had a depot at Monterey "well furnished with Goods for the market, with which they purchase grain and other Provisions for their Establishments. . . ."[49]

The Russians, of course, also had compelling reasons for wanting to trade. Not only was colonial provisionment generally haphazard but from 1818, when salaries in money and in kind (flour) were substituted for shares, the company was obligated by contract to provide a certain

---

* Often the ships called at Port Rumyantsev, too, to unload supplies (sugar, salt, tea, fish) and passengers for Ross Counter and to load agricultural products, furs, and passengers for New Archangel.
** When Khlebnikov left the colonies in 1832, he was replaced as commissary (1833) by an American merchant, William Hartnell. In 1834 Hartnell quit; his place was taken by Peter Kostromitinov, who was eventually succeeded by George Chernykh.

amount of provisions. So a regular supply of grain became essential. Hagemeister acknowledged in 1818: "When grain is supplied from California in sufficient quantity, a non-monetary outlay will be made to Russians in accordance with the head office's order, including flour provisions of one pood [36 pounds] each per month. . . ."[50] And Khlebnikov wrote in 1832 that "for 14 years, that is, from the time when the company was obligated to supply its promyshlenniks and then its other employees with grain provisions, wheat or flour and other foodstuffs were obtained primarily from California, where harvests were sometimes very abundant and sometimes meager but sufficient for the supply of the colonies with provisions. . . ."[51]

New Archangel imported provisions from Alta California's ports nearly every year from 1814 until 1848, when the area was annexed by the United States* (Table 10).

In addition, the company occasionally imported salt from both Alta and Baja California. The chief sources were Baja California's San Quintín and Carmen Island, where, in Khlebnikov's words, the salt was found in "great abundance" and was obtained "very conveniently and cheaply."[52]

For these provisions the company traded primarily manufactures, including textiles, metals, utensils, implements, cord, thread, canvas, tea, coffee, sugar, pepper, wax, candles, and other commodities such as shot and tobacco.[53] The cargos brought to San Francisco on the *Buldakov* in 1821 and the *Kyakhta* in 1828 consisted of mostly linens and woolens, stockings and hats, thread and buttons, lanterns and funnels, axes and files, and sugar and paper.[54]

The demand for such items attested the scarcity of manufactured goods in Alta California. In 1806 Rezanov marveled that Alta California lacked so many things that were so easily obtainable.[55] The province received some Chinese goods from Acapulco via the Manila galleons but, as Arrillaga told Rezanov, "only through the hands of the Mexicans, who, by two corvetas which are annually cruising along our coast from San Blas, send us goods at excessive prices, and we have to pay the piastres in advance, in order to obtain, the following year, the necessaries of life."[56] The last Manila galleon sailed in 1815. About the same year a promyshlennik observed that at San Francisco Mission the Spaniards

---

* Occasionally Russian Navy ships also obtained provisions at Alta California's ports for their own use. For example, in 1824 the *Cruiser* procured 2258 bushels of wheat (USNA, 29:55v.).

"used wooden ploughs to plough the fields and . . . they had scarcely any tools."[57] And several years later Khlebnikov noted that there was "hardly a skilled mechanic among them."[58] In 1824 Dmitry Zavalishin of the *Cruiser* observed that processing was so uncommon and expensive that flour cost 20 to 24 times as much as whole grain.[59] For this reason the company imported almost solely whole grain from Alta California. The province's needs were supplied mostly by the company, at least until the mid-1820s, when Zavalishin found that most of the European goods in the province originated with the company.[60]

The Russians also obtained provisions from the Espagnols via joint hunting in Alta California's waters and via barter with Fort Ross. From 1817 the company had tried in vain to persuade De Solá to allow joint hunting.* His successor, however, Luis Argüello, signed an agreement permitting such hunting between San Francisco and San Diego, with the catch being divided equally. The Russians were to exchange their share of the catch with Argüello for first-class wheat at 41½ bushels per pelt.[61]** In 1824, for example, the *Golovnin* exchanged fur seals at Monterey for 4896 bushels of wheat.[62] This arrangement lasted until 1834.

Trade at Fort Ross

At Fort Ross commercial relations with the missionaries and commandants of Alta California were established early. Golovnin asserted that the Californios "even helped the Russians, supplying them with their first acquisitions of cattle and horses, and afterwards they had friendly relations and trade with Mr. Kuskov. From him the missionaries purchased various goods for grain and money. . . ."[63] General Vallejo admitted that in the beginning the Russians bought as much wheat as they could, as well as butter and dried beef.[64] With the founding of San Rafael Mission (1817) and Sonoma Mission (1821), both of which needed materials and equipment, contacts with Fort Ross became very frequent. Under both Schmidt and Shelikhov Ross Counter's relations with the Californios were always friendly, and in times of need baidarkas were sent from Fort Ross to San Francisco, where they "always obtained tallow, lard, soap, and other requirements from the missions."[65]

---

* So the Russians poached instead at every opportunity.
** The signing of this agreement was timely for the company, whose catch of sea otters along the coast of New Albion had dropped from 877 in 1812–14 to only 43 in 1822–23 (*Materialy*, III, 139).

Table 10. Company Imports of Provisions from Alta California, 1814–48

Year	Ship	Port	Wheat (bu*)	Barley (bu*)	Flour (lbs*)	Beans and Peas (bu*)	Dried and Salted Meat (lbs*)	Tallow and Lard (lbs*)
1814	Pedlar	San Francisco	252	0	0	0	0	0
1814	Chirikov	San Francisco	909	0	0	0	0	0
1815	Chirikov	San Francisco	2,630	0	0	0	0	0
1816	Ilmen	San Francisco	1,037	0	0	0	0	0
1817	Kutuzov	San Francisco	808	578	4,590	263	0	5,177
1818	Kutuzov	Monterey and Santa Cruz	7,091**	1,128**	2,907	2,177	13,770	27,617
1820†	Buldakov	Monterey	3,105	564	6,111	392	6,565	9,848
1821	Golovnin	San Francisco	1,668	0	0	58	0	6,641
1821	Kutuzov	Monterey	2,618	677	0	738	18,407	12,120
1821	Buldakov	San Francisco	4,243	0	379	0	0	6,515
1822	Volga	Monterey	291	632	101	60	0	0
1822	Buldakov	Monterey	2,315	451	4,116	366	4,545	8,030
1822	Volga	Santa Cruz	1,173	0	0	289	0	152
1823	Rurik	Monterey	1,674	259	2,550	207	4,293	4,747
1824	Baikal	Monterey	2,972	903	0	0	0	12,878
1824	Kyakhta	Santa Cruz	2,970	0	0	60	4,570	2,437
1824	Buldakov	San Pedro	4,254	0	0	0	0	3,535
1825	Kyakhta	Monterey	3,408	0	0	94	0	6,515
1825	Baikal	San Pedro	1,196	14	0	0	0	556
1826	Baikal	San Pedro and San Diego	3,315	205	0	390	11,665	6,666
1826	Okhotsk	San Francisco	1,918	0	0	0	0	0
1827	Golovnin	Monterey	1,555	767	0	445	0	0
1827	Okhotsk	San Francisco	2,076	0	0	0	4,747	5,417
1827	Baikal	San Diego	1,334	293	2,020	72	0	5,353
1828	Kyakhta	San Francisco	2,339	63	0	31	3,358	5,479
1828	Okhotsk	Monterey and San Diego	1,406	7	0	177	1,263	1,010
1830	Baikal	Monterey and San Francisco	4,987	0	0	361	12,278	6,616
1831	Urup	Monterey and San Francisco	4,710	0	0	323	4,762	9,216
1832	Urup	San Francisco	5,511	0	0	89	1,986	0
1833	Urup	San Francisco	4,762	0	0	676	4,570	12,575
1834	Urup and Polifem	Monterey and San Francisco	9,352	?	?	?	some	?
1835	Polifem	?	2,800	0	0	0	0	0
1836	Sitka	?	0	0	59,586	0	0	0
1837	Sitka	?	4,949	0	0	0	?‡	0
1838	Sitka	?	9,033	0	0	0	?	0
1839	Helena	San Francisco	8,400	0	0	0	?	0

Year	Ship	Port	Wheat (bu*)	Barley (bu*)	Flour (lbs*)	Beans and Peas (bu*)	Dried and Salted Meat (lbs*)	Tallow and Lard (lbs*)
1839	?	San Francisco	4,767	0	0	0	?	0
1840	Baikal	?	13,230	0	0	0	0	0
1840	?	?						
1844	Alexander's Heir	?	4,246	?	?	?	?	?
1845	Baikal and Constantine	?	3,994 to 4,410	0	0	0	0	0
1846	Constantine	?	2,730*†	210	0	8	10,924	4,225 to 5,200
1846	Baikal	?	4,118	0	0	0	0	0
1847	Alexander's Heir	?	4,717*‡	0	0	some	130 head	some
1848	Okhotsk	?	0	0	0	0	18,075	0

* Through 1839 these conversions are based upon Khlebnikov's equivalents of 135½ pounds per *fanega* of wheat, 108⅓ pounds per *fanega* of barley, 144½ pounds per *fanega* of peas or beans, and 25½ pounds per *arroba* of flour, meat, tallow, or lard (Gibson, "Russian America," 7). From 1839 the conversions are based upon New Archangel's equivalent of 126 pounds per *fanega* of wheat or barley (USNA, 45: 263). Also, one sack of flour (or tallow) commonly weighed 325 pounds and one barrel of flour (or meat) commonly weighed about 198 pounds. One American bushel comprises 60 pounds of wheat, peas, or beans and 48 pounds of barley.

** Elsewhere the same author states that the *Kutuzov* obtained 271 tons of grain (9028 to 11,285 bushels of wheat and barley) (Khlebnikov, *Zhizneopisanie*, 173). The French navigator De Roquefeuil says Hagemeister procured 500 tons of grain (16,667 to 20,833 bushels of wheat and barley) (De Roquefeuil, *Voyage*, 108). The Russian officer Lütke asserts that Hagemeister acquired 325 tons (10,834 bushels) of wheat (Shur, *K beregam*, 140).

† In many instances the 1820–33 figures differ slightly from the figures for the same years listed elsewhere by the same author (see Khlebnikov, "Zapiski," 60–61 and *Materialy*, III, 12,79).

‡ According to the company doctor at New Archangel, in the late 1830s 16 to 24 tons of salted meat were imported annually from Alta California (Blaschke, *Topographia*, 53).

*† All of this wheat was received from Sutter in partial payment for Ross Counter (USNA, 52: 48ov.).

*‡ This total includes 517 bushels received from Sutter in partial payment for Ross Counter (USNA, 54: 18, 28ov.).

Sources: Gibson, "Russian America," 11; Khlebnikov, "Zapiski," 13v., 60; Tikhmenev, *Historical Review*, I, 406; USNA, 37: 137v., 38: 105, 283–83v., 39: 138v., 40: 51, 41: 338, 42: 86v., 43: 17, 33, 313, 50: 51, 51: 163, 286, 52: 133, 338v., 339v., 479v., 480v., 54: 280v., 282, 283, 55: 123v.

With their lack of artisans the Californios often sought the services of Russian craftsmen at Fort Ross. In 1824 Von Kotzebue noted during his second visit to San Francisco that the Spaniards "often find Ross very serviceable to them. For instance, there is no such thing as a smith in all California; consequently the making and repairing of all manner of iron implements here is a great accommodation to them, and affords lucrative employment to the Russians."[66]* In a letter to the governor of Alta California a manager at Ross Counter wrote that "through our work and equipment the missions along San Francisco Bay acquire rowboats. These missionaries and other inhabitants always come to our settlement with requests to repair rifles, locks, instruments, and the like."[67] The Californios especially needed small vessels. In 1806 Von Langsdorff was amazed by the "total want of vessels" at the missions of Santa Clara, San José, and San Francisco and at the presidio of San Francisco.[68] During Von Kotzebue's first visit to San Francisco in 1816 Von Chamisso noted that the Spaniards possessed "not a single boat in this glorious water-basin."[69] In 1823, 1826, and 1827 the Russians exchanged longboats with the Californios for provisions for both Russian California and Russian Alaska; for example, in 1823 an old longboat was sold to Commandant Martínez of San Francisco for 322 bushels of wheat, and in 1827 the padres of San José Mission paid 1129 bushels of wheat for a longboat.[70] Until the mid-1820s Ross Counter profited as much as 6000 rubles in some years from the sale of longboats, wheels, firearms, sabers, saddles, and pots and pans in Alta California.[71] Such swapping evidently continued through the 1830s, for in 1839 General Sutter recollected that Californios often went to Fort Ross to buy articles.[72] Manager Rotchev procured 3839 bushels of wheat from the missions in 1839 (1806 bushels) and 1840 (2033 bushels) for New Archangel.[73] General Vallejo was to recall many years later that the Russians at Fort Ross bought a good deal from the missions.[74]

Importance to the Russians

Together the California trade and the Boston trade sustained the colonies. The attempt to gain a foothold on the Sandwich Islands, a potential source of foodstuffs, had been thwarted in 1817. Furthermore, after

---

* The German traveler Adolf Erman noted in 1829 that company doctors and artisans regularly voyaged from New Archangel to Alta California to ply their skills (Erman, "Zufass-Bemerkungen," 254, 254n.).

1817, company employees were entitled to definite and substantial food rations, and in 1821 all foreign ships (including American vessels, which had been supplying the company's colonies since the beginning of the century) were barred from Russian America's ports. And by now Russian California's agriculture had not proved very productive. As an anonymous Russian stated in 1826, "Trade with California and the Americans (the civilized ones) furnishes plenty of everything, not only the necessities of life but even articles that make it pleasant and at very moderate prices in accordance with circumstances."[75] Khlebnikov declared that "if for some reason grain were not supplied from California, then the position of the colonies would be threatened with starvation,"[76] and a Mexican official asserted in 1824 that the Russians could not sustain themselves without California's abundant grain and beef.[77]

Mainly because of the California trade at New Archangel in the mid-1820s the company was able to distribute as rations more than five tons of flour in winter and four tons in summer, selling in addition up to four tons of flour in winter and two tons in summer.[78] In fact, Russian America became California's chief grain market. Governor Wrangel reported in 1834 that from the Californios the company bought "especially wheat, which nobody except us buys from them."[79] And in 1841 George Chernykh, the company's commissary in Alta California, stated that "The *chief market* for wheat from California has heretofore been our American colonies, for which 3000 to 4000 *fanegas* [6300 to 8400 bushels] of wheat have been bought annually."[80] California provisions were also inexpensive. At New Archangel in the late 1820s, bread made from California wheat cost ten kopecks per pound, whereas bread made from Siberian wheat cost twenty-five kopecks per pound.[81] So important was the California trade that the company tried long and hard to persuade the provincial authorities to sign a formal agreement on regular trade that would secure a steady and sufficient supply of provisions for the Kamchatka Peninsula and Okhotsk Seaboard as well as for Alaska. In early 1820 the head office even told Count Nesselrode, Russia's Minister of Foreign Affairs, that the company "would willingly abandon this establishment [of Fort Ross] . . . if it could compensate the loss of this possession with the constant trade with New California into which the entry of the foreigners is prohibited. . . ."[82] All Russian overtures were rejected, however, and the company never did negotiate a formal commercial pact with the Espagnols, probably because of lingering Mexican suspicion of Russian intentions.

Competition

At first the company made sizable profits on the California trade, since, apart from a few American and English smugglers, only Russian ships were importing goods into the province. In 1821, following the revolution in Mexico, Alta California's ports were opened to all foreign vessels. Governor Muravyov was jubilant. He now hoped to obtain 1445 tons of California grain, enough to feed both Alaska (361 tons) and the Kamchatka Peninsula and Okhotsk Seaboard (1084 tons) for three years.[83] Actually, however, he seldom procured enough for Alaska alone for one year, for more and more American and English trading vessels were now visiting Alta California, with the result that the Russians had to sell goods more cheaply and to buy provisions more dearly in the face of stiffer competition. In 1823 Muravyov reported that "as soon as California's ports were opened to the ships of all nations, English and American ships came with large cargos for trade, and we have already lost the advantage of high prices on our goods."[84] It was not long before Russian wares were being outsold by more and better British and American merchandise.* Consequently, the company had instead to use piasters, which were scarce, and letters of credit, which the Californios were reluctant to accept. In 1826 Governor Chistyakov complained that "our trade with the Californios is being hampered more and more by foreign visitors, who sell their goods more cheaply than ours, and soon it will be difficult to obtain wheat without piasters. . . ."[85] So in 1827 he asked the head office to send him 10,000 piasters.[86] In 1829 he reported that California grain could not be obtained with Russian goods, only with American goods, and that duties almost always had to be paid in piasters.[87] It was difficult, he noted, to find enough piasters to pay for imports; for example, in 1828 the company purchased 8428 rubles' worth

---

* In 1828 a Hudson's Bay Company report on American trade in Alta California noted that the Americans brought mainly clothing, hats, textiles (cottons, silks, lace), cutlery, spirits, and sugar, which were bartered for hides and tallow, chiefly from the missions, whose priests were anxious to profit before being expelled by the new government, to which they refused to swear allegiance. The Americans usually disposed of their cargos at a profit of 200 to 300 per cent if they evaded Alta California's duties (25 per cent on sales and a tonnage fee of $2.50 per ton). "In the present unsettled state of the Country," it was noted, "they succeed in doing [so] to a great extent . . . by distributing presents and bribes to the official Men." The captain or supercargo simply paid for a false list of sales, but to be able to do this he had to know both the language and the officials (HBC, D.4/121, 26–26v.).

of salt at San Diego, only 870 rubles' worth of which could be obtained for goods.[88] In order to obtain the precious specie Khlebnikov even rented an apartment in Monterey, from which he and his assistants conducted a petty trade that netted two or three piasters daily.[89] In 1832 Wrangel reported: "The purchase of grain is made for goods and piasters. The goods are assessed high duties, and foreigners bring almost every kind of merchandise in such quantity that it is not always advantageous for us to market goods."[90] He calculated that no fewer than 8000 piasters (40,000 rubles) per year were needed to pay for California imports.*[91]

From 1821 the numerous American and British vessels not only competed with the company for sales of goods but also for purchases of foodstuffs. For instance, whaling ships, up to 130 of which frequented the California coast, called for provisions.[92] In 1822 non-Russian ships took 1152 tons of grain from Alta California to Peru.[93] Prices rose with increasing demand and decreasing supply; for whole wheat and barley the company paid 5 kopecks and 2 kopecks per pound in 1805 and 12 kopecks and 10 kopecks per pound in 1820.[94] And during the next few years the average cost of whole wheat from California was 15 kopecks per pound in goods or 11 kopecks per pound in money.**[95] By 1826 the grain cost the company 14 kopecks per pound, and 10 per cent of it was sand and gravel.[96] In 1831 Wrangel wrote Governor Victoria that the company, which had decided to pay no more than 7 kopecks per pound, would buy grain in Chile if prices, as well as duty and anchorage charges, were not lowered. The threat worked; the cost dropped from 9 kopecks per pound in 1832 to 7½ kopecks in 1834.[97] The reduction was partly due to the fact that the company paid mostly in piasters and letters of credit, which, unlike goods, were not liable to import duties.† Also, by now grain supply had increased, thanks to the growing number of ranchos. After 1821, foreigners were admitted to Alta California not only to trade but also to settle, provided that they became Mexican citizens and Catholics. Many Americans, Irishmen, Germans, and French-

* The head office had to send piasters periodically to New Archangel; in 1834, for example, 5000 were sent.
** This differential, of course, made it even more difficult for the company to trade goods rather than piasters for provisions.
† Etholen persuaded the Californios in 1832 to accept letters of credit. In 1833 Wrangel ordered the annual California ship to try to barter one-quarter in goods and piasters and three-quarters in letters of credit because of the shortage of the former, especially piasters, in the colonies (USNA, 36:326, 328v).

men arrived and received land grants measuring 13½ sections. This multiplication of ranchos broke the monopoly of the missions on the growing and trading of grain and thereby lowered its price—for wheat from 3 to 4 piasters per fanega in the mid-1820s to 2 piasters in the mid-1830s and 1½ piasters in 1838.[98]

Problems

Not only grain prices but also harbor fees and custom duties gradually increased during the 1820s. First exacted in 1818, custom duties were doubled to 25 per cent on imports and 6 per cent on exports in 1821; in addition, an anchorage fee of 2½ piasters per ship was imposed.[99] Throughout the 1820s Russian trading vessels paid both an anchorage fee of 10 piasters per vessel and a tonnage fee of 2⅛ piasters per ton of capacity.[100] Chistyakov complained in 1827 that "trade with California is being hampered more and more by the government's imposition of frightful percentages on imported goods and by other shipping charges. It will soon be quite impossible to buy grain for goods."[101] By 1835 the anchorage fee had been abolished; instead, the tonnage fee was exacted for the right to anchor whether or not any trading occurred, and if ships anchored for more than two days, duty was imposed on their cargo whether or not any was sold. This duty was exacted partly in money.[102]

These restrictive measures progressively diminished trade; in 1835, for example, only two ships traded at Monterey.[103] Additional expenses and delays were incurred by long waits in the ports; Wrangel complained in 1831 that company ships trading at San Francisco had to spend two to three months there at "great expense."[104] And by 1833, ships were waiting up to five months.[105] Moreover, frequent political changes meant frequent changes in trade regulations. Thus rising costs plus the falling prices on Russian imports made the company's California trade more and more difficult and less and less profitable, although the company was sometimes exempted from certain fees. Profits steadily declined—from 254 per cent in 1817 to 150 per cent in 1818, 110 per cent in 1820, and 35 to 70 per cent thereafter.*[106] Even so, profits were suffi-

* In Alaska, however, the return amounted to more than 100 per cent. In 1832, for example, the company imported from Alta California provisions worth 58,964 rubles at New Archangel, of which 20,281 rubles were company profit (Vrangel, "Donesenie o plavanii," 3). Similarly, salt obtained from Carmen Island in 1842 cost the company 3½ kopecks a pound at New Archangel but was sold there for 11 kopecks for a profit of more than 200 per cent (USNA, 46:173–73v.).

cient to defray the cost of upkeep of company vessels plying between San Francisco and New Archangel.[107] According to Khlebnikov, however, the California trade was motivated not by profit but by necessity— the necessity of provisioning the company's colonies.[108]

The decreasing supply of California grain was due not only to greater demand but also to periodic crop failures, particularly during the last half of the 1820s. Harvest failures occurred in 1823, 1826, 1827, 1828, 1829, 1835, 1836, 1840, and 1845.[109]* The 1829 failure, caused by drought, was especially severe, with most of the grainland not returning the seed and one-third of the cattle dying in many places.[110] In that year Chistyakov, frustrated by four straight crop failures, reported:

> For four years I have had the experience of explaining the same reason why there has been no harvest there. Now I doubt that there will ever be a harvest. Truthfully I say again that it is not worthwhile to send for grain to California, where it is expensive. Ships are gone for five months, and they return almost empty.[111]

Following the failures of 1835 and 1836, Governor Kupreyanov told his assistant Etholen that "continual experiments have shown that the supply of the colonies from California is very dubious because of the crop failures that not infrequently occur in that country and the resultant very high prices on California grain and provisions in general. . . ."[112] In 1835 the Governor-General of Eastern Siberia asked Kupreyanov whether the company could supply Petropavlovsk and Okhotsk with grain from Alta California; Kupreyanov's reply was that the company could not even rely upon the province to meet the needs of Russian America, let alone those of the Russian Far East, on account of frequent harvest failures.[113]

Grain production was even more drastically reduced by the breakup of the company's main suppliers and main customers—the missions.** Secularization was implemented in Alta California from 1834 through 1836. In the words of a Russian witness, "In early 1834 the Indians were set free and the padres were removed from the missions, assigned a salary (in local products) of a thousand piasters a year, and appointed administrators."[114] The missions quickly decayed; they were abandoned by

---

* According to the company's agronomist in Ross Counter, George Chernykh, the main causes were rust, foraging by young mares, and burning by Indians (Chernykh, "O zemledelii," 258).

** Admittedly, the decline of the missions was partially offset by the growth of the ranchos.

the Indians and plundered by the rancheros. The lands went unculti-
vated and the herds were slaughtered, their meat and hides sold to foreign traders. Wrangel, appalled by the decline of the missions, wrote in
1835:

> In order to demonstrate the reason for the utter decline of the pros-
> perity of the missions in California it is sufficient to recall the change in
> administration of these establishments in 1834: the old padres—natives
> of Spain—were replaced by uneducated and self-interested Mexicans
> and the economic part of the administration was transferred to the gov-
> ernment, which for this [purpose] appointed civilian *administradores;*
> freedom was granted to the Indians and they were allotted land and
> given needed assistance in the form of cattle and implements for an
> economic beginning, and no obligation was imposed other than the
> cultivation of so-called common land, whose output was prescribed for
> the upkeep of public institutions—hospitals, schools, churches, and
> priests. It would seem that all of this was very good and humane; but
> unfortunately neither the executors nor the Indians themselves thought
> so. The administrators, lacking the power and the ability to manage
> the lazy and free Indians, found the only reward for their labor in the
> securing of their own position; and the Indians, for whom freedom had
> no other meaning than the carefree life of an idler, abandoned them-
> selves completely to this sweet *fare vientes,* some of them making for
> their former woods, while those who stayed at the missions or in the
> pueblos—either because of an unaccustomedness to nomadic life or an
> attachment to liquor—did not find any better use for their earnings
> than to spend them on drink.[115]

And in 1841 George Chernykh noted sadly:

> at the missions, where formerly 100 to 300 fanegas [210 to 630 bush-
> els] were sown, almost nothing is sown now, for all of the Indians left
> the missions when their emancipation was declared and they now oc-
> cupy themselves in horsemanship: they drive the herds of horses away
> from the *thinking people* [*razones* or Californios, as distinguished from
> the *gentiles* or Indians] and commit plunder.[116]

Results

Not surprisingly, Alta California seldom met Russian America's food
needs. From 1817 through 1840 the California trade satisfied Alaska's
annual grain needs (6000 to 7500 bushels) in only seven different years
(1818, 1821, 1824, 1834, 1838, 1839, and 1840) and its annual beef needs
(no fewer than 14,445 pounds) in only one year (1821; possibly in the

late 1830s, too).* As Chistyakov reported in 1827, the company's California trade became worse and worse.[117] By 1828 California provisionment had become so unreliable that the company's head office decided to send up to 72 tons of flour annually to New Archangel via Okhotsk.[118] This meant that Alta California was supplying at most only about 60 per cent of the 181 tons of grain needed each year by the colonies. In 1828 Chistyakov reported that enough provisions could be obtained in Alta California to last one year only, despite "every effort" over the years to secure enough for two years in advance.[119] It was not until 1831 that Wrangel was able to procure more than a year's supply. In the mid-1830s the California trade furnished only about 60 per cent of the 271 tons of grain required annually by Russian America,[120] although in 1835 only one-third and in 1836 only one-half of the necessary amount of grain was provided.[121] In the latter year Wrangel complained to the Mexican government that the company's grain trade with Alta California had become so expensive and so dilatory that it was more advantageous to trade with Chile. Russian ships had to call at Monterey first to obtain permission to trade and then wait for the delivery of grain.[122]

As early as 1829, in fact, the company did trade in Chile, buying 5622 bushels of Chilean wheat, which was half as expensive and, being free of sand,[123] ten times better than California wheat. With the lowering of the price of California wheat to 2 piasters per fanega in 1832, however, Chilean wheat was no longer a bargain, for then the former cost 9 kopecks per pound at its source and 10 kopecks per pound after delivery to New Archangel while the latter cost 7 kopecks per pound at its source and 9½ kopecks per pound after delivery.[124]** Consequently, there is almost no advantage in going to Chile for wheat," Wrangel concluded.[125] Old Mexico was also seen as an alternative supplier. In 1832 Khlebnikov had advised Wrangel that although wheat was not grown in abundance along the coast of Mexico, it was possible to buy a "considerable amount" of flour at Guaymas, where it was brought from the interior;[126] in 1836 the company bought 30 tons of flour and 181 tons of salt in Mexico.[127] In the same year the company also exchanged 2750 piasters' worth of timber for up to 312 tons of whole wheat and flour at Valparaiso.[128]

---

* In the early 1830s the company wanted to obtain 9 tons of salted beef annually from California (USNA, 33:312) but got nowhere near that amount.
** In addition, in the spring of 1831 the Chilean wheat at New Archangel had been found to contain many midges (USNA, 33:213).

Decline and Revival

From the sale of Ross Counter in 1841 until the end of California's gold rush in the mid-1850s, company trade with California was slight. During the 1840s Russian America was amply provisioned by the Hudson's Bay Company. Nevertheless, the California trade continued, albeit on a reduced scale, because the company wanted a large stock of provisions on hand for emergencies. It also wanted to provision Kamchatka. In 1844 Etholen stated that the company desired 9033 bushels of wheat annually from California;[129] two years later, however, Governor Tebenkov reported that it could not expect expect to obtain this amount, owing to the large influx of Americans into California.[130] With the discovery of gold at Sutter's Mill in 1848, hordes of gold seekers created a food deficit in California, and late in the same year Tebenkov wryly reported that "Having an inestimable wealth of gold, California has almost none of life's necessities. . . ."[131] In that year the company's food supply became critical because (1) the importation of provisions from California collapsed with the abandonment of agriculture and the skyrocketing of food prices occasioned by the gold rush, and (2) the Hudson's Bay Company declined to renew the provisionment clause in its 1839 agreement (because of the loss of the fertile lower Columbia basin to the United States in 1846 and the flight of many of its agricultural settlers to the California gold fields).[132] For the same reasons farming declined and food prices increased in other agrarian countries on the Pacific coast, such as Chile and Colombia, and California was not replaced as a food supplier for Alaska. In fact, in 1849 California itself had to import grain from Chile; at the same time the Russians even tried to sell flour in California.* In 1850 Tebenkov reported that the "discovery of gold in California has greatly increased prices on all local products—grain, salt, cattle, etc.—and has made the acquisition of these products from there very disadvantageous for us at present."[133] So in the late 1840s and early 1850s Russian America was provisioned by sea from Europe. By the mid-1850s the gold fever had subsided and agriculture had recovered to the extent that California again produced a surplus of food. From 1855 the company annually bought flour, salted beef, butter, vegetables, hay,

---

* They did not succeed; instead, a schooner, a warehouse, fish, timber, and manufactures worth 243,782 rubles were sold for a net profit of 124,789 rubles (USNA, 55:276–77).

and salt in California, paying for them with the money received from the sale of ice and fish and taking them back to New Archangel on the same ships that brought ice and fish to San Francisco.* In 1855 Governor Voyevodsky observed:

> With the present development of grain cultivation in California and Oregon (which is confirmed by a letter received from Mr. Sanders [the company's banker in San Francisco]) I consider it most reliable and most advantageous in all respects to obtain provisions for the colonies from San Francisco rather than from other places, even Chile, from which our last shipment . . . of flour was very expensive. In this I am also keeping in mind that in obtaining provisions in instalments it is more advantageous to buy them when the opportunity arises, more convenient to deliver them on ships arriving here for ice, and more secure to obtain supplies in case of a blockade or other unforeseen circumstance. . . .[134]

Voyevodsky later noted that "in California grain can sometimes be bought at a very cheap price, especially in the fall with a good harvest, and its delivery to the colonies on ships used to transport ice also cannot be expensive, so that grain imported by the colonies in this way can cost less than that supplied by any other means."[135] Twice, however, the company was forced to go to Chile, just as it had done before American annexation—in 1854 for 201 tons of flour and in 1858 for fifty-three tons.[136] American California's provisions were high in quality but also high in price; around 1860 beef and butter from California cost the company twice as much and one and one-half times as much, respectively, as beef from Ayan and butter from Yakutsk.[137] But, because California grain was cheaper, the company in 1861 decided to buy from California rather than from Russia. In 1860 the head office had already instructed Governor Furguhelm that "in the future these provisions [wheat, flour, peas, and butter] must be bought at San Francisco and that they will no longer be sent to the colonies from Europe without a special request from you."[138] This revival of Russian-California trade, however, was fairly short-lived, ending with the sale of Alaska in 1867.

---

* To facilitate this renewed trade the company maintained a commercial agent (Peter Kostromitinov, former manager of Ross Counter) at San Francisco from 1851 through 1861.

Readings

Chernykh, E. L., "Agriculture of Upper California," *The Pacific Historian*, Winter 1967, 10–28.

Gentilcore, R. Louis, "Missions and Mission Lands of Alta California," *Annals* of the Association of American Geographers, March 1961, 46–72.

Khlebnikov, K. T., "Memoirs of California," trans. by Anatole G. Mazour, *Pacific Historical Review*, September 1940, 307–36.

Pierce, Richard A., ed., *Rezanov Reconnoiters California, 1806,* San Francisco, 1972.

Taylor, George P., "Spanish-Russian Rivalry in the Pacific, 1769–1820," *The Americas,* 1958, 109–27.

Vallejo, Guadalupe, "Ranch and Mission Days in Alta California," *Century Magazine,* 1890, 183–92.

11 TRADE WITH KING GEORGE'S MEN

Our attention on this side the Continent has been hitherto directed to the business of the Interior Country, but we have it now in view to extend it to the Trade of the Coast, and to connect therewith the discovery and Settlement of the interior Country up to our most Northern limits. This will place us so near each other as to afford frequent and facile opportunities of communication, and will I trust enable us to cultivate to Friendship, an acquaintance which we have long been desirous of forming, our wish being to establish with you an intercourse which may have for its end, the promotion of each others interests, while we are exceedingly anxious that our proximity should not give rise to any feelings of Rivalship or Competition in Trade which could not fail of being highly injurious to the interests of both parties.

Governor George Simpson to Governor Chistyakov, March 21, 1829.

British Competition

Russian trade with the "King George's men" of the Hudson's Bay Company, like that with the Boston men, arose partly from disagreement over hunting-trading rights on the Northwest Coast. Following the merger with the North West Company in 1821 and the reorganizational work of George Simpson in the last half of the 1820s, the "new Concern" loomed larger and larger on the Pacific slope, both onshore and offshore. Its domination of the coastal trade by the early 1830s moved Governor Wrangel to advise the head office that he could not compete with the

British traders because they had more and better trade goods (tobacco, cinnabar [vermilion], blankets, shirts, and dresses).[1] He wrote:

> For the excellent quality and abundance of the merchandise of the English constitute an attraction to the Kolosh which we have no means to compete with, and there is no doubt whatever that if the Board of Directors does not find means to supply the colonies with merchandise of such quality and in such quantity as to be able to hold out against the Hudson Bay Company, this company will be in possession of the whole fur trade in northwestern America from Cross Sound or even from a more northern point to the south as far as the coast of California.[2]

In 1833 and 1834 the Russians attempted to trade directly with the Koloshes in the straits but the latter demanded high prices and the British offered stiff competition. The Russian-American Company labored under two disadvantages: (1) trade goods cost much more because of higher transport costs; and (2) the British did not strictly observe the ban (1825) placed upon trading firearms and spirits to the Koloshes.[3] Trade goods sent to New Archangel via Cronstadt or Okhotsk cost twice as much as the same goods sent to Fort Vancouver from England, with the result that the Hudson's Bay Company was able to pay the Koloshes two to three times as much for furs as was the Russian-American Company.[4] No wonder Governor Kupreyanov reported in 1839 that "Year by year I see the Koloshes drawn more and more from our places to the English frontier. . . ."[5]

RAPPROCHEMENT

Meanwhile, the competition between the two companies had erupted into conflict and near warfare. In 1834 the Russians at St. Dionysius Redoubt at the mouth of the Stikine River prevented the Hudson's Bay Company ship *Dryad* from ascending the river to establish a post upstream. Claiming a breach of the Anglo-Russian Convention of 1825, the British demanded 22,150 pounds sterling in damages. In resolving this matter both sides decided that concord was less dangerous and more profitable than conflict. In 1838 the Ministry of Finance ordered the Russian-American Company to reach a "peaceful agreement" with the Hudson's Bay Company,[6] and Baron Wrangel, fresh from the governorship of Russian America, began to correspond with the Hudson's Bay Company in London with a view to "rapprochement . . . agreement on mutual interests, and avoidance of hostile conflict in the future."[7] The

British expressed a desire to rent the *lisière* (coastal strip) north and south of the Stikine River for an annual payment of furs and to supply Alaska annually with goods and provisions at moderate prices. In this way the Honourable Company would exclude both the Russians and the Americans from the coastal trade, which it alone would control. For their part the Russians would no longer have to rely on the shrewd Americans for supplies and would be able to abandon the increasingly burdensome counter of Ross. Moreover, the supply of wheat from Alta California, according to Governor Etholen, was "sometimes precarious."[8] In September 1838 at St. Petersburg, Governor Pelly of the Hudson's Bay Company proposed to Wrangel that the British sell manufactures and provisions to the Russians, thereby blocking the Americans from the coastal trade and lessening the sale of arms, ammunition, and liquor to the Indians. Both monopolies, he contended, would save money by reducing the number of posts, ships, and men needed to protect the trade.[9] The Russian-American Company, however, hesitated because it was obtaining wares and foodstuffs from Chile "on very moderate terms and by means of their own [Russian] ships" and because its second twenty-year charter was about to expire.[10] But this hesitation did not last long under official pressure. In January 1839, with the tsar's approval, the Russian-American Company dispatched Wrangel to negotiate with George Simpson. The two representatives met halfway at Hamburg, where they signed an agreement that was to be valid for 10 years from June 1, 1840.

AGREEMENT

The Russians agreed to abandon St. Dionysius Redoubt and to lease the coast between Cape Spencer and Cross Sound (54° 40′ N) for an annual rent of 2000 river otters.* They also agreed to discourage American ships from visiting Alaska to sell goods, except in emergencies. In return the British agreed to drop their claim for damages in the *Dryad* affair and to sell annually at New Archangel 2000 river otters bagged west of the Rockies at 23 shillings each and 3000 river otters bagged east of the Rockies at 32 shillings each, as well as 8400 bushels of wheat

---

* The Hudson's Bay Company thus came to monopolize the hunting of the valuable Stikine River otters, which in 1835 brought 78 rubles each at Kyakhta as against 45 rubles each for ordinary river otters from Alaska (USNA, 9:380). The abandonment of St. Dionysius Redoubt released twenty-three men for the remaining undermanned Russian posts (USNA, 46:223v.).

(4200 bushels in 1840) at 6⅔ shillings a bushel, 8 tons of wheat flour, 6½ tons of barley groats, 6½ tons of peas, 15 tons of salted beef, 1½ tons of ham, and 8 tons of butter, plus various manufactures at 13 pounds per ton.[11] Except for butter and perhaps salted beef, which were also obtainable from Yakutsk, these provisions were sufficient to meet colonial needs (Table 5). They were produced at the Hudson's Bay Company farms in the Oregon Country (Forts Vancouver, Victoria, and Langley).

The company even formed a special affiliate, the Puget's Sound Agricultural Company, with farms at Cowlitz and Nisqually (in present-day Washington state) to meet Article 4, the provisionment clause, of the Hamburg agreement. Significantly, the founding meeting of the Puget's Sound Agricultural Company was held in London on February 29, 1839, upon Simpson's return from Germany. Just as significantly, the Russian-American Company's decision to relinguish Russian California was taken two months after the conclusion of the Hamburg accord. In the words of George Simpson:

> After the loss of that profitable branch of trade [hunting], and the recent arrangement with the Hon[ble] Company, enabling them to obtain grain and other farm produce for the use of their northern establishments, cheaper than they could raise it, the Russian American Company very wisely determined on withdrawing from California, and by that resolution have benefitted their Association to the amount of upwards of £5,000 per annum.[12]

Also in 1839 New Archangel placed its last order for supplies with a Boston ship. In 1840 the *Vancouver* reached New Archangel with the first shipment of Hudson's Bay Company provisions, plus 4045 pounds of gunpowder and 200 blankets.[13] Thereafter one or two British ships arrived annually with contracted supplies (Table 11).

Origins

Actually, the 1839 agreement had been suggested a decade earlier. As early as 1824, as he began reorganizing the Columbia Department, Governor Simpson foresaw the time when his company would supplant the Bostonians and Californios as suppliers of the Russian American colonies. He declared:

> The Russian Settlements have hitherto been principally supplied with goods for their trade by the American adventurers on this coast

Table 11. Provisions shipped to Russian America from the Oregon Country by the Hudson's Bay Company, 1840–49

Year	Barque	Wheat (bu.)	Flour (lbs.)	Biscuits (lbs.)	Peas (lbs.)	Pork (lbs.)	Beef (lbs.)	Butter (lbs.)	Hops (lbs.)
1840	Vancouver	3,206	0	0	0	0	0	2,664	0
1841*	Columbia	?	?	?	?	?	?	?	?
1842**	Vancouver	?	?	?	?	?	?	?	?
1843	Vancouver and Columbia	9,314	41,200	0	17,584	0	33,456	5,448	48
1844†	Columbia and Cowlitz	15,600	39,200	0	17,300	6,000	33,725	4,592	90
1845	Vancouver	8,016	39,200	0	17,300	0	33,600	4,584	90
1846‡	Columbia	17,021	79,968	0	16,349	0	32,400	3,360	90
1847	Cowlitz	13,068	51,548	336	16,240	3,000	33,400	3,416	0
1848	Cowlitz	8,446	51,352	336	19,775	4,500	32,400	3,360	37
1849	Columbia	7,875	51,352	336	19,110	0	29,600	3,360	0

* Comprising £3,502' worth of provisions and manufactures (USN, 45: 361v.).
** Comprising £2,472' worth of provisions and manufactures (USNA, 46: 327v.).
† Plus 2 kegs of pickles, 269 pounds of dried apples, and 1878 gallons of molasses.
‡ Plus 3154 pounds of mutton.

Sources: HBC, B.223/d/133, 38d; /150, 35d; /158, 76d; /161, 39; /166, 9d; /179, 8d, 9; /183a, 11d; /190, 15.

payable by Bills on St Petersburg or in furs; but if we conduct our business with good management according to the present plans that channel will be shut up as we ought to be able to put down all competition on the Coast in which case 'tis probable we should be enabled to do business with the Russians on advantageous terms.[14]

In 1828 Simpson reported to headquarters: "We could . . . furnish them with Provisions, say Grain, Beef & Pork, as the Farm at [Fort] Vancouver can be made to produce, much more than we require: indeed, we know that they now pay 3$ p. Bushel for wheat in California, which we can raise at 2/-p. Bushel."[15] Not only was the Columbia Department now able to begin exporting foodstuffs; at the same time Alta California's agricultural surpluses were being reduced by droughts. It was reported in 1829 that "Wheat, other Grain and Provisions are articles they [the Russians] would readily purchase from the Company if they could supply it in any quantity and at a moderate price, as they find their supplies from California very precarious so much so that he

[Governor Chistyakov] intended to send a vessel to Chili for Grain this year."[16] In 1829 Simpson proposed that Hudson's Bay Company ships annually supply New Archangel with 50 to 100 or more tons of manufactures from England and 4000 to 5000 bushels of grain and 4 to 5 tons of salted beef and pork from the Columbia in exchange for furs or bills of exchange payable at London or St. Petersburg.[17] The Bay Company offered to deliver wheat at 2½ piasters per fanega, pease at 2 piasters per fanega, and corn at 1¾ piasters per fanega.[18] The Russian-American Company was skeptical, however; although the British could undoubtedly supply textiles more cheaply than the Americans and grain more cheaply than the Californios or Siberians, it would not want to bother shipping such a small amount of textiles (five tons). Furthermore, the Russian colonists would not want to rely on a foreign competitor for such a basic item as grain.[19] And Wrangel asserted that the prices of British goods would be much higher than those paid to Americans for the same articles.[20] By the late 1830s, however, these objections were outweighed by the stronger competition of the British and the weaker competition of the Americans and by the decreasing supply and increasing price of California grain. These exigencies facilitated the agreement of 1839.

Advantages

This pact enabled the Russian-American Company to provision not only Alaska but also Kamchatka. The added responsibility, which the Russian government had long desired (and which the Russian-American Company had temporarily and unsuccessfully shouldered in the early 1820s), was incorporated into its third charter (1842). In 1841 the Hudson's Bay Company informed Governor Simpson:

> it appears the Russian American Company are about to enter into a contract with the Imperial Government to furnish the Province of Kamschatka for a term of ten years, deliverable at the harbour of St. Peter and St. Paul, with grain and other supplies, usually provided by subjects of the United States and other strangers: and that the Russian American Company are disposed to take Grain and other farm produce, that would be required by them to fulfil that Contract from the Company, deliverable at Sitka, in addition to the contract entered into thro' you at Hamburg under date 6th February 1839.[21]

Simpson told Chief Factor John McLoughlin of Fort Vancouver in 1842 that the Bay Company had agreed to sell the Russians an additional 10 tons of flour at 1½ pence per pound.[22] The next year McLoughlin recommended that for Kamchatka the Russian-American Company be furnished an additional 10,000 bushels (300 tons) of wheat.[23] By then the farms of the Puget's Sound Agricultural Company were productive enough to enable the parent company to exceed the amount of foodstuffs stipulated by the 1839 accord. So by 1847 the Russian-American Company had become Kamchatka's chief provisioner and had underpriced foreign suppliers, whose ships no longer visited the peninsula.[24]*

Although at first the Russians occasionally complained that a wrong assortment, an insufficient quantity, or an inadequate quality of merchandise was received at New Archangel, or that it arrived too late for forwarding to the other counters and to Kamchatka,** generally they were very satisfied with both the manufactures (from Russia and England) and the provisions (from Old Oregon). The Russians felt that the agreement favored them, since the leased *lisière* was "very poor" in sea otters, the British delivered supplies at "very moderate" prices and in "reliable" fashion, the supplies were payable in bills of exchange on St. Petersburg, and the agreement would still be valid in case of a rift between Russia and England.[25] Columbia wheat was no more expensive (at about 4 shillings per bushel or 2 piasters per fanega†) than California wheat.[26] Columbia provisions, especially wheat, were also of better quality than California provisions.[27] In 1840 Etholen reported that the "wheat delivered this year on the *Vancouver* is extremely clean and the kernels are fairly large, in short, better than we ever obtained from California."[28] Also, provisions from the Columbia were more readily obtainable, entailing less waiting, than those from California.[29] Because Columbia provisions were delivered on Hudson's Bay Company ships, Russian-American Company ships were freed for other operations.†† Moreover, as Governor Tebenkov admitted in 1846, two sources of pro-

---

* The company's Kamchatka trade continued until 1855, when the administrative center of the Russian Far East was transferred from Petropavlovsk to Nikolayevsk at the mouth of the Amur, by then the focus of Russian attention on the Pacific.

** These initial difficulties stemmed largely from a temporary shortage of Hudson's Bay Company ships.

† The Columbia fanega contained 126 pounds of wheat, the same as the California and Chilean fanegas from 1839. The English and American bushels held 60 pounds of wheat.

†† This had the further advantage of halting the desertion of Russian sailors from company ships in California ports. For example, in 1806 two men deserted at San Francisco from the *Juno,* the very first Russian ship to visit Alta California, and in 1836 seven men deserted from the *Sitka* in California (Tikhmenev, *Historical Review,* I, 181; USNA, 39:139).

visions were better than one because they made for a more reliable and less expensive supply.[30] Certainly abundant provisions were now regularly available to Alaska for the first time. In 1840, after meeting the annual needs of the colonial counters and the Okhotsk factory, the company still had 734 tons of grain left, enough for two years.[31] In 1841, after all of the colonial counters had been provisioned and 36 tons (1204 bushels) of wheat had been sent to Okhotsk, there still remained at New Archangel and Fort Ross 542 tons (18,057 bushels), enough to meet the company's needs for one year.[32] So many provisions were received from the Columbia that in 1843 Chief Director Wrangel felt that the company could supply Kamchatka with 117 tons of flour annually.[33] By 1845 the Hudson's Bay Company was supplying the Russian-American Company with 20,000 bushels of wheat annually.[34]

The manufactures supplied by the Honourable Company were also high in quality and low in price; in fact, it was reported in 1839 that they were of the "best quality" and "incomparably cheaper" than those supplied by American vessels.[35] The British also delivered goods at lower rates (57 to 83 rubles per ton) than the Russians were able to charge on goods shipped from Cronstadt (170 to 224 rubles per ton) or via Okhotsk (474 to 554 rubles per ton).[36]

The Hudson's Bay Company was also very satisfied with the 1839 pact, for it profited on the delivery and sale of supplies and on the hunting of furs. It bought the grain in the Oregon Country (from both the farms of the Puget's Sound Agricultural Company and the Willamette settlers) for 3 shillings per bushel (paid in goods) and sold it at New Archangel for 5⅓ shillings per bushel, less freight costs (about half a shilling per bushel); this profit amounted to some £750 annually.[37] For freight on English manufactures the Bay Company charged the Russians £10 per ton, while it paid less than half that sum for freighting the same manufactures from England on chartered ships; the freight profit totaled nearly £4000 in 1844.[38] Hunting was even more profitable, with returns from the rental of the *lisière* bringing in $8000 to $10,000 annually.[39] In 1843 the company procured 12,343 pelts in the *lisière* valued at some £8000.[40]

Problems

By the late 1840s, however, circumstances had changed radically. First, the Oregon Treaty of 1846 had resolved the territorial dispute between

Great Britain and the United States over the Pacific Northwest with a
so-called compromise settlement—the 49th parallel from the Rockies to
the Pacific. This demarcation deprived the Hudson's Bay Company of
its most productive farm at Fort Vancouver and both farms of the
Puget's Sound Agricultural Company, leaving sizable farms at Forts Victoria and Langley only.* The treaty did guarantee the Bay Company's
property and navigational rights in the lower Columbia basin but squat-
ting settlers and spiteful officials frequently disregarded these rights.
Second, the California gold rush of 1848, with its promise of overnight
riches, deprived the Oregon Country and the Hudson's Bay Company
of many agricultural settlers, who abandoned their plows and headed
south. About 1848 Chief Factor James Douglas wrote Governor Tebenkov that it would be "very difficult" for the Bay Company to furnish the
amount of provisions required by the Russians because almost the entire
white population of the Pacific Northwest (including two-thirds of the
white population of Oregon) had abandoned their farms and left for
California.[41] Third, the Russian-American Company had found that
goods could be obtained more cheaply from Russia, Germany, and England on chartered ships—mainly out of Abo (Turku)—than from the Bay
Company.** Consequently, when the 1839 agreement was renewed in
1849 for nine years, it did not include a clause on provisions (or on
manufactures†). In the words of the head office: "The refusal of the
English to supply the colonies with provisions is based upon quite valid
reasons. . . ."[42] The Russians relied upon provisionment from Cronstadt
—for which four ships were acquired in 1850–53—at least until the revival of agriculture in California in the mid-1850s. Meanwhile, the
diluted agreement between the two companies was renewed until May
31, 1859, when the Bay Company's privileges were due to expire. The
Russians again leased the *lisière* for an annual rent of 2000 river otters

* In fact, in 1848 and 1849 the provisionment clause of the 1839 contract was met
largely by Forts Victoria and Langley.
** In 1851 the head office learned from the Hudson's Bay Company that the gold
fever was abating in California and that immigrants were re-entering Oregon to
farm, so it instructed Governor Rosenburg to determine whether Oregon could again
meet Russian America's grain needs and thereby obviate the need for provisionment
from Cronstadt (USNA, 19:579–82, 57:580v.–81). However, by the time Oregon's
agriculture had recovered, so had California's. The latter's output proved larger and
cheaper, so that eventually the Russian-American Company returned to California
rather than to Oregon.
† So in 1850 the Russian-American Company shifted its buying of dry goods for the
colonies from London to Hamburg (Tikhmenev, *Historical Review*, II, 177).

(later, 1500 river otters, and later still, cash). In 1859 the accord was renewed again for four years, and once again for another two years. By then the territorial futures of both companies were clearly limited. The Hudson's Bay Company sold Rupert's Land to the new nation of Canada in 1869, just two years after the Russian-American Company sold Alaska to the United States. These last grand acts by two powerful rivals sealed the basic political geography of much of North America.

Readings

Davidson, Donald C., "Relations of the Hudson's Bay Company with the Russian American Company on the Northwest Coast, 1829–1867," *British Columbia Historical Quarterly*, January 1941, 33–51.

Jackson, C. Ian, "The Stikine Territory Lease and Its Relevance to the Alaska Purchase," *Pacific Historical Review*, August 1967, 289–306.

Saw, Reginald, "Treaty with the Russians," *The Beaver*, December 1948, 30–33.

Williams, Glyndwr, ed., *London Correspondence Inward from Sir George Simpson 1841–42*, London, 1973.

12 TRADE WITH KANAKAS

The group of Sandwich Islands is very commodious for all ships going to the north-west coast of America, to the Aleutian Islands, or to Kamschatka, to touch at; it has very secure bays. Here may be procured abundance of swine, bread-fruit, bananas, cocoa-nuts, taro, yams, batatas [sweet potatoes], salt, wood, water, and other things particularly desirable for ship stores.

G. H. Von Langsdorff

Until the mid-1840s the Russian-American Company traded irregularly with the Kanakas (Sandwich Islanders). Sandalwood, salt, and taro were the articles in which the islands abounded, and it was these products, not foodstuffs, that the company usually obtained from the distant archipelago.

The Sandwich Islands became important toward the end of the eighteenth century as a stopover for American and British vessels plying the Pacific between the Orient and the Northwest Coast; there they could rest their crews and obtain fresh water, fresh food, and capable seamen (Kanakas) and, later, sandalwood as well. In 1804 the first Russian round-the-world expedition visited the islands and noted their commercial possibilities. Korobitsyn, a member of the *Hope's* crew, described the agricultural resources:

The edible fruits and other products that grow on that island [Hawaii] include a considerable quantity of bananas and coconuts, as well as breadfruit, potatoes, ayebua roots, water-melons, cabbage and radishes, and a fair amount of sugarcane. They raise an adequate number of pigs and goats, as well as chickens. Occasionally they also have horned cattle: bulls and cows which had been left by the English navigator Cook for breeding purposes.[1]

In 1806 King Tomi-omi (Kamehameha) sent an American sailor, George Clark, to New Archangel to negotiate a commercial treaty with Governor Baranov whereby Hawaiian taro, breadfruit, coconuts, breadstuffs, pigs, and rope would be exchanged for Russian textiles, timber, and iron, beginning in 1807.[2] Evidently the only result of this overture was the voyage of one Sysoy Slobodchikov, who bartered furs in the islands in 1807 for provisions for the company.[3] A year later, Hagemeister, leader of the second Russian circumnavigation, visited the islands and exchanged 1805 fur seals and some walrus tusks for twenty-two tons of salt and some sandalwood, pearls, salted pork, and dried taro, which were taken to Kodiak.[4] Hagemeister reported to the head office that although any of the Sandwich Islands could provide everything that Russian America needed, including sugarcane, taro, and wheat, trade would not be advantageous because all Hawaiian commerce was personally controlled by King Tomi-omi, who demanded high prices; moreover, Hawaiian foodstuffs had become expensive because of the heavy demand by American ships en route to Canton.[5] But in late 1814 King Tomari (Kaumuali), Tomi-omi's rival, wrote Baranov, offering to trade sandalwood, taro, candlenuts, and "anything that is on the island [Kauai] that you want" for firearms, ammunition, gunpowder, cloth, stills, blacksmithing equipment, carpentering tools, and a ship.[6] Baranov's response led to the abortive Schaffer affair.

For some time thereafter company trade with the islands was stymied by the hostility of its kings, especially Tomari, and by the need to prepare taro beforehand.* Besides, Hawaiian provisions were no longer cheap, owing to the growing demand of American ships. By 1821 provisions cost more at Honolulu than they did at Boston. In 1822 the head office advised Governor Muravyov that "experience has shown that of the products of the islands none can be obtained for the colonies other than salt, which is obtainable more profitably and more closely in California together with grain."[7] Although the company did procure 51 to 54

---

* Taro is the nutritious edible tuber of the tropical plant of the same name. It had to be dried and pounded into flour.

tons of salt in 1824 and 59 to 90 tons in 1825,[8] Alta California and Old Oregon provisioned the Russian colonies until the late 1840s.

Then the temporary collapse of American agriculture on the West Coast during California's gold rush prompted the company to resume and expand its trade with the islands. For ten straight years (1845–54) it traded with the islands, exchanging mostly timber and fish for salt, which by now was much cheaper than that from Baja California. In 1847 Governor Tebenkov recommended that the company's Hawaiian trade be expanded to the extent of an annual turnover of no less than 200,000 rubles by acquiring two ships and establishing a commercial agent on the islands; he estimated that this measure would reduce the cost of up-keep of the colonies by 25 per cent or 200,000 rubles through the sale of fur seals to the islanders.[9] So in 1848 the company concluded an agreement with the Sandwich Islands, promising to exchange 15,000 to 30,000 feet of timber and 200 to 500 barrels of fish annually for three years for salt, sugar, coffee, and other products.[10] No sooner had this deal been concluded, however, when the archipelago was depopulated (by the ravages of an epidemic, which claimed 12,000 lives, and by the lure of California's gold rush).[11] The resultant fall in supply and rise in price of island products discouraged company trade, which ceased altogether with the recovery of California agriculture in the mid-1850s. *

Readings

Pierce, Richard A., *Russia's Hawaiian Adventure, 1815–1817*, Berkeley, Calif., 1965.

---

* In 1865 and 1866 the company again bartered salted fish for salt, sugar, molasses, coffee, and rice. For example, in 1865 53 tons of salt, 125 sacks and 102 barrels of sugar, 50 barrels of molasses, 6 sacks of coffee, and 204 sacks of rice were obtained (USNA, 65:pt. 1, 62v.).

AFTERWORD

According to the latest reports to me from all counters, the colonies of the Russian-American Company are fine, peace and harmony have been maintained with the neighboring savage tribes, and there have been no extraordinary diseases.

Annual message of the Governor of Russian America to the head office of the Russian-American Company.

This sanguine message, which was sent almost every year, obviously oversimplified the realities of life in Russian America, especially the problem of supply. The company labored long and hard—with middling success—to satisfy the food needs of its colonies. These efforts, which were geographically manifested in local agriculture and domestic and foreign trade, formed a changing and overlapping pattern in response to interrelated physical, economic, and political conditions. At first most provisions were received from Siberia via Okhotsk. Although this old supply line was entirely under Russian control, it was very long and very hazardous—especially the packhorse link between Yakutsk and Okhotsk—and limited provisions were delivered at great cost. The complete breakdown of this channel at the beginning of the 1800s led to a shift to supply by sea from Cronstadt on company and navy ships and from Boston on Yankee vessels. Although they served other purposes besides provisionment, Russian voyages around the world were expensive and infrequent. Trade with the Bostonians provided considerable supplies but deprived the Russians of too many sea otter and fur seal pelts; besides, the company did not like having to rely upon an unscrupulous competitor for basic necessities. So in the 1810s it turned briefly to the Arcadian Sandwich Islands but more determinedly to bountiful Alta California, where an agricultural colony was founded while trade was attempted with the Californios. Agriculture did prove much more productive in Russian California than in Russian Alaska, where it had been introduced early but had been thwarted by a raw climate and a scarcity of labor; nonetheless, farming around Fort Ross was inadequate, being much less successful than at the California missions and ranchos. So when Alta California's ports were opened to foreign traders in 1821, the company traded less with the Bostonians and more with the Espagnols. At least the Espagnols did not poach and smuggle in Alaskan waters. But both sources were equally subject to change. Just as the Boston trade declined with the depletion of the precious fur bearers in the 1810s, so the California trade withered with the disappearance of the fertile missions in the 1830s. The company then turned to another competitor, the Hudson's Bay Company, which provisioned Alaska amply and regularly during the 1840s from its Oregon Country farms. This arrangement also permitted the Russians to relinquish Russian California and to discontinue the Boston trade. California's gold rush, however, temporarily decimated agricultural production on the West Coast, forcing the Russian colonies to return to supply from Europe and even to reopen trade with the Sandwich Islands. But by the mid-1850s California agriculture had recovered, and it met Alaska's food needs until the American purchase in 1867, when Russia withdrew from North America to concentrate upon expansion in Asia.

These multimodal efforts were indifferently successful. Seldom did the colonies have ample provisions, and not infrequently the meager provisions they did receive were low in quality. Food shortages were severe; for example, in the very first years of the 1800s, in the early 1820s, and in the mid-1850s. New Archangel's residents often complained that "We are hungry, bring us grain soon."[1] During the late 1700s and the early 1800s grain was so scarce that the clerics of the Kodiak Mission (1794–1837) were permitted by the Holy Synod to eat meat during Lent.[2] Around 1820 Governor Yanovsky commented:

> It should be noted that for the maintenance of the missionaries and other Russian employees grain was supplied from the magazines of the [Russian-] American Company; but sometimes there was no grain. Grain was neither sown nor grown there, and rye was imported 10 thousand versts [6629 miles] from Irkutsk, so that rye flour was 12

paper rubles per pood [36 pounds] there; or wheat was imported two thousand versts [1,326 miles] from California, and wheat flour was 5 paper rubles per pood; but sometimes the ship was wrecked or delayed; then they suffered from a shortage of grain, so there they ate fish, various kinds of which were very abundant in summer; in addition, they ate the flesh of all sea animals.[3]

Indeed, fish and grain were the staple foods of Russian America,[4] and fresh, dried, and salted fish often saved the colonies from starvation.* But not even fish were always plentiful.**

Usually there were enough provisions to meet the salaries in kind of company employees. Governor Yanovsky, however, observed in 1820 that the grain salary of 36 pounds per month was most insufficient for a worker, who consequently had to buy much additional flour—up to 144 pounds—from the company's stock.[5]† Sometimes, however, the shortage of grain forced the company to halt these sales of extra flour, resulting in "hardship," as in 1820.[6] Governor Wrangel reported in 1831 that a company worker's monthly ration included 36 pounds of flour and some fish at New Archangel but 66 pounds of flour, 6½ pounds of groats, 22½ pounds of beef, one pound of butter, and 2 pounds of salt, besides fish and vegetables, at Okhotsk.[7] Moreover, Russian America's fewer provisions cost much more; butter, for example, cost 47 kopecks per pound at Okhotsk but 77½ kopecks per pound at New Archangel.[8] Wrangel added that company employees at the colonial capital had to buy fish, fowl, and slugs from the neighboring Koloshes at high prices for want of beef and butter.[9] Indeed, mountain sheep, grouse, and halibut constituted virtually the only fresh food at the capital in winter.[10]†† During the 1850s up to 400 mountain sheep and up to 1000 grouse were consumed annually at New Archangel.[11] The Koloshes also furnished berries and roots in summer and potatoes in fall. But despite these increments, basic necessities were often scarce. Privation was the rule, not the exception. Wrangel was not exaggerating or overgeneralizing in 1834 when he decried the "wretched state of the customary scarcity of the most neces-

* Dried fish—yukola—was so basic that it was called "Kamchatka bread."
** Occasionally, too, there was a shortage of salt for preserving fish. Sometimes the company had to precipitate salt from sea water in large boilers. And there was a dearth of sunshine for drying fish.
† This was a major source of employee indebtedness.
†† The Dall mountain sheep were clubbed along the seashore, where they sought refuge from low snow in the mountains.

sary articles."[12] Doctor Edward Blaschke, the company's physician at New Archangel in the last half of the 1830s, observed that food was often difficult to obtain and limited mostly to fish.[13] In the mid-1850s supply became precarious when shipping was interrupted by the Crimean War. Fish runs were also light and vegetable yields low, causing Governor Voyevodsky to report that in 1855 and 1856 provisionment was unusually meager.[14] By 1860 Russian America was importing 542 tons of grain, 27 to 36 tons of beef, 36 tons of butter, and 181 tons of salt annually, with half being used at New Archangel and half elsewhere.[15] But each inhabitant of the colonies theoretically received less grain in one year than a Russian Navy sailor received in one month.[16]

Even when enough provisions were delivered to New Archangel, some were lost by wastage in storage. There were three kinds of wastage: (1) natural—from temperature and humidity changes; (2) direct—from consumption by rats, leakage, spillage, breakage, and so forth; and (3) arbitrary—from incorrect measurement.[17] The dank climate and the crude wooden construction must have facilitated considerable spoilage of both provisions and manufactures, and of course rats were numerous at Russian America's ports, as they were at ports throughout the world. At the company's Okhotsk factory, rats devoured 1870 pounds of flour in 1834 and 1569 pounds in 1835.[18] From all causes 3611 pounds of grain were wasted in company storehouses in the colonies in 1825, and in 1837 one-sixth of the flour stored in Kodiak Counter alone was wasted.[19] The company could ill afford such losses.

Not surprisingly, the diet of colonial personnel—with the probable exception of officials and officers*—was nutritionally deficient. The dominance of salted fish, salted beef, and grain and the dearth of fresh fruits and vegetables meant a lack of vitamins B and C, especially the latter. In 1860 it was admitted that the chief foods were salted fish and salted meat; even salted wild mutton was given to the workers only three or four times during the year (mainly during Easter).[20] The only fresh meat was some wild mutton and halibut in winter and the only fresh vegetables were potatoes, turnips, and rutabagas in summer. Scurvy was common, especially in late winter and early spring, after fresh stores had been exhausted. In the winter of 1796–97 thirty of the 80 inhabitants of Slavorossiya died of scurvy.[21] And in 1818 Captain Golovnin noted that many employees at New Archangel were scorbutic and that "no

---

* Apparently promyshlenniks did not eat as well as officials and officers, who received bread, butter, tea, wine, rum, and sugar.

small number" of them died every year.[22] In 1853 scurvy was particularly fierce.*

But scurvy was only the most common of several diseases that were
promoted by malnutrition and the cold, wet climate. The smallpox out-
break of 1835–38 was the worst of a number of epidemics that periodically ravaged the colonies. A measles epidemic raged from 1847 through
1849. And during the eight-year stint (1851–58) of one Doctor Govorlivy in Russian America there were six epidemics: malaria on his way to
New Archangel aboard the *Nicholas I* in 1850–51, scurvy in early 1853,
influenza in late 1855, typhoid fever and whooping cough in 1857 and
1858, and German measles in late 1858.[23] The doctor found that the
most common afflictions at New Archangel were rheumatism and ca-
tarrh, which resulted from the changeable weather and the excessive
drinking.[24]**

These debilitating diseases seriously impaired the colonial labor force,
which was insufficient even when all of its members were healthy. In the
spring of 1819 Governor Yanovsky reported that at New Archangel one
out of every six men were sick because of the shortage of fresh food and
the unhealthfulness of the climate.[25] At the colonial capital in 1838–40,
at the end of the smallpox epidemic, 25 to 30 men were sick daily in
summer and 40 to 60 in fall, winter, and spring.[26] The sick, of course,
contributed to the large number of unfit workers. In 1846, for instance, it
was reported that 150 of the 400 workers at New Archangel and Ozyorsk
Redoubt were "useless."[27]

Thus, the shortfall of provisions was partly responsible for the debili-
tation of colonial manpower, which in turn was less able to operate ef-
fectively against foreign competitors and native opponents.† Certainly,
imperfect provisionment was a major feature of the over-all plight that
disposed the Russian government to part with Russian America. The
company had always been aware of the seriousness of the food supply
problem and had energetically attempted various solutions; indeed, it
had exhausted all possibilities. But by trying several approaches the
company at least lessened the monovariate risk of total failure and prob-

* From the mid-1850s the incidence of scurvy was reduced by the importation of
dried preserves from Paris (ORAK, 1860:74–75).
** Alcoholism has long been a major social problem in Russia (Tsarist and Soviet).
† Russian competition was further weakened by the company's chronic shortage of
trade goods and trading vessels, with the result that fewer pelts were forthcoming
from the Indians and longer storage (and more risk of spoilage) was needed for the
returns.

ably lowered the competitive cost of provisions. The only drawback to this pluralistic approach was the fact that foreign sources, which proved to be relatively the most bountiful, were beyond the company's control. But it really had no other choice, for Russian America's harsh environment was not conducive to productive agriculture and its distant location was not amenable to easy delivery. These two hard realities persistently conditioned the geography and history of Russia's only overseas colony. Their impact, as well as that of the unfamiliar maritime mold of the colony, the restrictive monopolistic character of the company, and the traditional administrative and technological backwardness of the colonizers, help to explain why Alaska did not remain a Russian colony.

Readings

Gibson, James R., "The Significance of Siberia to Tsarist Russia," *Canadian Slavonic Papers*, Autumn 1972, 442–53.

Kerner, Robert J., "Russian Expansion to America, Its Bibliographical Foundations," *Papers of the Bibliographical Society of America*, 1931, 111–29.

ABBREVIATIONS

AGO—Archive of the Geographical Society of the USSR (Leningrad)
AVPR—Archive of the Foreign Policy of Russia (Moscow)
car.—carton
d.—*delo* (file or dossier)
f.—*fond* (fund or stock)
HBC—Archive of the Hudson's Bay Company (Ottawa)
op.—*opis* (inventory or account)
ORAK—Annual Reports of the Russian-American Company
raz.—*razryad* (category or class)
ROLL—Manuscript Division of the Lenin Library (Moscow)
supp.—supplement
TsGADA—Central State Archive of Ancient Acts (Moscow)
TsGIAL—Central State Historical Archive in Leningrad
USNA—United States National Archives (Washington, D.C.)
v.—verso

LOCATION OF LIBRARIES

Baker Library—Cambridge, Mass.
Bancroft Library—Berkeley, Calif.
Beinecke Library—New Haven, Conn.
Göttingen University Library—Göttingen, Germany
Saltykov-Shchedrin State Public Library—Leningrad

NOTES

Chapter 1

1. Makarova, *Russkie,* 113, 182–88.
2. Andreyev, *Russkie otkrytiya,* 208.
3. Iosaf, "Kratkiya obyasneniya," 2.
4. Andreyev, *Russkie otkrytiya,* 350, 354.
5. Berkh, "Izvestie," 257.
6. Vila Vilar, *Los Rusos,* 75–80.
7. AVPR, f. RAK, d. 154, 5, 31; Iosaf, "Kratkiya obyasneniya," 3.
8. Shur, *K beregam,* 145.
9. Lazarev, *Zapiski,* 186, 235.
10. Sauer, *An Account,* 171.
11. Berkh, "Izvestie," 98.
12. Khlebnikov, "Zapiski," 9, 36.
13. Tikhmenev, *Historical Review,* I, 45, 285.
14. Valaam Monastery, *Ocherk,* 228.
15. Khlebnikov, *Baranov,* 34.
16. Golovnin, *Puteshestvie,* 140.
17. Glavnoye Pravlenie Rossiisko-Amerikanskoy Kompanii, "Doneseniya," 10.
18. Pavlov, *K istorii,* 158; Tikhmenev, *Historical Review,* I, 145.
19. Anonymous, "Obozrenie," 66, 86; Pavlov, *K istorii,* 19–20, 27–32, 34–35.
20. Tikhmenev, *Historical Review,* I, 306.
21. Lazarev, *Plavanie,* 161.
22. USNA, 57: 331.
23. Khlebnikov, "Zapiski," 9.
24. Tikhmenev, *Historical Review,* I, 284.
25. *Ibid.,* I, 178, 184.
26. Pavlov, *K istorii,* 114.
27. Anonymous, "Kratkaya Istoricheskaya Zapiska," 1.

28. Tikhmenev, *Historical Review,* I, 90, 169.

29. *Ibid.,* I, 310.

30. Irving, *Astoria,* 420.

31. USNA, 26: 20.

32. USNA, 4: 417.

33. USNA, 6: 101v.

34. USNA, 37: 258–58v.

35. Blaschke, *Topographia,* 40.

36. Khlebnikov, "Zapiski," 40–41.

37. *Ibid.,* 125.

38. USNA, 32: 124v.

39. USNA, 30: 196.

40. Anonymous, "Kratkaya Istoricheskaya Zapiska," 3.

41. Tikhmenev, *Historical Review,* I, 385–89.

42. *Ibid.,* I, 441.

43. USNA, 14: 110v.–111.

44. USNA, 46: 363.

45. USNA, 61: 49.

46. ORAK, 1859: 120.

47. Tikhmenev, *Historical Review,* II, 328.

48. Berkh, "Izvestie," 263.

49. Blaschke, *Topographia,* 8, 40.

50. Simpson, *Narrative,* II, 190.

51. USNA, 51: 427.

52. USNA, 62: 66v.

53. USNA, 50: 270–70v.

54. Fyodorova, *Russkoye naselenie,* 173.

55. AVPR, f. RAK, d. 410, 16–16v.

56. Andreyev, *Russkie otkrytiya,* 282.

Chapter 2

1. Khlebnikov, "Zapiski," 36.

2. Cowdin, "The Northwest Fur Trade," 534.

3. Berkh "Izvestie," 105; Khlebnikov, "Zapiski," 36v.

4. Khlebnikov, "Zapiski," 36v.

5. *Ibid.,* 36.

6. *Ibid.,* 120v.–21, 122.

7. USNA, 6: 101.

8. Vrangel, "O pushnykh tovarakh," 510.

9. Khlebnikov, "Zapiski," 355–355v.; Table 7.

10. ORAK, 1842: 37.

11. Von Wrangell, *Statistische und ethnographische Nachrichten,* 51.

12. Anonymous, "Obozrenie," 55.

13. Pavlov, *K istorii,* 33–34.

14. USNA, 9: 110v.

15. Anonymous, "Obozrenie," 100; Tikhmenev, *Historical Review*, I, 290, 310.

16. Ministerstvo inostrannykh del SSR, *Vneshnyaya politika Rossii*, VII, 396–97.

17. Tikhmenev, *Historical Review*, I, 169.

18. USNA, 20: 639.

19. ORAK, 1842: 33.

20. ORAK, 1845: 41, 1846: 34, 1847: 34, 1848: 29, 1849: 28.

21. USNA, 30: 25v.

22. Von Wrangell, *Statistische und ethnographische Nachrichten*, 19–20.

23. *Doklad komiteta*, II, supp. 9; USNA, 40: 170v.

24. Anonymous, "Obozrenie," 111.

25. *Doklad komiteta*, II, 407–8.

26. Tikhmenev, *Historical Review*, I, 151.

27. *Doklad komiteta*, II, 201, 411; ORAK, 1862: 43.

28. *Doklad komiteta*, II, supp. 18.

Chapter 3

1. United States, *Proceedings*, II, 24.

2. USNA, 52: 482.

3. USNA, 32: 63v.

4. [Khlebnikov], "Zapiski," 96v.–98v.

5. [Khlebnikov], "Vzglyad," 305.

6. USNA, 37: 75v.

7. Khlebnikov, "Zapiski," 135v.

8. Valaam Monastery, *Ocherk*, 137, 156.

9. Khlebnikov, "Zapiski," 118v.

10. Blashke, "Neskolko zamechany," 116.

11. USNA, 39: 235v.

12. USNA, 51: 426, 55: 136v.

13. USNA, 4: 448v.

14. Tikhmenev, *Historical Review*, I, 177.

15. AVPR, f. 341, op. 888, d. 194, 13–14.

16. Barsukov, *Innokenty*, 10.

17. USNA, 20: 21.

18. *Materialy*, I, 8.

19. USNA, 31: 6ov., 389v.

20. ORAK, 1842: 25.

21. USNA, 34: 141v.

22. Golovin, "Obzor," 50.

23. *Doklad komiteta*, II, 101.

24. USNA, 35: 64.

25. AVPR, f. 341, op. 888, d. 411, 39.

26. Alaska History Research Project, *Documents*, IV, 138.

27. USNA, 27: 122, 28: 138v.

28. Pavlov, *K istorii,* 158.

29. USNA, 37: 74v.

30. *Doklad komiteta,* II, 92; Khlebnikov, "Zapiski," 50v–51; USNA, 61: pt. 2, 113.

31. USNA, 47: 457, 459v., 48: 400.

32. USNA, 3: 171, 172–72v.

33. USNA, 58: 186.

Chapter 4

1. Minitsky, "Opisanie," 159.

2. Miller, "Moy put," 259.

3. Shch., *Poyezdka,* 106.

4. *Ibid.,* 24, 141.

5. Anonymous, "Opisanie," 34–36.

6. Andreyev, *Russian Discoveries,* 92.

7. Andreyev, *Russkie otkrytiya,* 264; AVPR, f. RAK, d. 133, 6–10, 12–19 and d. 377, 9v.–10; USNA, 47:201v.

8. Alaska History Research Project, *Documents,* III, 217; USNA, 46: 153v.

9. USNA, 14: 192–92v.

10. Anonymous, "Kratkaya Istoricheskaya Zapiska," 1–1v.

11. USNA, 10: 328–28v.

12. Dobell, *Travels,* II, 79.

13. Zagoskin, *Puteshestviya,* 340.

14. Vrangel, "Putevia zapiski," 172.

15. Cochrane, *Narrative,* 251, 318.

16. USNA, 7: 223.

17. USNA, 12: 247.

18. USNA, 3: 165.

19. USNA, 32: 165v.–66.

20. Andreyev, *Russkie otkrytiya,* 365.

21. Bilbasov, *Arkhiv,* III, 577.

22. USNA, 14: 179–80.

23. Bilbasov, *Arkhiv,* III, 571.

24. Tikhmenev, *Supplement,* 287.

25. Alaska History Research Project, *Documents,* III, 178.

26. Tikhmenev, *Historical Review,* I, 284: Von Wrangell, *Statistische und ethnographische Nachrichten,* 19–20.

27. De La Perouse, *Voyage,* III, 40.

28. Tikhmenev, *Supplement,* 156.

29. Okun, *The Russian American Company,* 99.

30. Alaska History Research Project, *Documents,* III, 178.

31. Von Wrangell, *Statistische und ethnographische Nachrichten,* 21.

32. Rowand, *Notes,* 22.

33. Dobell, *Travels,* I, 297–98.

34. Pavlov, *K istorii,* 20–21.

35. Kruzenshtern, *Puteshestvie*, 6.
36. Von Wrangell, *Statistische und ethnographische Nachrichten*, 21.
37. Anonymous, "Kratkaya Istoricheskaya Zapiska," 1–1v.
38. Von Wrangell, *Statistische und ethnographische Nachrichten*, 21.
39. Andreyev, *Russkie otkrytiya*, 251.
40. Dobell, *Travels*, II, 24–26.
41. *Doklad komiteta*, I, 124 and II, 94.
42. USNA, 34: 196v.
43. USNA, 58: 517–17v., 59: 215v.
44. USNA, 47: 205.
45. Andreyev, *Russkie otkrytiya*, 278, 280, 365–67.
46. USNA, 8: 175–76.
47. Mamyshev, "Amerikanskiya vladeniya," 285.
48. USNA, 47: 227.
49. USNA, 50: 251.
50. Tolstoy, "Missionerskaya deyatelnost," 283.
51. USNA, 52: 360.
52. ORAK, 1856: 7–8, 1858: 8, 1859: 7–8; USNA, 22: 16, 159, 62: pt. 1, 103v.
53. Bilbasov, *Arkhiv*, VI, 673.

Chapter 5

1. Sgibnev, "Istorichesky ocherk," 58.
2. Alaska History Research Project, *Documents*, III, 270.
3. Von Krusenstern, *Voyage*, I, xxvi.
4. Ministerstvo inostrannykh del SSSR, *Vneshnyaya politika Rossii*, II, 297–98.
5. Zubov, *Otechestvennie moreplavateli-issledovateli*, 143.
6. Sokolov, "Prigotovlenie krugosvetnoy ekspeditsii," 147–49, 189.
7. Sirotkin, "Dokumenty," 87.
8. Tikhmenev, *Historical Review*, I, 123.
9. *Doklad komiteta*, II, 426; Tikhmenev, *Historical Review*, II, 176, 176n.
10. Anonymous, "Kratkaya Istoricheskaya Zapiska," 3v.–4.
11. AVPR, f. RAK, d. 291, 2.
12. ORAK, 1850: 7–8.
13. Pervy sibirsky komitet, "O predpolozheniyakh," 76v., 87v.
14. USNA, 2: 164.
15. Pervy sibirsky komitet, "O predpolozheniyakh," 77v., 88.
16. USNA, 3: 165–65v.
17. Anonymous, "Kratkaya Istoricheskaya Zapiska," 10.
18. USNA, 39: 186.
19. USNA, 30: 260v.
20. USNA, 9: 125, 36: 349v.–50.
21. ORAK, 1850: 10.
22. USNA, 30: 260v.

23. USNA, 5: 103v.–4.
24. Tikhmenev, *Historical Review*, I, 434.
25. Lazarev, *Zapiski*, 233; Tikhmenev, *Historical Review*, I, 434.
26. *Doklad komiteta*, I, 123, 133, II, 212.
27. Okun, *The Russian American Company*, 68.
28. USNA, 36: 48v., 52.
29. ORAK, 1842: 23.
30. Tikhmenev, *Historical Review*, I, 437.
31. Shiroky, "Iz istorii," 218.
32. USNA, 5: 103v.
33. USNA, 5: 103v.
34. USNA, 63: pt. 2, 88.

Chapter 6

1. [Shelikhov], "Voyage," 16.
2. Andreyev, *Russian Discoveries*, 80.
3. Sauer, *An Account*, 173.
4. Andreyev, *Russian Discoveries*, 93.
5. *Ibid.*, 90, 93.
6. Russia, Gosudarstvenny sovet, *Arkhiv*, I, pt. 2, 666–67.
7. Russia, *Polnoye sobranie*, 1st series, XXXIII, No. 17, 171, 478.
8. Alaska History Research Project, *Documents*, III, 161.
9. *Ibid.*
10. Berkh, "Izvestie," 105–06; Tikhmenev, *Historical Review*, I, 53; Tikhmenev, *Supplement*, 154–55, 339.
11. Tikhmenev, *Historical Review*, I, 53.
12. *Ibid.*, I, supplements, 4.
13. Pavlov, *K istorii*, 31.
14. USNA, 65: pt. 1, 121v.
15. USNA, 34: 182.
16. USNA, 54: 258v.–59, 324v.–25.
17. Khlebnikov, "Kadyaksky otdel," 3v.
18. Valaam Monastery, *Ocherk*, 201.
19. Khlebnikov, "Zapiski," 131.
20. USNA, 34: 168.
21. USNA, 47: 463v.–64.
22. ORAK, 1858: 24, 1859: 73.
23. *Doklad komiteta*, II, supp. 3.
24. Von Kotzebue, *A New Voyage*, II, 43–44.
25. USNA, 48: 332v., 50: 344, 51: 187v.
26. USNA, 48: 571–72v.
27. USNA, 54: 253.
28. USNA, 63: pt. 1, 191v.
29. Valaam Monastery, *Ocherk*, 98.
30. *Ibid.*

31. Khlebnikov, "Zapiski," 134.
32. USNA, 33: 356v.
33. [Shelikhov], "Voyage," 33–34.
34. Tikhmenev, *Supplement,* 117.
35. Khlebnikov, "Kadyaksky otdel," 3v.; Tikhmenev, *Supplement,* 137.
36. Khlebnikov, "Zapiski," 135v.
37. ORAK, 1860: 24.
38. Valaam Monastery, *Ocherk,* 155.
39. USNA, 62: pt. 2, 72, 63: pt. 1, 76v.
40. USNA, 37: 91.
41. *Materialy,* III, 126–27.
42. Von Wrangell, *Statistische und ethnographische Nachrichten,* 13.
43. Veniaminov, *Zapiski,* I, 63.
44. USNA, 32: 60v.
45. Anonymous, "Obozrenie," 115–16.
46. Tikhmenev, *Historical Review,* I, 151.
47. *Doklad komiteta,* II, 146; Khlebnikov, *Zhizneopisanie,* 203; Von Wrangell, *Statistische und ethnographische Nachrichten,* 18.
48. *Doklad komiteta,* II, 325; *Materialy,* III, 163.
49. ORAK, 1860: 26.
50. AVPR, f. RAK, d. 284, 3.
51. USNA, 63: pt. 1, 191v.–92.
52. *Doklad komiteta,* II, 570.
53. Golovin, "Iz putevykh pisem," 181–82.
54. Khlebnikov, "Zapiski," 236v.
55. [Khlebnikov], "Zapiski," 125; USNA, 37: 177v.
56. Von Wrangell and Von Wrangell, "Briefe," 361.
57. USNA, 63: pt. 1, 191v.
58. ORAK, 1860: 24–25.
59. USNA, 43: 221.
60. Iosaf, "Kratkiya obyasneniya," 9.
61. Lisiansky, *Voyage,* 190.
62. Golovnin, *Puteshestvie,* I, 194.
63. *Ibid.,* I, 211–12.
64. Veniaminov, *Zapiski,* I, 62.
65. ORAK, 1860: 24–25.
66. Tikhmenev, *Historical Review,* I, 150.
67. Lazarev, *Zapiski,* 239.
68. Zavalishin, "Krugosvetnoye plavanie," 151.
69. USNA, 51: 187.
70. United States, Congress, House of Representatives, *Russian America,* 22.
71. D., "Russkiya poseleniya," 830.
72. Khlebnikov, "Kadyaksky otdel," 4.
73. USNA, 63: pt. 1, 192, 65: pt. 1, 113–13v.
74. USNA, 52: 444v.

75. USNA, 34: 175; Veniaminov, *Zapiski*, I, 72.

76. USNA, 63: pt. 1, 191v.–92.

77. USNA, 33: 122–22v.

78. USNA, 34: 168v.

79. *Materialy*, III, 127.

80. USNA, 63: pt. 1, 123.

81. *Doklad komiteta*, II, 503.

82. USNA, 27: 284v., 34: 168.

83. USNA, 32: 266–66v.

84. USNA, 54: 243v.–44.

85. Alaska History Research Project, *Documents*, III, 145; Tikhmenev, *Supplement*, 138; Von Langsdorff, *Voyages and Travels*, II, 228.

86. Golder, "Attitude," 272; Shashkov, *Sobranie*, II, 644.

87. Khlebnikov, "Zapiski," 76–77, 104–4v.

88. Alaska History Research Project, *Documents*, III, 176.

89. Khlebnikov, "Zapiski," 134–34v.

90. Alaska History Research Project, *Documents*, III, 145; Tikhmenev, *Supplement*, 137.

91. Von Langsdorff, *Voyages and Travels*, II, 228.

92. Veniaminov, *Zapiski*, I, 62.

93. USNA, 33: 200.

94. USNA, 54: 245–46.

95. Andreyev, *Russian Discoveries*, 92.

96. Von Wrangell, *Statistische und ethnographische Nachrichten*, 26n.

97. USNA, 31: 72.

98. USNA, 65: pt. 1, 113v.

99. Tikhmenev, *Supplement*, 428.

100. Zavalishin, "Delo," 39.

101. *Doklad komiteta*, I, 132, II, 310–11.

102. Khlebnikov, "Kadyaksky otdel," 3.

103. *Doklad komiteta*, II, 147.

104. United States, Congress, House of Representatives, *Russian America*, 49.

105. Khlebnikov, "Kadyaksky otdel," 3v.

106. Anonymous, "Kratkoye opisanie," 95.

107. ORAK, 1859: 72–73.

Chapter 7

1. United States, Congress, Senate, *Proceedings*, II, 23.

2. Kusov and Severin, "Istoricheskaya zapiska," 1.

3. Ministerstvo inostrannykh del SSSR, *Vneshnyaya politika Rossii*, VI, 280.

4. Gibson, "Russia in California," 207.

5. Choris, *Voyage*, 7.

6. Golovnin, *Puteshestvie*, I, 281.

7. USNA, 1: 67v.–68.

8. USNA, 29: 97v.–98.

9. USNA, 29: 119v.

10. Potekhin, "Selenie Ross," 30–31.

11. Carter, "Duhaut-Cilly's Account," 326.

12. Gibson, "Russia in California," 210.

13. Glavnoye pravlenie Rossiisko-Amerikanskoy kompanii, "O selenii Ross," 1.

14. *Ibid.*

15. USNA, 4: 424v.

16. [Duflot De Mofras], *Travels*, II, 253; Du Four, Essig, *et al.*, "The Russians in California," Documentary Appendix, 258–59; [Sutter], "Inventaire," 26v.

17. [Duflot De Mofras], *Travels*, II, 253; Du Four, Essig, *et al.*, "The Russians in California," Documentary Appendix, 258; [Sutter], "Inventaire," 26–26v.

18. USNA, 41: 251.

19. [Duflot De Mofras], *Travels*, II, 254; Du Four, Essig, *et al.*, "The Russians in California," Documentary Appendix, 259; [Sutter], "Inventaire," 26v.–27.

20. [Duflot De Mofras], *Travels*, II, 251–52; Du Four, Essig, *et al.*, "The Russians in California," Documentary Appendix, 257–58; [Sutter], "Inventaire," 25v.

21. Vallejo, "Informe," 98.

22. Vallejo, "Establecimientos Rusos," 7.

23. Sutter, "Personal Reminiscences," 24.

24. USNA, 14: 345–45v.

25. Sutter, "Personal Reminiscences," 24.

26. Gibson, "Two New Chernykh Letters," 60.

27. Khlebnikov, "Donesenie o obozrenii," 2.

28. Gibson, "Russia in California," 210; Khlebnikov, "Donesenie o obozrenii," 2; USNA, 37: 322.

29. USNA, 30: 160.

30. Tikhmenev, *Historical Review*, I, 417.

31. Gibson, "Two New Chernykh Letters," 54.

32. USNA, 41: 249.

33. Nunis, *California Diary*, 106.

34. Bilbasov, *Arkhiv*, VI, 671; *Materialy*, III, 169.

35. Gentilcore, "Missions and Mission Lands," 61; Kusov and Severin, "Istoricheskaya zapiska," 3; Potekhin, "Selenie Ross," 28.

36. Khlebnikov, "Zapiski o Kalifornii," 281.

37. Kusov and Severin, "Istoricheskaya zapiska," 2.

38. Gibson, "Russia in California," 208.

39. *Materialy*, III, 155.

40. *Ibid.*

41. *Materialy*, III, 155; Potekhin, "Selenie Ross," 12; Tikhmenev, *Historical Review*, I, 254; Von Kotzebue, *A New Voyage*, II, 125.

42. Corney, *Voyages*, 82.
43. Von Kotzebue, *A New Voyage*, II, 125.
44. Golovnin, *Puteshestvie*, I, 279.
45. Khlebnikov, "Donesenie o obozrenii," 2, 7v.
46. Potekhin, "Selenie Ross," 29.
47. Khlebnikov, "Donesenie o obozrenii," 2; Vallejo, "Informe," 107.
48. Potekhin, "Selenie Ross," 29.
49. *Ibid.*, 13; Tikhmenev, *Historical Review*, I, 257.
50. Davis, *Seventy-Five Years*, 31; Thompson, *Historical and Descriptive Sketch*, 23.
51. Golovnin, *Puteshestvie*, I, 280; *Materialy*, III, 153.
52. USNA, 33: 236.
53. Khlebnikov, "Donesenie o obozrenii," 4.
54. *Ibid.*
55. *Materialy*, III, 154, 156.
56. Golovnin, *Puteshestvie*, I, 280.
57. Von Wrangell, *Statistische und ethnographische Nachrichten*, 18–19.
58. USNA, 30: 252.
59. Gibson, "Russia in California," 208; Potekhin, "Selenie Ross," 28; Tikhmenev, *Historical Review*, I, 415–16.
60. USNA, 7: 22, 31: 358, 41: 340v.
61. Kupreyanov, "Donesenie o nyneshnem sostoyanii," 3; Tikhmenev, *Historical Review*, I, 417.
62. Gibson, "Russia in California," 209; Tikhmenev, *Historical Review*, I, 418.
63. Tikhmenev, *Historical Review*, I, 254.
64. USNA, 36: 107.
65. Tikhmenev, *Historical Review*, I, 423.
66. USNA, 6: 302.
67. USNA, 32: 99v.
68. Tchitchinoff, *Adventures*, 9.
69. *Ibid.*, 9–10.
70. Carter, "Duhaut-Cilly's Account," 326.
71. USNA, 30: 160.
72. Khlebnikov, "Donesenie o obozrenii," 3–3v.
73. USNA, 4: 424.
74. Rotchev, "Vospominaniya," 103.
75. Bilbasov, *Arkhiv*, VI, 671; *Materialy*, III, 169.
76. USNA, 30: 158v.
77. USNA, 39: 249–49v.
78. USNA, 40: 189.
79. USNA, 42: 101.
80. Mahr, *Visit*, 43 [309], 65 [331]; Von Chamisso, *Sojourn*, 10.
81. Gibson, "A Russian," 66, n. 10.
82. Khlebnikov, "Zapiski o Kalifornii," 224.
83. USNA, 28: 58v., 87v., 29: 207.

84. USNA, 28: 95v.
85. Gibson, "Russia in California," 210–11.
86. USNA, 31: 291.
87. Gibson, "Russia in California," 207.
88. Tarakanoff, *Statement*, 35.
89. *Materialy*, III, 153.
90. Von Chamisso, *Sojourn*, 11.
91. Choris, *Voyage*, 7.
92. Von Kotzebue, *A New Voyage*, II, 125.
93. USNA, 28: 290.
94. USNA, 29: 100.
95. USNA, 30: 272, 31: 46v.
96. Gibson, "Russia in California," 208.
97. Shur, *K beregam*, 159.
98. Tikhmenev, *Historical Review*, I, 255.
99. Von Krusenstern, *Voyage*, II, 110.
100. Von Langsdorff, *Voyages and Travels*, II, 67–68.
101. Zavalishin, "Delo," 52–53.
102. Gibson, "Russia in California," 208.
103. USNA, 5: 45–46.
104. USNA, 30: 363.
105. USNA, 5: 45.
106. Tarakanoff, *Statement*, 4–5.
107. Tchitchinoff, *Adventures*, 3–4.
108. Khlebnikov, "Donesenie o obozrenii," 3v.–4.
109. *Ibid.*, 4.
110. *Ibid.*, 3v.
111. Vallejo, "Informe," 109.
112. USNA, 41: 253, 42: 94.
113. Gibson, "Two New Chernykh Letters," 56, 58.
114. *Ibid.*, 55.
115. USNA, 40: 72v.
116. Mahr, *Visit*, 117 [383].
117. Tarakanoff, *Statement*, 36.
118. Gibson, "Russia in California," 208.
119. *Materialy*, III, 153.
120. Storie and Weir, *Generalized Soil Map*, 40, Tables 16, 20.
121. USNA, 30: 343v.
122. USNA, 30: 343v.–44.
123. Glavnoye pravlenie Rossiisko-Amerikanskoy kompanii, "O selenii Ross," 1v.; *Materialy*, III, 151.
124. Gibson, "Two New Cherynkh Letters," 52.
125. Gibson, "Russia in California," 208.
126. USNA, 34: 430v.
127. Tikhmenev, *Historical Review*, I, 256.
128. Gibson, "A Russian," 66, n. 13.

129. Gibson, "Two New Chernykh Letters," 54–56.
130. Gibson, "Russia in California," 208.
131. USNA, 29: 210.
132. Tikhmenev, *Historical Review*, I, 418.
133. USNA, 41: 254, 341–41v.
134. Gibson, "Two New Chernykh Letters," 59.
135. Khlebnikov, "Donesenie o obozrenii," 7v.
136. Tikhmenev, *Historical Review*, I, 254.
137. USNA, 12: 425v.
138. Gibson, "Russia in California," 212.
139. USNA, 12: 426.
140. Tikhmenev, *Historical Review*, I, 422.
141. [Duflot De Mofras], *Travels*, II, 249.
142. Tikhmenev, *Historical Review*, I, 422.
143. [Duflot De Mofras], *Travels*, II, 4.
144. USNA, 43: 17v.
145. USNA, 12: 185.
146. USNA, 12: 185–86.
147. USNA, 12: 426v.–27.
148. USNA, 45: 362v.
149. USNA, 46: 166v.
150. USNA, 46: 167.

Chapter 8

1. Okun, *The Russian American Company*, 153.
2. Berkh, "Nechto," 159–60.
3. Andreyev, *Russian Discoveries*, 165–66; Berkh, "Nechto," 160.
4. Berkh, "Nechto," 162.
5. Rossiisko-Amerikanskaya kompaniya, *Sheffer Papers*, [11–12].
6. Campbell, *Voyage*, 81.
7. Khlebnikov, *Zhizneopisanie*, 161–62.
8. Pierce, *Russia's Hawaiian Adventure*, 172–73.
9. *Ibid.*, 191.
10. *Ibid.*, 194–95.
11. *Ibid.*, 195.
12. *Ibid.*
13. *Ibid.*
14. *Ibid.*, 196.
15. *Ibid.*, 196–97.
16. *Ibid.*, 186.
17. Tarakanoff, *Statement*, 29.
18. Pierce, *Russia's Hawaiian Adventure*, 127.
19. Okun, "Tsarskaya Rossiya," 174; Pierce, *Russia's Hawaiian Adventure*, 194–95; USNA, 1: 250v.–51.
20. Tarakanoff, *Statement*, 31.

21. *Ibid.*
22. Pierce, *Russia's Hawaiian Adventure,* 151, 187.
23. Khlebnikov, "Zapiski," 21.
24. Tarakanoff, *Statement,* 32.
25. USNA, 1: 242v.–43v.
26. Rossiisko-Amerikanskaya kompaniya, *Sheffer Papers,* [127].
27. Khelbnikov, *Zhizneopisanie,* 168; Okun, "Tsarskaya Rossiya," 173; Pierce, *Russia's Hawaiian Adventure,* 138; Shur, *K beregam,* 63; Tikhmenev, *Historical Review,* I, 232; Tumarkin, *Vtorzhenie,* 162.
28. USNA, 1: 257v.–58.
29. Tikhmenev, *Historical Review,* I, 233.

Chapter 9

1. United States, Congress, Senate, *Proceedings,* II, 24.
2. Alaska History Research Project, *Documents,* III, 179–80.
3. *Materialy,* III, 74.
4. Cook [and King], *Voyage,* III, 437.
5. Howay, "Outline Sketch," 7.
6. Anonymous, "Early Commerce," 1–3.
7. Anonymous, "Zapiski," 3, 5v.
8. Sturgis, "Extracts," I, 1, 11, II, 1.
9. [Phelps], "Solid men," 9, 77.
10. Cowdin, "The Northwest Fur Trade," 537.
11. [Phelps], "Solid men," 77.
12. Alaska History Research Project, *Documents,* III, 163.
13. Anonymous, "Kratkaya Istoricheskaya Zapiska," 3.
14. Khlebnikov, *Zhizneopisanie,* 64.
15. D'Wolf, *Voyage,* 39–40; Von Langsdorff, *Voyages and Travels,* II, 89.
16. Alaska History Research Project, *Documents,* III, 203.
17. *Materialy,* III, 4, 13.
18. USNA, 28: 140.
19. Anonymous, "Kratkaya Istoricheskaya Zapiska," 2v.–3.
20. Ministerstvo inostrannykh del SSSR, *Vneshnyaya politika Rossii,* IV, 241.
21. AVPR, f. RAK, d. 314, 3.
22. Anonymous, "Zapiski," 5.
23. *Ibid.,* 2–2v.
24. United States, Congress, American State Papers, 439.
25. Anonymous, "Zapiski," 6v.–7.
26. Ministerstvo inostrannykh del SSSR, *Vneshnyaya politika Rossii,* VI, 279.
27. *Ibid.,* V, 270.
28. *Ibid.,* V, 273.
29. AVPR, f. Glavny Arkhiv II–3, d. 8, 90.
30. Irving, *Astoria,* 386–87.

31. Anonymous, "Zapiski," 9v.–10; Tikhmenev, *Historical Review*, I, 222.
32. AVPR, f. Kantselyariya, d. 3,646, 21v.–22.
33. *Ibid.*, 22.
34. Astor, "Astor Papers," Box 20.
35. Choris, *Voyage*, 8.
36. USNA, 28: 244v.
37. USNA, 28: 244v.
38. Choris, *Voyage*, 9.
39. AVPR, f. RAK, d. 284, 5.
40. Anonymous, "Kratkaya Istoricheskaya Zapiska," 5v.
41. *Doklad komiteta*, I, 28–29; United States, Congress, Senate, *Proceedings*, II, 25.
42. Anonymous, "Kratkaya Istoricheskaya Zapiska," 6v.
43. *Ibid.*
44. *Ibid.*, 6v.–7.
45. *Ibid.*, 7.
46. *Ibid.*
47. *Ibid.*
48. *Ibid.*, 7v.
49. *Ibid.*, 7v.–8.
50. *Ibid.*, 8.
51. *Ibid.*
52. *Ibid.*, 8–8v.
53. *Ibid.*, 8v.–9.
54. *Ibid.*, 9.
55. *Ibid.*, 10.
56. *Ibid.*, 10–10v.
57. *Ibid.*, 10v.
58. *Ibid.*, 11.
59. USNA, 4: 6.
60. *Materialy*, III, 91.
61. USNA, 31: 76.
62. ORAK, 1842: 37.
63. USNA, 36: 51, 52v.
64. Tikhmenev, *Historical Review*, I, 435.
65. HBC, D.4/123, 19v.; Merk, *Fur Trade*, 317; Rich, *Part of Dispatch*, 75.
66. USNA, 32: 45–46v.
67. USNA, 54: 53v.–54.
68. USNA, 7: 12–13.
69. USNA, 8: 328.
70. USNA, 8: 89v.
71. USNA, 36: 52v.–53.
72. USNA, 36: 53–53v.
73. Howay, "Outline Sketch," 14; Lütke, *Voyage*, I, 131.
74. United States, Congress, Senate, *Proceedings*, II, 235.
75. USNA, 32: 255v.

76. USNA, 44: 7.

77. USNA, 44: 125v.

78. Khlebnikov, "Zapiski," 17.

79. [Khlebnikov], "Zapiski," 102; USNA, 7: 13v.

80. USNA, 7: 20v.

81. USNA, 31: 326v.

82. USNA, 31: 327.

83. Tikhmenev, *Historical Review*, I, 397.

84. Lütke, *Voyage*, I, 128.

Chapter 10

1. Golovnin, *Puteshestvie*, I, supplement, Table B.

2. Khlebnikov, "Zapiski o Kalifornii," 283.

3. Khlebnikov, "Donesenie o obozrenii," 6.

4. Khlebnikov, "Zapiski o Kalifornii," 282.

5. Golovnin, *Puteshestvie*, I, supplement, Table B.

6. De Roquefeuil, *Journal*, II, 267.

7. Shur, *K beregam*, 198.

8. Tikhmenev, *Historical Review*, I, 198.

9. Von Langsdorff, *Voyages and Travels*, II, 99.

10. *Ibid.*, II, 93.

11. Rezanov, *Rezanov Voyage*, 5.

12. Tikhmenev, *Historical Review*, I, 184; Tikhmenev, *Supplement*, 427; Von Langsdorff, *Voyages and Travels*, II, 94, 136.

13. Von Langsdorff, *Voyages and Travels*, II, 97.

14. Tikhmenev, *Supplement*, 334–35.

15. *Materialy*, III, 137.

16. Alaska History Research Project, *Documents*, III, 311.

17. Tikhmenev, *Supplement*, 396; Rezanov, *Rezanov Voyage*, 26.

18. Rezanov, *Rezanov Voyage*, 31.

19. Ministerstvo inostrannykh del SSSR, *Vneshnyaya politika Rossii*, IV, 164, VII, 696.

20. Tikhmenev, *Supplement*, 395.

21. Khlebnikov, *Zhizneopisanie*, 105; *Materialy*, III, 145–46; Tikhmenev, *Historical Review*, I, 184; Tikhmenev, *Supplement*, 406.

22. Khlebnikov, *Zhizneopisanie*, 105.

23. Von Langsdorff, *Voyages and Travels*, II, 215.

24. Tikhmenev, *Historical Review*, I, 186–87.

25. Ministerstvo inostrannykh del SSSR, *Vneshnyaya politika Rossii*, III, 692.

26. Tikhmenev, *Supplement*, 407.

27. Tikhmenev, *Historical Review*, I, 187.

28. AVPR, f. Glavny Arkhiv II–3, d. 8, 10v.–11; Ministerstvo inostrannykh del SSSR, *Vneshnyaya politika Rossii*, IV, 163–64; Rossiisko-Amerikanskaya Kompaniya, "Obrashchenie direktorov."

29. Rossiisko-Amerikanskaya Kompaniya, "Obrashchenie direktorov."

30. Alaska History Research Project, *Documents*, III, 311–12; AVPR, f. Glavny Arkhiv II–3, d. 8, 13v.; Rossiisko-Amerikanskaya Kompaniya, Glavnoye pravlenie, "Predstavlenie," 311–12; Tikhmenev, *Historical Review*, I, 247–48.

31. Rossiisko-Amerikanskaya Kompaniya, Glavnoye pravlenie, "Donesenie," 11.

32. Alaska History Research Project, *Documents*, III, 311; Rossiisko-Amerikanskaya Kompaniya, Glavnoye pravlenie, "Predstavlenie," 7.

33. Ministerstvo inostrannykh del SSSR, *Vneshnyaya politika Rossii*, VI, 281.

34. Rossiisko-Amerikanskaya Kompaniya, "Obrashchenie glavnovo pravleniya," 143v.

35. Rossiisko-Amerikanskaya Kompaniya, Glavnoye pravlenie, "Predstavlenie," 7.

36. Alaska History Research Project, *Documents*, III, 312; Rossiisko-Amerikanskaya Kompaniya, Glavnoye pravlenie, "Predstavlenie," 8–9.

37. Ministerstvo inostrannykh del SSSR, *Vneshnyaya politika Rossii*, VI, 728; Potekhin, "Selenie Ross," 13; Tikhmenev, *Historical Review*, I, 257.

38. Potekhin, "Selenie Ross," 13; Tikhmenev, *Historical Review*, I, 257.

39. Von Chamisso, *Sojourn*, 3.

40. *Ibid.*, 4.

41. Volkl, *Russland*, 126.

42. Shur, *K beregam*, 304.

43. Zavalishin, "Delo," 61.

44. *Materialy*, III, 78; Potekhin, "Selenie Ross," 22; Tikhmenev, *Historical Review*, I, 264–65.

45. Shur, *K beregam*, 140–41.

46. Khlebnikov, "Zapiski o Kalifornii," 402–03; *Materialy*, III, 78, 148.

47. Khlebnikov, "Zapiski o Kalifornii," 402.

48. USNA, 3: 83.

49. HBC, D.4/121, 22.

50. USNA, 36: 34v.

51. [Khlebnikov], "Zapiski," 126v.

52. Khlebnikov, "Donesenie o raztorzhke," 2v.

53. Lütke, *Voyage*, I, 125; *Materialy*, III, 81–82.

54. *Vallejo Documentos*, I, nos. 56–56A, 155D–155H.

55. Rezanov, *Rezanov Voyage*, 49.

56. *Ibid.*, 50–51.

57. Tarakanoff, *Statement*, 15.

58. Khlebnikov, "Zapiski o Kalifornii," 399.

59. Zavalishin, "Kaliforniya," 357.

60. *Ibid.*, 348.

61. Fernandez, "Cosas," 25–26.

62. Tikhmenev, *Historical Review*, I, 394.

63. Golovnin, *Puteshestvie*, I, 274.

64. Vallejo, "Establecimientos Rusos," 2.

65. Khlebnikov, "Donesenie o raztorzhke," 2.

66. Von Kotzebue, *A New Voyage*, II, 123.

67. Zavalishin, "Delo," 62.

68. Von Langsdorff, *Voyages and Travels*, II, 187–88.

69. Von Chamisso, *Sojourn*, 1.

70. *Materialy*, III, 148–49; USNA, 31: 46.

71. Tikhmenev, *Historical Review*, I, 420; USNA, 36: 66v.–67, 81.

72. Sutter, "Personal Reminiscences," 24.

73. Tikhmenev, *Historical Review*, I, 408; USNA, 43: 313.

74. Vallejo, "Ranch and Mission Days," 187.

75. L., "Vypiska," [3].

76. *Materialy*, III, 129.

77. Mexico, Junta del Fomento de las Californias, "Exposición," 8.

78. *Materialy*, III, 69.

79. USNA, 36: 325v.

80. Chernykh, "O zemledelii," 260.

81. Erman, "Zufass-Bermerkungen," 251.

82. Tikhmenev, *Historical Review*, I, 268–69.

83. USNA, 3: 85, 163v.

84. USNA, 28: 201v.

85. USNA, 30: 54–54v.

86. USNA, 30: 286v.

87. USNA, 31: 330.

88. Chistyakov, "Donesenie," 1.

89. *Ibid.*, 1–2.

90. Vrangel, "Donesenie o zakupke," 2–3.

91. *Ibid.*, 3.

92. Tikhmenev, *Historical Review*, I, 401.

93. USNA, 28: 201v.

94. USNA, 3: 164.

95. *Materialy*, III, 83–84; Tikhmenev, *Historical Review*, I, 267.

96. USNA, 30: 55.

97. USNA, 34: 121, 35: 69v., 37: 138; Vrangel, "Donesenie o plavanii," 3.

98. Chernykh, "O zemledelii," 261.

99. Lütke, *Voyage*, I, 124; *Materialy*, III, 83; Tikhmenev, *Historical Review*, I, 400.

100. Shur, *K beregam*, 197–98.

101. USNA, 30: 286v.

102. Shur, *K beregam*, 198.

103. *Ibid.*

104. Zavalishin, "Delo," 59.

105. Vrangel, "Donesenie o plavanii," 2.

106. *Materialy*, III, 82–83.

107. Lütke, *Voyage*, I, 127.

108. *Materialy*, III, 84.

109. USNA, 28: 418, 29: 11, 53v., 30: 252, 31: 40, 291, 32: 68v.–69, 70v., 37: 325v., 38: 105v., 51: 286.
110. USNA, 32: 69.
111. USNA, 31: 358–58v.
112. USNA, 38: 359.
113. USNA, 39: 53v.–54v., 126–27.
114. Shur, *K beregam*, 308–09.
115. *Ibid.*, 196–97.
116. Chernykh, "O zemledelii," 261.
117. USNA, 6: 123.
118. USNA, 6: 157, 31: 359, 368v.
119. USNA, 31: 61v.
120. Von Wrangell, *Statistische und ethnographische Nachrichten*, 12.
121. Tikhmenev, *Historical Review*, I, 404.
122. Shur, *K beregam*, 234–35.
123. Tikhmenev, *Historical Review*, I, 403; USNA, 32: 164v.–65.
124. USNA, 34: 121v.; Vrangel, "Donesenie o zakupke," 2.
125. Vrangel, "Donesenie o zakupke," 2.
126. Khlebnikov, "Donesenie o raztorzhke," 2v.
127. Tikhmenev, *Historical Review*, I, 405.
128. *Ibid.;* USNA, 10: 483–83v., 11: 277v., 39: 354, 358v.
129. USNA, 48: 447v., 455.
130. USNA, 52: 133–33v.
131. USNA, 54: 440v.
132. ORAK, 1848: 36–37.
133. USNA, 56: 71–71v.
134. USNA, 60: 116.
135. USNA, 61: pt. 2, 111v.
136. USNA, 60: 48v., 62: pt. 1, 136.
137. *Doklad komiteta*, II, 326; Tikhmenev, *Historical Review*, II, 267–68.
138. USNA, 23: 113.

Chapter 11

1. USNA, 34: 104–4v.
2. United States, Congress, Senate, *Proceedings*, II, 264–65.
3. USNA, 8: 327v.
4. USNA, 8: 327v.–28, 330v.
5. USNA, 42: 446.
6. USNA, 12: 278–78v.
7. USNA, 12: 278v.
8. HBC, B.223/b/12, 23.
9. HBC, F.29/2, 144–46.
10. HBC, F.29/2, 146–47.
11. AVPR, f. RAK, d. 368, 13–13v.; HBC, F.29/2, 162–70, 174–77v.; Tikhmenev, *Historical Review*, II, 411–12.

12. Schafer, "Letters," 85.
13. USNA, 44: 84.
14. Merk, *Fur Trade*, 86.
15. Rich, *Part of Dispatch*, 85.
16. HBC, D.4/123, 19.
17. Barker, *Letters*, 17; Merk, *Fur Trade*, 312; USNA, 7: 26–26v.
18. USNA, 35: 19v.
19. USNA, 7: 20–22.
20. USNA, 34: 103.
21. Rich, *Letters*, II, 54n.
22. *Ibid.*, II, 54.
23. *Ibid.*, II, 125.
24. Tikhmenev, *Historical Review*, II, 183.
25. USNA, 12: 287v.–89v.
26. USNA, 52: 6v.
27. USNA, 52: 7.
28. USNA, 44: 85.
29. USNA, 52: 7.
30. USNA, 51: 227v., 52: 7–7v.
31. USNA, 43: 313v., 44: 84v.
32. Tikhmenev, *Historical Review*, I, 406.
33. USNA, 48: 566, 638.
34. HBC, B.223/z/4, 208.
35. USNA, 46: 136, 253.
36. Tikhmenev, *Historical Review*, I, 436–37.
37. HBC, A.12/2, 292v., D.4/66, 53.
38. HBC, A.12/2, 292v., D.4/66, 53.
39. Davidson, "Relations," 49.
40. HBC, A.12/2, 292, D.4/66, 52v.
41. USNA, 55: 150v.
42. USNA, 18: 102.

Chapter 12

1. Andreyev, *Russian Discoveries*, 162.
2. Rezanov, *Rezanov Voyage*, 75; Tikhmenev, *Supplement*, 432; Von Langsdorff, *Voyages and Travels*, I, 188.
3. Tikhmenev, *Historical Review*, I, 206.
4. Campbell, *Voyage*, 90; Tikhmenev, *Historical Review*, I, 204.
5. Rossiisko-Amerikanskaya Kompaniya, "Sheffer Papers," [1], [5]; Tikhmenev, *Historical Review*, I, 203.
6. Pierce, *Russia's Hawaiian Adventure*, 40–41.
7. USNA, 3: 83.
8. Gibson, "Russian America," 7–8; USNA, 31: 304–4v.
9. USNA, 52: 486v.–99.
10. ORAK, 1848: 39-40.

11. Cordes, "Letters," 111; ORAK, 1850: 28–29; Tikhmenev, *Historical Review*, II, 193.

Afterword

1. Vishnevsky, *Puteshestvennik*, 36.
2. Valaam Monastery, *Ocherk*, 140.
3. *Ibid.*
4. Blaschke, *Topographia*, 51; *Doklad komiteta*, I, 119, II, 96; Khlebnikov, "Zapiski," 51v.; Lütke, *Voyage*, I, 144; *Materialy*, III, 69; Von Wrangell, *Statistische und ethnographische Nachrichten*, 12.
5. USNA, 27: 122, 28: 138v.
6. USNA, 27: 122.
7. USNA, 33: 115.
8. USNA, 33: 117.
9. USNA, 33: 3–3v., 114v.
10. Khlebnikov, "Zapiski," 38; Tikhmenev, *Historical Review*, II, 275.
11. *Doklad komiteta*, II, 95, supp. 17.
12. USNA, 36: 43v.
13. Blaschke, *Topographia*, 53.
14. USNA, 61: pt. 1, 85v.
15. *Doklad komiteta*, I, 117, II, 92–94, 99, 323, 326.
16. *Ibid.*, II, 102.
17. USNA, 13: 220–20v.
18. USNA, 13: 222.
19. USNA, 13: 219.
20. ORAK, 1860: 74; USNA, 63, pt. 2, 44v.
21. *Materialy*, III, 2n.; Tikhmenev, *Supplement*, 193–94.
22. Golovnin, *Puteshestvie*, I, 141.
23. ORAK, 1860: 85.
24. ORAK, 1860: 94.
25. USNA, 2: 14.
26. USNA, 42: 306v., 43: 221.
27. USNA, 51: 426.

BIBLIOGRAPHY

Alaska History Research Project, *Documents Relative to the History of Alaska*, College, Alaska, 1936–38, III–IV.

Andreyev, A. I., ed., *Russian Discoveries in the Pacific and in North America in the Eighteenth and Nineteenth Centuries*, trans. by Carl Ginsburg, Ann Arbor, Mich., 1952.

————, ed., *Russkie otkrytiya v Tikhom okeane i Severnoy Amerike v XVIII veke [Russian Discoveries in the Pacific Ocean and in North America in the 18th Century]*, Moscow, 1948.

Anonymous, "Early Commerce in the North Pacific," Bancroft Library, Ms P–K 29.

Anonymous, "Kratkaya Istoricheskaya Zapiska o sostoyanii Rossiisko-Amerikanskoy Kompanii" ["A Brief Historical Note on the Condition of the Russian-American Company"], AGO, raz. 99, op. 1, no. 29.

Anonymous [Archmandrite Bolotov], "Kratkoye opisanie ob Amerikanskom ostrove Kadyake" ["A Brief Description of the American Island of Kodiak"], *Drug prosveshcheniya*, October 1805, 89–106.

Anonymous, "Obozrenie sostoyaniya deistvy Rossiisko-Amerikanskoy Kompanii s 1797 po 1819 god" ["A Review of the Condition of the Russian-American Company's Activities from 1797 to 1819"], *Zhurnal manufaktur i torgovli*, 1835, 12–124.

Anonymous, "Opisanie Yakutskoy Provintsii" ["A Description of Yakutsk Province"], Saltykov-Shchedrin State Public Library, Ermitazhnoye sobranie, Ms 238 6–f.

Anonymous, "Vzglyad na torgovlyu, proizvodimuyu chrez Okhotsky port" ["A Glance at the Trade Conducted through Okhotsk Port"], *Severny arkhiv*, 1823, 28–45.

Anonymous, "Zapiski o torgovle severo-amerikantsev v russkikh koloniyakh v Amerike, dekabrya 23 dnya 1816 goda" ["Notes on the Trade of the North Americans in the Russian Colonies in America, December 23, 1816"], AVPR, f. Kantselyariya, d. 12, 182.

Astor, John Jacob, "Astor Papers," Baker Library, Box 20.

AVPR, f. Glavny Arkhiv II–3, d. 8; f. Kantselyariya, d. 3,646; f. RAK, d. 133, d. 154, d. 183, d. 284, d. 291, d. 301, d. 314, d. 318, d. 368, d. 410; f. 341, op. 888, d. 181, d. 411.

Barker, Burt Brown, ed., *Letters of Dr. John McLoughlin Written at Fort Vancouver 1829–1832*, Portland, Oreg., 1948.

Barsukov, Ivan, *Innokentii Mitropolit Moskovsky i Kolomensky po yevo sochineniyam, pismam i razskazam sovremennikov [Metropolitan Innocent of Moscow and Koloma According to His Writings and Letters and the Accounts of Contemporaries]*, Moscow, 1883.

Berkh, V., "Izvestie o mekhovoy torgovle, proizvodimoy Rossiyanami pri ostrovakh Kurilskikh, Aleutskikh i severozapadnom beregu Ameriki" ["Information on the Russian Fur Trade along the Kurile and Aleutian Islands and the Northwest Coast of America"], *Syn otechestva*, 1823, pt. 88, 243–64, pt. 89, 97–106, 165, table between 178 and 179.

——— "Nechto o Sandvichevykh ostrovakh" ["A Few Words on the Sandwich Islands"], *Syn otechestva*, 1818, 158–65.

Bilbasov, V. A., ed., *Arkhiv grafov Mordvinovykh [The Archive of the Counts Mordvinov]*, St. Petersburg, 1902, VI.

Blaschke, E., "Neskolko zamechany o plavanii v baidarkakh i o Lisyevskikh Aleyutakh" ["Some Remarks on Boating in Kayaks and the Fox Island Aleuts"], *Morskoy sbornik*, 1848, 115–24, 160–65.

———, *Topographia Medica Portus Novi-Archangelscensis [A Medical Description of Port New Archangel]*, Petropoli, 1842.

Campbell, Archibald, *A Voyage Round the World, from 1806 to 1812*, 2nd ed., New York, 1819 (reprint 1970).

Carter, Charles Franklin, trans., "Duhaut-Cilly's Account of California in the Years 1827–1828," *California Historical Quarterly*, December 1929, 306–36.

Chernykh, Ye., "O zemledelii v verkhney Kalifornii" ["Concerning Agriculture in Upper California"], *Zhurnal selskavo khozyaistva i ovtsevodstva*, 1841, 234–65.

Chistyakov, Pyotr, "Donesenie o selenii Ross, No. 46, Marta 16 dnya 1829 goda" ["A Report on Ross Settlement, No. 46, March 16, 1829"], AGO, raz. 99, op. 1, d. 36.

Choris, M. Louis, *Voyage pittoresque autour du monde*, Paris, 1822.

Cochrane, Capt. John Dundas, *Narrative of a Pedestrian Journey through Russia and Siberian Tartary, from the Frontiers of China to the Frozen Sea and Kamtchatka*, Philadelphia, 1824 (reprint 1970).

Cook, Captain James [and King, Captain James], *A Voyage to the Pacific Ocean*, London, 1784, III.

Cordes, Frederick C., "Letters of A. Rotchev, Last Commandant at Fort Ross And the Résumé of the Report of the Russian-American Company for the Year 1850–51," *California Historical Quarterly*, June 1960, 97–115.

Corney, Peter, *Voyages in the Northern Pacific*, Honolulu, 1896 (reprint 1966).

Cowdin, Elliot C., "The Northwest Fur Trade," *Hunt's Merchants' Magazine*, June 1846, 532–39.

D., "Russkiya poseleniya v Amerike" ["Russian Settlements in America"], *Sanktpeterburgskiya vedomosti*, August 21/September 2, 1836, 830.

Dana, Richard Henry, *Two Years Before the Mast*, Garden City, N.Y., n.d.

Davidson, Donald C., "Relations of the Hudson's Bay Company with the Russian American Company on the Northwest Coast, 1829–1867," *British Columbia Historical Quarterly*, January 1941, 33–51.

Davis, William Heath, *Seventy-five Years in California*, San Francisco, 1929 (reprint 1967).

Davydov, G. I., *Dvukratnoye puteshestvie v Ameriku morskikh ofitserov Khvostova i Davydova [The Duplicate Voyage to America of the Naval Officers Khvostov and Davydov]*, St. Petersburg, 1810, I–II.

De La Perouse, J. F. G., *A Voyage Round the World*, London, 1798, III (reprint 1968).

De Roquefeuil, Camille, *Journal d'un voyage autour du monde*, Paris, 1823, I–II.

Dobell, Peter, *Travels in Kamtchatka and Siberia*, London, 1830, I–II (reprint 1970).

Doklad komiteta ob ustroistve russkikh amerikanskikh kolony [Report of the Committee on the Organization of the Russian-American Colonies], St. Petersburg, 1863–64, I–II.

[Duflot de Mofras, Eugene], *Duflot de Mofras' Travels on the Pacific Coast*, trans. by Marguerite Eyer Wilbur, Santa Ana, Calif., 1937, II.

Dufour, Clarence John, E. O. Essig, *et al.*, "The Russians in California," *California Historical Quarterly*, September 1933.

D'Wolf, Captain John, *A Voyage to the North Pacific and A Journey through Siberia*, Cambridge, Mass., 1861 (reprint 1968).

Erman, Adolf, "Zufass-Bemerkungen über Neu Californien" ["Additional Remarks on New California"], *Annalen der Erd-, Volker- und Staatenkunde*, series 2, June 1833, 240–60.

Fernandez, Captain José, "Cosas de California" ["Facts about California"], Bancroft Library, Ms C–D 10.

Fyodorova, S. F., *Russkoye naselenie Alyaski i Kalifornii [The Russian Population of Alaska and California]*, Moscow, 1971.

Gentilcore, R. Louis, "Missions and Mission Lands of Alta California," *Annals of the Association of American Geographers*, March 1961, 46–72.

Gibson, James R., "Russia in California, 1833: Report of Governor Wrangel," *Pacific Northwest Quarterly*, October 1969, 205–15.

———, "Russian America in 1833: The Survey of Kirill Khlebnikov," *Pacific Northwest Quarterly*, January 1972, 1–13.

———, "A Russian Orthodox Priest in a Mexican Catholic Parish," *The Pacific Historian*, Summer 1971, 57–66.

———, "Two New Chernykh Letters," *The Pacific Historian*, Summer 1968, 48–56, Fall 1968, 55–60.

Golder, Frank A., "The Attitude of the Russian Government toward Alaska," in H. Morse Stephens, and Herbert E. Bolton, eds., *The Pacific Ocean in History*, New York, 1917, 269–75.

Golovin, P. N., "Iz putevykh pisem P. N. Golovina" ["From the Travel Letters of P. N. Golovin"], *Morskoy sbornik*, May 1863, 101–82, June 1863, 275–340.

———, "Obzor russkikh kolony v Severnoy Amerike" ["A Survey of the Russian Colonies in North America"], *Morskoy sbornik*, January 1862, 19–192.

Golovnin, Fleet Lieutenant, *Puteshestvie na shlyupe "Diana" iz Kronshtadta v Kamchatku* [*A Voyage on the Sloop "Diana" from Cronstadt to Kamchatka*], Moscow, 1961.

HBC, A.12/2, B.223/b/12, B.223/z/4, D.4/66, D.4/123, F.29/2.

Howay, F. W., "An Outline Sketch of the Maritime Fur Trade," *Annual Report of the Canadian Historical Association*, 1932, 5–14.

Iosaf, Archmandrite, "Kratkiya obyasneniya" ["Brief Explanations"], Göttingen University Library, Ms, Codex Asch 216.

Irving, Washington, *Astoria*, Clatsop Edition, Portland, Oreg., n.d.

Ivashintsov, N., "Russkiya krugosvetnia puteshestviya" ["Russian Round-the-World Voyages"], *Zapiski Gidrograficheskavo Departamenta*, 1849, 1–116, 1850, 1–190.

Khlebnikov, K. T., *Baranov*, trans. by Colin Bearne, Kingston, Ontario, 1973.

———, "Donesenie o obozrenii del po kontore v Rosse" ["A Report on a Survey of Affairs in Ross Counter"], AVPR, f. RAK, d. 323.

———, "Donesenie o raztorzhke v Kalifornii" ["A Report on Trade in California"], AVPR, f. RAK, d. 346.

———, "Kadyaksky otdel. Ostrov Kadyak" ["The Kodiak District. Kodiak Island"], AGO, raz, 99, op. 1, no. 60.

[———], "Vzglyad no polveka moyey zhizni" ["A Glance at the Half-Century of My Life"], *Syn otechestva*, 1836, 299–324, 345–73, 413–28.

———, "Zapiski o Kalifornii" ["Notes on California"], *Syn otechestva i severny arkhiv*, 1829, no. 2, 208–27, 276–88, 336–47, 400–410, no. 3, 25–35.

[———], "Zapiski o Koloniyakh v Amerike Rossiisko-Amerikanskoy kompanii" ["Notes on the Colonies of the Russian-American Company in America"], pt. 1, AGO, raz, 99, op. 1, no. 111.

———, "Zapiski o Koloniyakh Rossiisko-Amerikanskoy Kompanii" ["Notes on the Colonies of the Russian-American Company"], AGO, raz. 99, op. 1, no. 112.

———, *Zhizneopisanie Aleksandra Andreyevicha Baranova* [*Biography of Alexander Andreyevich Baranov*], St. Petersburg, 1835.

Kruzenshtern, I. F., *Puteshestvie vokrug sveta* [*A Voyage Around the World*], Moscow, 1950.

Kupreyanov, Ivan, "Donesenie o nyneshnem sostoyanii Seleniya Ross, s prilozheniem odnovo dokumenta, No. 321, 15 Iyunya 1837 goda" ["A Report on the Present Condition of Ross Settlement, with an Enclosure of One Document, No. 321, June 15, 1837"], AGO, raz. 99, op. 1, d. 36.

Kusov, Nikolay, and Andrey Severin, "Istoricheskaya zapiska o selenii Ross na beregakh novavo Albiona" ["An Historical Note on Ross Settlement on the Coast of New Albion"], AVPR, f. RAK, d. 363.

L., "Vypiska iz pisma iz Novo-Arkhangelska, na severa-zapadnom beregu Ameriki" ["An Extract from a Letter from New Archangel on the Northwest Coast of America"], *Severnaya pchela*, October 20/November 1, 1828 [3–4].

Lazarev, Andrey, *Plavanie vokrug sveta na shlyupe Ladoge v 1822, 1823 i 1824 godakh* [*A Voyage Around the World on the Sloop Ladoga in 1822, 1823, and 1824*], St. Petersburg, 1832.

———, *Zapiski o plavanii voyennovo shloopa Blagonamerennovo v Beringov proliv i vokrug sveta dlya otkryty v 1819, 1820, 1821 i 1822 godakh* [*Notes on the Voyage of the Naval Sloop Loyal to Bering Strait and Around the World for Discoveries in 1819, 1820, 1821, and 1822*], Moscow, 1950.

Lisiansky, Urey, *A Voyage Round the World in the Years 1803, 4, 5, & 6*, trans. by the author, London, 1814 (reprint 1968).

Lütke, Frédéric, *Voyage autour du monde*, Paris, 1835, I–II (reprint 1971).

Mahr, August C., *The Visit of the "Rurik" to San Francisco in 1816*, Stanford University Publications in History, Economics, and Political Science, II, Palo Alto, Calif., 1932 (reprint 1972).

Makarova, R. V., *Russkie na Tikhom okeane vo vtoroy polovine XVIII v.* [*Russians on the Pacific Ocean in the Second Half of the 18th Century*], Moscow, 1968.

Mamyshev, V., "Amerikanskiya vladeniya Rossii" ["Russia's American Possessions"], *Biblioteka dlya chteniya*, March-April 1855, 205–92.

Materialy dlya istorii russkikh zaselenii po beregam vostochnavo okeana [*Materials for the History of Russian Settlement on the Shores of the Eastern Ocean*], St. Petersburg, 1861, III.

Merk, Frederick, ed., *Fur Trade and Empire: George Simpson's Journal*, Cambridge, Mass., 1931 (revised edition 1968).

Mexico, Junta del Fomento de las Californias, "Exposición echa a la Junta en 26 de Marzo de 1825 par el Sr. D. Francisco de Paula Famariz Pre. la recuperación del Puerto de la Bodega ocupado par los Rusos" ["Explanation Given to the Junta on March 26, 1825 by Mr. D. Francisco de Paula Famariz about the Recovery of the Port of Bodega Occupied by the Russians"], Beinecke Library, Ms S–667.

Miller, Ivan, "Moy put iz Irkutska v Kirensk (v 1814 godu)" ["My Route from Irkutsk to Kirensk (in 1814)"], *Kazanskaya izvestiya*, June 28/July 10, 1816, 258–60.

Minitsky, Rear-Admiral, "Opisanie Okhotskavo porta" ["A Description of Okhotsk Port"], *Syn otechestva i severny arkhiv*, 1829, 136–53, 206–21.

Nunis, Doyce B., Jr., *The California Diary of Faxon Dean Atherton 1836–1839*, San Francisco, 1964.

Okun, S. B., *The Russian American Company*, trans. by Carl Ginsburg, Cambridge, Mass., 1951.

———, ed. "Tsarskaya Rossiya i Gavaiskie ostrova" ["Tsarist Russia and the Hawaiian Islands"], *Krasny arkhiv*, 1936, 161–86.

Pavlov, P. N., ed., *K istorii Rossiisko-Amerikanskoy kompanii: sbornik dokumentalnykh materialov [Towards a History of the Russian-American Company: A Collection of Documentary Materials]*, Krasnoyarsk, 1957.

[Phelps, William Dane], "Solid Men of Boston in the Northwest," Bancroft Library, Ms P–C 31.

Pierce, Richard A., *Russia's Hawaiian Adventure, 1815–1817*, Berkeley, Calif. 1965.

Potekhin, V., "Selenie Ross" ["Ross Settlement"], *Zhurnal manufaktur i torgovli*, 1859, 1–42.

Rezanov, Nikolai Petrovich, *The Rezanov Voyage to Nueva California in 1806*, trans. by Thomas C. Russell, San Francisco, 1926.

Rich, E. E., ed., *The Letters of John McLoughlin . . .* , second series (1839–44), The Publications of the Champlain Society; Hudson's Bay Company Series, VI, Toronto, 1943.

——— ed., *Part of Dispatch from George Simpson Esqr Governor of Ruperts Land to the Governor & Committee of the Hudson's Bay Company London,* The Publications of the Champlain Society: Hudson's Bay Company Series, X, Toronto, 1947.

Rossiisko-Amerikanskaya Kompaniya, "Obrashchenie direktorov Kompanii k naseleniyu Kaliforniyey o vygodakh vzaimnykh torgovykh snosheny" ["An Appeal of the Directors of the Company to the Population of California on the Advantages of Mutual Trade Relations"], ROLL, f. 205, car. 15, no. 34.

——— "Obrashchenie glavnovo pravleniya Rossiisko-Amerikanskoy kompanii k 'blagorodnym gospodam gishpantsam, zhivushchim v Kalifornii' " ["An Appeal of the Head Office of the Russian-American Company to the 'Noble Spanish Gentlemen Living in California' "], ROLL, f. 204, car. 32, no. 36.

——— *Otchyot Rossiisko-Amerikanskoy Kompanii Glavnavo Pravleniva za odin god . . . [Report of the Head Office of the Russian-American Company for One Year . . .]*, St. Petersburg, 1843–65, I–XXI.

———, "Sheffer Papers," trans. by George Lantzeff, Bancroft Library, Ms P–N 4.

———, Glavnoye Pravlenie, "Doneseniya Glavnovo pravleniya Rossiisko-Amerikanskoy kompanii Aleksandru I o deyatelnosti Baranova Aleksandra Andreyevicha po rasshireniyu torgovli kompanii" ["Reports of the Head Office of the Russian-American Company to Alexander I on the Activity of Alexander Andreyevich Baranov in the Expansion of the Company's Trade"], TsGADA, f. 796, op. 1, d. 161.

———, Glavnoye Pravlenie, "Predstavlenie Soveta Rossiisko-Amerikanskoy kompanii Aleksandru I o tseli soobraznosti zaklyucheniya torgovovo dogovora s Ispanskoy Kaliforniyey dlya snabzheniya kolony kompanii" ["The Submission of the Council of the Russian-American Company to Alexander I on the Purpose of the Conclusion of a Trade Agreement

with Spanish California for Supplying the Company's Colonies"], TsGADA, f. 796, op. 1, d. 163.
————, Glavnoye Pravlenie, "O selenii Ross i torgovle s Kaliforniyey" ["Concerning Ross Settlement and Trade with California"], AGO, raz. 99, op. 1, d. 32.
Rotchev, A. G., "Vospominaniya russkavo puteshestvennika o Vest-Indii, Kalifornii i Ost-Indii" ["Recollections of a Russian Traveler on the West Indies, California, and the East Indies"], Panteon, 1854, no. 1, 79–108, no. 2, 93–114.
Rowand, Alexander, Notes of a Journey in Russian America and Siberia, During the Years 1841 and 1842, [Edinburgh?], n.d.
Ruschenberger, W. S. W., A Voyage Round the World, Philadelphia, 1838.
Russia, Polnoye sobranie zakonov rossiiskoy imperii [A Complete Collection of Laws of the Russian Empire], first series (1649–1825), St. Petersburg, 1830, XXIII.
————, Gosudarstvenny sovet, Arkhiv Gosudarstvennavo soveta [The Archive of the State Council], St. Petersburg, 1869, I.
————, Pervy sibirsky komitet, "O predpolozheniyakh Nachalnika Kamchatki ob ustroistve sevo kraya" ["Concerning the Proposals of the Commandant of Kamchatka on the Organization of His Territory"], pt. 3, TsGIAL, f. 1,264, op. 1, d. 168.
Sauer, Martin, An Account of a Geographical and Astronomical Expedition to the Northern Parts of Russia, London, 1802 (reprint 1972).
Schafer, Joseph, "Letters of Sir George Simpson, 1841–1843," American Historical Review, October 1908, 70–94.
Sgibnev, A., "Istorichesky ocherk glavneishikh sobyty v Kamchatke" ["An Historical Sketch of the Main Events in Kamchatka"], pt. 5, Morskoy sbornik, August 1869, 33–110.
Shashkov, S. S., "Rossiisko-Amerikanskaya Kompaniya" ["The Russian-American Company"], in idem., Sobranie sochineny S. S. Shashkova, St. Petersburg, 1898, II, 632–52.
Shch. [Shchukin], N., Poyezdka v Yakutsk [A Journey to Yakutsk], St. Petersburg, 1833,
[Shelikhov, Gregory], "The Voyage of Gregory Shelekhof," trans. by William Tooke, Varieties of Literature, 1795, 1–42.
Shiroky, V. F., "Iz istorii khozyaistvennoy deyatelnosti Rossiisko-Amerikanskoy kompanii" ["From the History of the Economic Activities of the Russian-American Company"], Istoricheskie zapiski, 1942, 207–21.
Shur, L. A., K beregam Novovo Sveta [To the Shores of the New World], Moscow, 1971.
Simpson, Sir George, Narrative of a Journey Round the World, London, 1847, I–II.
Sirotkin, V. G., "Dokumenty o politike Rossii na Dalnem Vostoke v nachale XIX v." ["Documents on Russia's Policy in the Far East at the Beginning of the 19th Century"], Istorichesky zapiski, November–December 1962, 85–99.

Sokolov, A., "Prigotovlenie krugosvetnoy ekspeditsii 1787 goda, pod nachalst-vom Mulovskavo" ["The Readying of the Round-the-World Expedition of 1787 Under the Command of Mulovsky"], *Zapiski Gidrografi-cheskavo departamenta*, 1848, 142–91.

Storie, R. Earl and Weir, Walter W., *Generalized Soil Map of California*, University of California College of Agriculture Publications, Manual 6, Berkeley, Calif., n.d.

Sturgis, William, "Extracts from Sturgis' Manuscript," Bancroft Library, Ms P–K 33.

[Sutter, John A.], "Inventaire des biens meubles et immeubles qui se trouvent au Port Bodego, à l'establissement de Ross et aux ranchos de la Compagnie Russe-Américaine" ["Inventory of Real and Personal Property Located at the Port of Bodega, the Settlement of Ross, and the Ranchos of the Russian-American Company"], in *idem.*, ["Correspondence and Papers, 1846–1870"], Bancroft Library, Ms C–B 631.

———, "Personal Reminiscences," Bancroft Library, Ms.

Tarakanoff, Vassili Petrovitch, *Statement of My Captivity Among the Californians*, Los Angeles, 1953.

Tchitchinoff, Zakahar, *Adventures in California*, Los Angeles, 1956.

Thompson, Robert A., *Historical and Descriptive Sketch of Sonoma County, California*, Philadelphia, 1877.

Tikhmenev, P., *The Historical Review of Formation of the Russian-American Company*, trans. by Dimitri Krenov, Seattle, 1939–40, I–II.

———, *Supplement of Some Historical Documents to the Historical Review of the Formation of the Russian-American Company*, trans. by Dimitri Krenov, Seattle, 1938.

Tolstoy, Graf M., "Missionerskaya deyatelnost pokoinavo mitropolita Innokentiya" ["The Missionary Activity of the Late Metropolitan Innocent"], *Russky arkhiv*, 1879, 273–303.

Tumarkin, D. D., *Vtorzhenie kolonizatorov v "kray vechnoy vesny"* [*The Invasion of the "Land of Eternal Spring" by Colonizers*], Moscow, 1964.

Union of Soviet Socialist Republics, Ministerstvo Inostrannykh del, *Vneshnyaya politika Rossii XIX i nachala XX veka* [*The Foreign Policy of Russia of the 19th and Early 20th Centuries*], first series, Moscow, 1961–70, II–VII.

———, Ministerstvo Oborony, *Morskoy atlas* [*Marine Atlas*], Moscow [?], 1958, III.

United States, Congress, *American State Papers*, Foreign Relations, Washington, D.C., 1858, V.

———, Congress, House of Representatives, *Russian America*, 40th Congress, 2nd Session, Executive Document No. 177, Washington, D.C., 1868.

———, Congress, Senate, *Proceedings of the Alaskan Boundary Tribunal*, Washington, D.C., 1904, II.

———, Congress, Senate, *Russian Administration of Alaska and the Status of the Alaskan Natives*, 81st Congress, 2nd Session, Senate Document No. 152, Washington, D.C., 1950.

———, General Services Administration, National Archives, "Records of the

Russian-American Company 1802–1867: Correspondence of Governors General," File Microcopies of Records in the National Archives: No. 11, Washington, D.C., 1942, reels 1–65 (vols. 1–49).

Vagin, V., *Istoricheskiya svedeniya o deyatelnosti grafa M. M. Speranskavo v Sibiri s 1819 po 1822 god* [*Historical Information on Count M. M. Speransky's Activity in Siberia from 1819 to 1822*], St. Petersburg, 1872, I–II.

Valaam Monastery, *Ocherk iz istorii Amerikanskoy pravoslavnoy dukhovnoy missii (Kadyakskoy missii 1794–1837 gg.)* [*A Sketch from the History of the American Orthodox Ecclesiastical Mission (The Kodiak Mission, 1794–1837)*], St. Petersburg, 1894.

Vallejo, M. G., "Establecimientos Rusos de California" ["The Russian Establishments of California"], Bancroft Library, Ms.

———, "Informe . . . Mariano G. Vallejo (Reservado)" ["Report . . . of Mariano G. Vallejo (Confidential)"], Bancroft Library, Ms C–A 53.

———, "Ranch and Mission Days in Alta California," *Century Magazine*, 1890, 183–92.

Vallejo Documentos, Bancroft Library, I, X.

Veniaminov, I., *Zapiski ob ustrovakh Unalashkinskavo otdela* [*Notes on the Islands of the Unalaska District*], St. Petersburg, 1840, I–II.

Vila Vilar, Enriqueta, *Los rusos en America* [*The Russians in America*], Seville, Spain, 1966.

Vishnevsky, B. N., *Puteshestvennik Kirill Khlebnikov* [*The Traveler Cyril Khlebnikov*], Perm, U.S.S.R., 1957.

Volkl, Ekkehard, *Russland und Lateinamerika 1741–1841*, Wiesbaden, Germany, 1968.

Von Chamisso, Adelbert, *A Sojourn at San Francisco Bay 1816*, San Francisco, 1936.

Von Kotzebue, Otto, *A New Voyage Round the World, in the Years 1823, 24, 25, and 26*, London, 1830, I–II (reprint 1967).

———, *A Voyage of Discovery into the South Sea and Beering's Straits*, London, 1821, I–III (reprint 1969).

Von Krusenstern, Captain A. J., *Voyage Round the World in the Years 1803, 1804, 1805, & 1806*, trans. by Richard Belgrave Hoppner, London, 1813 (reprint 1968).

Von Langsdorff, G. H., *Voyages and Travels in Various Parts of the World*, London, 1814, I–II (reprint 1968).

Von Wrangell, Contre-Admiral, *Statistische und ethnographische Nachrichten über die russischen Besitzungen an der Nordwestküste von Amerika* [*Statistical and Ethnographical Report on the Russian Possessions on the Northwest Coast of America*], St. Petersburg, 1839.

Von Wrangell, Baron F., and Baronin E. Von Wrangell, "Briefe aus Sibirien und den russischen Niederlassungen in Amerika" ["Letters on Siberia and the Russian Establishments in America"], *Dorpater Jahrbücher für Litteratur, Statistik und Kunst, besonders Russlands*, 1833–34, I, 169–80, 263–66, 353–74, II, 179–86, 356–64.

Vrangel, Kapitan F., "Donesenie o plavanii Shloopa Urupa v Kaliforniyu za pokupkoyu pshenitsy i proch. s prilozheniem kopii s raporta Kap.-Leit. Etolina i s kontrakta zaklyuchennavo s G. Kuperom na promysel bo- brov v Kalifornii, No. 133, 1-vo maya 1833 goda" ["A Report on the Voyage of the Sloop *Urup* to California for the Purchase of Wheat, etc., with a Copy of the Report of Capt.-Lieut. Etholen and the Contract Concluded with Mr. Cooper for Hunting Sea Otters in California, No. 133, May 1, 1833"], AGO, raz. 99, op. 1, d. 36.

————, "Donesenie o zakupke pshenitsy v Kalifornii v kontse proshedshavo goda, s prilozheniem vedomosti, No. 139, 6 maya 1832 goda" ["A Re- port on the Purchase of Wheat in California at the End of Last Year, with a Record, No. 139, May 6, 1832"], AGO, raz. 99, op. 1, d. 36.

————, "O pushnykh tovarakh Severo-Amerikanskikh Rossiiskikh vladeny" ["Concerning the Furs of the Russian North American Possessions"], *Teleskop,* 1835, 496–518.

————, "Putevia zapiski admirala barona F. P. Vrangelya" ["The Travel Notes of Admiral Baron F. P. Wrangel"], *Istorichesky vestnik,* 1884, 162–80.

Zagoskin, L. A., *Puteshestviya i issledovaniya leitenanta Lavrentiya Zagoskina v Russkoy Amerike v 1842–1844 g.g.* [*Travels and Explorations of Lieutenant Lawrence Zagoskin in Russian America in the Years 1842– 1844*], Moscow, 1956.

Zavalishin, Dimitry, "Delo o kolonii Ross" ["The Ross Colony Affair"], *Russky vestnik,* 1866, 36–65.

————, "Kaliforniya v 1824 godu" ["California in 1824"], *Russky vestnik,* 1865, 322–68.

————, "Krugosvetnoye plavanie fregata 'Kreiser' v 1822–1825 gg. pod ko- mandoyu Mikhaila Petrovicha Lazareva" ["The Round-the-World Voyage of the Frigate *Cruiser* Under the Command of Michael Petro- vich Lazarev"], *Drevnyaya i novaya Rossiya,* 1877, no. 5, 54–67, no. 6, 115–25, no. 7, 199–214, no. 10, 143–58, no. 11, 210–23.

Zubov, N. N., *Otechestvennie moreplavateli-issledovateli morey i okeanov* [*Native Navigators-Explorers of the Seas and Oceans*], Moscow, 1954.

INDEX

Afognak Island, 6, 98
Ainus, 32, 46, 95
Alaska: Russian population, 7; sale, 25, 29, 197, 208; shortage of Aleuts, 47n, 127; shift of Russian interest, 71; climatic change, 103n; unattractiveness, 107; temporal conflict of farming and hunting, 110; Russian California grain imports, 122, 124; beef needs, 125; grain needs, 190, 194
Alaska Panhandle, 10, 24, 25, 37, 45, 72
Alaska Peninsula, 4, 18, 19
Aldan River, 58, 61, 71
Aleutian Islands: fur-trading voyages, 3; Near group, 3, 19; Andreanof group, 7, 19; Fox group, 18, 106, 106n; Rat group, 19
Aleuts: hunting expertise, 7–8, 32–33; exploitation, 8, 32; depopulation, 8; killing of, 14, 159; staple food, 19–20; use of sea lions, 19–20, 35; agricultural ignorance, 46, 129–130; smallpox toll, 47; shortage of, 47n; adoption of agriculture, 98-99, 109
Alexander I, 15, 21, 36n, 74, 134, 145, 178
Alexander Archipelago, 10
Alexander Island (see Urup Island)
Alexander Redoubt, 6
Alexandrovsk, 147
Alta California: regularization of company trade, 21, 83, 183; decline of agriculture, 69, 117, 168; opening of ports, 116, 117, 163, 183, 190, 213; grain yields, 121–22; agricultural productivity, 174–75; trade, 175; scarcity of manufactures, 176, 184; weakness of Mexican Revolution, 180n; American trade, 190n; foreign settlers, 191; secularization of missions, 193; droughts, 203
American California, 197
American Company, 4
American Fur Company, 160, 161
American-Russian Commercial Company, 41, 42
American-Russian convention, 17, 22, 167
Amur River, 29, 71, 71n, 72, 77, 84, 205n
Amur Valley, 25
Amuria, 6, 51, 71, 76, 84n, 87n
Anglo-Russian convention, 22, 23, 167, 200
"apostle of Alaska," 15
Archangel, 75
Archangel St. Michael (see New Archangel and Sitka)
"Arctic Hansa," 10
Argüello, Concepción, 177
Arrillaga, José, 176, 177, 179, 181, 184
Arroyo de Fumalancia, 117
artels, 11
Astor, John Jacob, 160, 161, 162
Astoria, 160, 161
Astorians, 11, 172
Atka Counter, 11, 18, 19, 39
Atka Island, 7, 38, 59n, 96, 166
Atuvai, 143, 144, 145, 146, 147, 148
Avacha River, 117

Ayan: transfer of Okhotsk factory, 25, 69; advantages and disadvantages, 69–71; attack, 77
Ayan Bay, 69, 70
Ayan Road, 70

baidara, 107
baidarka, 7, 107
Baikalia, 57, 58
Baja California, 32, 39, 51, 184, 211
Banner, Ivan, 143
Baranof Island, 10, 12, 38, 40, 96, 102
Baranov, Alexander: founding of St. Paul's Harbor, 6; expansionist policy, 10, 112–13, 141, 143; plot against, 14; death of replacements, 14; described, 15; conflict with Lazarev, 65n, 143n; Boston trade, 161n, 162n; replacement, 162, 182
Barclay, 147
Bellingshausen, Faddey, 75, 84
Bering, Vitus, 58, 68
Bering Bay (ses Yakutat Bay)
Bering Island, 96, 98
Bering Strait, 17
Berkh, Basil, 142
Big Shantar Island, 16
Billings Expedition, 76, 94
Blaschke, Edward, 215
Boardman Co., 167
Bodega Bay, 11, 113, 115
Bodega Corners, 118
Bornovolokov, Terty, 14
Boston men (Bostonians), 9, 24, 156, 161, 162, 166, 212–13
Boston trade, 161, 165, 166, 168, 188, 213
Bristol Bay, 16, 18
Buldakov, Michael, 73, 158, 178, 179
burduk, 18
Buryats, 57

California: company trade, 25–26, 41, 42; Russian desertions, 48, 205n; gold rush, 83, 196, 207, 211, 213; New Archangel's hay imports, 106; cost and quality of grain, 117, 191, 195, 203, 205; earthquakes, 137; joint hunting, 157, 159; agricultural productivity, 178–79; lack of manufactures, 179; crop failures, 193; decline of missions, 194; recovery of agriculture, 196–97, 207n, 211; Russian withdrawal, 202
California trade, 188, 189, 190, 193, 194, 195, 196, 213
Californios: opening of trade, 21; shortage of manufactures, 116, 188; Spanish neglect, 181
Camino Real, 174
Camp Holitna, 16
Canton: Russian inaccessibility, 8; disposal of American furs, 156
Cape Drake, 113
Cape Fairweather, 9
Cape of Good Hope, 23, 52, 72, 76, 76–77, 77, 156, 164
Cape Horn, 52, 72, 75, 76, 77, 159n
Cape Mendocino, 113
Cape St. Elias, 94, 95n
Cape Spencer, 201
Captain's Harbor, 5, 19, 102
Carmen Island, 184, 192n
Catherine II, 29, 67n
Chechenev, Zachary, 125
Chernykh, George, 118n, 131, 132, 135, 135n, 137, 183n, 189, 193n, 194
Chernykh Rancho, 118, 123, 137
Chile, 39, 178, 191, 195, 196, 197, 204
China, 23, 33, 36, 37, 71, 74, 75, 146, 155
China trade, 9, 156
Chiniatsk, 96, 97
Chistyakov, Peter: on the conduct of subordinates, 45; transport from Siberia, 62; farming at New Archangel, 101; Aleut cattlemen, 109; Yakut cattlemen, 109n; California trade, 117, 190, 192, 193, 195; private farming in Russian California, 126; Paul Shelikhov, 129; Boston trade, 165–66
Choris, Louis, 162
Chugach Inlet (see Chuvash Inlet)
Chukchi, 13
Chuvash Inlet, 4, 7, 18, 95
Clark, George, 210
Coal Bay, 41
Coast Ranges, 113
Cochrane, John, 62
"colonial citizens," 98
"colonial products," 18
"colonial supplies," 39, 48
Columbia Basin, 196, 207

Columbia Department, 24, 202, 203, 204, 205, 206
Columbia River, 11, 160, 176, 179
Commander Islands, 3, 16, 19, 35, 38, 96, 157n
Cook, James, 9, 75, 155, 210
Cook Inlet (see Kenai Inlet)
Corney, Peter, 122
"counters," 11
Cowlitz, 202
Creoles: defined, 10, 12; numbers, 11, 17; role, 12; increase, 26, 51; agricultural ineptness, 109, 130
Crimean War, 26, 28, 28n, 77, 84n, 85, 215
Cronstadt: function, 73; location, 73; cost of supply, 87, 87n, 200, 206
Cross Sound: 200, 201

Dall Island, 98n
Dall mountain sheep, 214n
Dana, Richard Henry, 65n
Dashkov, Andrew, 159, 160
De Roquefeuil, Camille, 175
De Solá, Pablo, 132, 181, 182, 183, 185
Decembrist Revolt, 134
Delarov, Yevstrat, 93–94, 95
Dixon Entrance, 98n
Dobell, Peter, 60, 67
Doldrums, 44
Don River, 147
Doroshin, Peter, 41
Douglas, James, 207
Dry Creek, 118
Dryad affair, 23, 24n, 201
Duflot De Mofras, Eugène, 138
Duhaut-Cilly, Auguste, 116, 126
Dutch Harbor, 103n
D'Wolf, John, 157

East India Company, 9, 10, 75, 155, 157n
Elizabetinsk, 147
English Bay, 41
Eskimos, 46
Espagnols, 155n, 174, 180, 183, 185, 189, 213
Estero Americano, 117
Etholen, Adolph, 16, 24, 68, 70, 98, 167, 191n, 193, 196, 201, 205

Farallon Islands, 11
Farnham Co., 167
First Channel, 59
First Kamchatka Expedition, 68
Fiutinje, 118
Fiutuye, 118
Fort George, 161
Fort Langley, 202, 207, 207n
Fort Ross: founding, 11, 15; purpose, 11; establishment of shipyard, 39; brick production, 41; sale, 47; transfer of Aleuts, 47n; site, 113; described of, 114; farm, 118; grain yields, 120, 121; grain exports, 122, 124; gardening and orcharding, 123; introduction of livestock, 123; poultry, 124; Baranov's and Kuskov's views, 125; working conditions, 128; measle toll, 128; scurvy, 130; activities of Cherynkh, 131–32; defensibility, 132; blocking of expansion, 134; fogs, 135; earthquakes, 137, 137n; Spanish suspicion, 181, 181n; Spanish trade, 185, 188; inadequacy of farming, 213
Fort Ross Cove, 115
Fort St. George, 7
Fort Vancouver, 200, 202, 203, 204, 207
Fort Victoria, 202, 207, 207n
French Co., 167
frontera del norte, 118, 182
Fur Seal Islands (see Pribilof Islands)
Furguhelm, Ivan, 88, 99, 103, 105, 197

Gideon, Father, 96, 99
Gizhiga, 11
Glazunov, Andrew, 17
Golikov, Ivan, 4, 5
Golikov-Shelikhov Company, 5n, 8, 46, 59, 60, 64, 66, 93, 156
Golovin, Nicholas, 75
Golovnin, Basil, 10, 15, 102, 104, 104n, 116, 122, 124, 162, 185, 215
Golovnin, P. N., 28
Goncharov, Ivan, 84
Govorlivy, 216
Grudinin, Basil, 64
Gualala River, 130
Guaymas, 195
Gulf of Alaska, 3, 6, 10, 59, 64, 73, 94, 99, 113, 157, 163

Hagemeister, Leon: 16, 129, 142, 143, 148, 162, 182, 183, 184, 210
Haida Indians, 98
Halfway House, 118
Hanalei, 147
Hanalei Valley, 147
Hanapepe River, 147
Hanna, James, 9, 155
Hartnell, William, 183n
Hawaii, 10, 25, 38, 39, 111, 209
Hawaiian Islands, 11, 142
Hawaiians, 48, 148
Herman, Father, 99
Hinchinbrook Island (see Nuchek Island)
Hokkaido, 32
Holy Alliance, 29
Honolulu, 144, 145, 148, 210
Horse Latitudes, 44
Hudson's Bay Company: encroachment, 15–16, 22–23, 37, 167, 200; Russian-American Company agreement, 24, 83, 139, 196, 201–02, 204–06; sale of territory, 29, 208; farms, 202, 207
Hunt, Wilson, 144

Icy Cape, 9
Igatsk: 96, 97
Innocent, Bishop, 70
Irkutsk, 10, 11, 21, 36, 37, 44n, 51, 57, 59n, 60, 67, 76, 213
Irkutsk Company, 4

Jacobi, Ivan, 9, 67n, 75
Johanson, 64
Jorge Rancho, 118
Joseph, Archimandrite, 13, 103–104, 108

Kachuga Landing, 57, 60
Kaigansk, 98, 98n
Kalsinsk, 97
Kamchatka Agricultural Company, 131
"Kamchatka bread," 214n
Kamchatka Peninsula: disappearance of sea otters, 4; reopening of company business, 25; company provisionment, 38, 51, 204, 205, 205n, 206
Kamehameha, 142, 210
kamleikas, 19
Kanakas, 48, 155n, 209
Kashevarov, Alexander, 17
Katmai, 108
Kauai, 142, 143, 146, 210
Kaumauli, 142, 210
Kenai Inlet, 6, 7, 10, 18, 39, 94, 95, 95n, 96
Kenai Mining Expedition, 41
Kenai Peninsula, 17, 41, 42, 46, 96, 98, 102, 103, 105
Khlebnikov, Cyril: on New Archangel's climate, 46; wheat yields of California missions, 122; private farming at Fort Ross, 126; desertions from Fort Ross, 128; Indian farm workers at Fort Ross, 130; soil at Fort Ross, 132; California trade, 183, 184, 189, 193; lack of craftsmen in California, 185; provisionment from Mexico, 195
Khlebnikov Plain, 118
Khlebnikov Rancho, 117
Khromchenko, Basil, 16
Khvostov, Nicholas, 63
King, James, 155
King George Archipelago, 10
King George's men, 9, 155n, 199
Koch, Johann, 14
Kodiak, 103, 103n
Kodiak Counter: composition, 18; decline of sea otter catch, 34; debts of company employees, 50; grain consumption, 51, farming, 96–97; colonial citizens, 98, 105; livestock, 102, 106, 107; flour wastage, 215
Kodiak Eskimos, 26
Kodiak Island: economy, 18; fishing, 40; brick making, 41; ice production, 42; earthquakes, 46; 1819 epidemic, 47; company farming, 96–97, 100, 101, 102; native gardening, 99; mission farming, 99; climate, 104; abundance of grass, 105; hay shortage, 105, 105n, livestock, 106, 107, 109; Yakut herders, 109n; obstacles to cultivation, 110–11
Kodiak Mission, 13, 213
Kodiaks, 32
Kolmakov Redoubt, 16
Kolosh Indians: resistance, 12–13, 13n, 14, 34, 74, 99, 109–10, 159, 161;

provisionment, 13, 98, 102, 102n, 109, 214; provisionment of, 48–49; adoption of farming, 98, 109; American trade, 165; British trade, 200
Kolosh Straits, 16, 39
Konyagas, 26, 32, 93, 109, 111
Korobitsyn, Nicholas, 209
Korsakov, Peter, 16
Kostlivtsev, Sergey, 28
Kostromitinov, Peter, 42, 117, 118, 120, 127, 129, 130, 183n, 197n
Kostromitinov Rancho, 118
Kotzebue Sound, 17
Kramer, Benedict, 158
Kropotkin, Peter, 71
Kruzenstern, Ivan, 67, 74, 75–76, 76, 84, 85, 129
Kuchelbecker, Wilhelm, 84
Kukhtui River, 62, 69
kumiss, 71n
Kupreyanov, Ivan, 86, 106n, 127, 131, 138, 193, 200
Kurile District, 18, 19, 25, 39
Kurile Islands, 3, 4, 7, 14, 16, 38, 45, 59, 94, 95, 103, 163
Kurile Straits, 66
Kurilians, 32
Kuskokwim River, 16
Kuskov, Ivan, 11, 14, 113, 116, 120, 122, 125, 129, 143, 181, 182, 185
Kuskovo, 113n
Kusov, Nicholas, 24
Kvikpak River, 16, 17
Kyakhta, 8, 11, 14, 21, 33, 36, 36n, 37, 59n, 74, 85, 86, 156, 201n

Lake Baikal, 57
Lanai, 144
lavtaks, 36
Lazarev, Michael, 65n, 75, 84, 143n, 162
Lebedev Islands (see Pribilof Islands)
Lebedev-Lastochkin Company, 7, 93
Lena River, 57, 58, 60, 61, 67
lisière, 201, 205, 206, 207
Lisyansky, Yury, 76, 104
Long Island (Kodiak Counter), 96, 108
Lopatka Channel, 59
López de Haro, Gonzalo, 7
"lords of the Pacific," 161
Lütke, Frederick, 65n

Maksutov, Dmitry, 101n, 109
Malakhov, Peter, 17
Manila galleon, 182, 184
marine Cossacks, 32–33
Marmot Island (Kodiak Counter), 96, 108
Martínez, Esteban, 7
Martínez, Ignacio, 188
Maya River, 58, 69, 71
McLoughlin, John, 204, 205
McNeill, William, 165
meshchanins, 12
Mexican California, 24, 122, 138, 168
Minitsky, Michael, 66
Missions: Sonoma, 123, 134, 185; San Rafael, 134, 185; San Juan Capistrano, 137; Santa Ynez, 137; San Francisco, 176, 184, 188; Santa Clara, 188; San José, 189
Molakai, 143
Monterey, 9, 123, 127, 176, 178, 181, 182, 185, 191, 192, 195
Moraga, José, 123, 181
Mordvinov, Nicholas, 72
Moscow Agricultural School, 131
Mulovsky, Gregory, 9, 75, 76
Muravyov, Matthew: on cattle raising on Kodiak, 106; economic priorities at Fort Ross, 116; desertions from Fort Ross, 128; Carl Schmidt, 129; Creoles as farmers, 130; Boston trade, 158, 161, 164–65; voyage of the Helena, 164
Mylnikov, Nicholas, 4

Nanaimo, 42
Nedelkovich, Dmitry, 28
Nelkan, 59
Nesselrode, Carl, 189
Netsvetov, Jacob, 64
Nevelskoy, Gennady, 84
New Albion, 11, 16, 113, 141, 154, 185n
New Alexander Redoubt, 16, 25, 41
New Archangel: founding, 10; purpose, 10; importance, 10, 18; population, 10, 18, 26; described, 10–11, 26; Kolosh threat, 12–13, 74, 109–10, 159; starvation, 14, 175–76, 213, 215; contemplated demotion, 17; Boston trade, 22, 161, 166–67, 168–72, 168n, 202; wood exports,

New Archangel: (*Cont.*)
    25–26; shipping, 26, 38–39, 157;
    occupational diversity, 38; barrel
    making, 38*n;* shipbuilding, 39–40;
    fishing, 40; flour milling, 40–41;
    brick needs, 41; ice production, 42;
    remoteness, 44, 45; climate, 46,
    104; sickness, 48, 216; rations, 51,
    214; markup on imports, 87; farm-
    ing, 96, 100, 101; Kolosh provision-
    ment, 98, 102, 102*n*, 214; livestock,
    102; limited farmland, 104–05; hay
    shortage, 106, 106*n;* California
    trade, 181, 183, 184, 188, 189;
    scurvy, 215–16
New Archangel Counter, 11, 18, 20, 50,
    126, 167
New California, 177, 189
New Islands (see Pribilof Islands)
New Rancho, 118
New Russia (Kurile District), 100
New Valaam, 99
Nicholas I, 134
Nikolayevsk, 77, 205*n*
Ninilchik, 103
Nisqually, 202
Nootka Sound, 9, 10, 36*n*, 74, 113
Nootka Sound Controversy, 9
North West Company, 16, 161, 172, 199
Northeastern American Company, 5
Northern District, 11, 18, 19
"northern expedition," 16
Northern Islands (see Pribilof Islands)
Northern Land Expedition, 16
Northwest Coast, 9, 10, 24, 40, 75, 83,
    113, 146, 153, 155, 159, 160, 163,
    165, 167, 172, 199, 209
Northwest Coast Indians, 33, 98, 155,
    156
Northwest trade, 155, 160, 162, 167
Norton Sound, 17, 19
Novo Arkhangelsk, 148
Nuchek Island (Kodiak Counter), 7
Nushagak, 41
Nushagak River, 16

Oahu, 144
odinochkas, 11
Okhota River, 61, 62, 69
Okhotsk: transfer of company factory,
    25, 25*n*, 55, 69–70; shipbuilding,
    39, 63–64; site, 62; population, 62;

character, 62; flooding, 62; reloca-
    tion, 62, 69; harbor, 62–63; aboli-
    tion of port, 71; cost of supply via,
    87, 87*n*, 200, 206
Okhotsk Road, 61, 71
Okhotsk Seaboard, 73, 75, 76, 116, 141,
    164, 189, 190
Okhotsk-Kamchatka Kray, 179
Oregon Country, 24, 84, 202, 206, 207,
    213
Oregon Treaty, 206
Orlovsk (see Igatsk)
Ozyorsk Redoubt, 13, 18, 38, 40, 41,
    216

Pacific Fur Company, 160
Pelly, John, 201
peredovshiks, 8
Petaluma Rancho, 124
Peters, William, 75, 157*n*
Petropavlovsk, 11, 25*n*, 28*n*, 51, 71, 75,
    77, 156, 157*n*, 164, 165, 178, 193,
    205*n*
Philippine Islands, 154, 178
Pil, Ivan, 94, 157
Podushkin, Jacob, 143, 144
Pomo Indians, 119, 130
Pomorye, 7, 55
Port Rumyantsev, 11, 39, 113, 115, 117,
    118, 123, 183*n*
Preamuria, 71
Pribilof Islands, 3, 4, 14, 19, 35, 36, 37,
    39, 39*n*, 45
Prince William Sound (see Chuvash
    Inlet)
Puget Sound, 113
Puget's Sound Agricultural Company,
    202, 205, 206, 207

Queen Charlotte Islands, 10, 36*n*, 72,
    98, 112–13

Rannoa, 144
razones, 175, 194
Regulations of 1821, 172
Rezanov, Nicholas: death, 14, 45, 178;
    inspection tour, 15, 113, 153; on

peopling of the colonies, 47; on colonial shipbuilding, 64; on colonial shipping, 65; advocacy of overseas supply by, 76; on colonial underpopulation, 108; on Kolosh threat to New Archangel, 109; on cultivation on Kodiak, 110; on establishment of a colony in New Albion, 113; on colonial trade, 153-54; visit to California, 175–78; on California's lacks, 184

Rikord, Peter, 85

Rosenberg, Nicholas, 12, 207n

Ross, 16, 113, 123, 125, 128, 135, 138, 139, 188

Ross Counter: character, 20; scarcity of fish, 40n; superior livestock potential, 96; extent, 113; chief harbor, 115; first manager, 116; agricultural expansion, 117; primary function, 118; grain production, 122; pre-eminent livestock rank, 123; grain exports, 124; livestock numbers, 125; earthquakes, 137; losses, 139; sale, 139n, 196, 201; relations with California, 185; profits on California trade, 188

Ross Rancho, 123

Rotchev, Alexander, 118, 127, 129, 132, 188

Rotchev River, 118

Rowand, Alexander, 66

Rudakov, Alexander, 38

Ruiz, José, 180

Rumyantsev, Nicholas, 74, 76, 159

Rupert's Land, 208

Russian California: founding, 11; character, 20; provisionment, 20n; sale, 24, 139, 202, 213; lumbering, 38; shipping, 39; payment for, 51; agricultural performance, 69; extent, 113; population, 115; pre-eminence of agriculture, 116; number of farms, 118; seasonal agricultural round, 119; grain yields, 120–22; orcharding, 123; livestock numbers, 123; grain exports, 124; beef exports, 125; loss of men, 127; inexperience of farm workers, 129; modernization of farming, 131; physical obstacles to farming, 132; agricultural expansion, 134; cost of wheat growing, 138; agricultural failure, 139, 164, 189, 213

Russian Hawaii, 52, 148

Russian River, 117

"Russian supplies," 48

Russian-American Company: formation, 4–5, 10, 73; first charter, 9, 112, 153; character, 10; strength, 11; Creole employees, 12; difficulties, 15; northward shift, 16; governmental connection, 29; liquidation, 29n; third charter, 32n; Chinese tea imports, 37; first headquarters, 44n; employees, 48; Okhotsk factory, 55; trade goods, 56n; investigation of Yakutsk-Udsk route, 69; use of Amur route, 71; Hudson's Bay Company agreement, 83, 201; priority of fur trade, 110; pre-eminence of provisions in trade, 154; 1812 American Fur Company agreement, 160–61; increased coastal trade, 167; Monterey depot, 183; competitive disadvantages in coastal trade, 200; disposal of Russian California, 202; provisionment of Kamchatka, 204–05; Hudson's Bay Company wheat imports, 206; sale of Alaska, 208; Hawaiian trade, 209

Russian-Finnish Whaling Company, 28

St. Constantine Redoubt, 7

St. Dionysius Redoubt, 25, 41, 47, 200, 201, 201n

St. George Island (Pribilofs), 20, 35, 36, 166

St. Michael Redoubt, 17

St. Nicholas Redoubt, 7, 18, 41, 96, 99, 100, 102, 103

St. Paul Island (Pribilofs), 20, 35

St. Paul's Harbor, 6, 10, 17, 18, 42, 44n, 96, 96n, 97, 103, 109

St. Peter and St. Paul, 204

Sakhalin, 25, 39, 71

San Andreas Fault, 137

San Blas, 9, 184

San Diego, 9, 174, 178, 183, 185, 191

San Francisco: founding, 9; ice trade, 25, 41n; Russian commercial agency and vice-consulate, 28, 42, 197n; Rezanov's visit, 113, 176–77

San Francisco Bay, 11, 127, 188

San Francisco Presidio, 177, 188

San Pedro, 183

San Pedro Bay, 174
San Quintín, 183, 184
Sandwich Islanders, 149, 155n, 209
Sandwich Islands, 15, 16, 38, 141, 142,
    144, 145, 146, 147, 148, 149, 156,
    188, 209, 210, 211, 213
Santa Cruz, 183
Sapozhnikov, Jacob, 96n, 100
Sapozhnikov River, 100
Sapozhnikova (see Chiniatsk)
sarana, 18
Sarychev, Gabriel, 76
Saskatchewan River, 61n
Schaffer, George, 143, 143n, 144, 145,
    146, 147, 147n, 148, 149, 210
Schaffer Valley, 147
Schmidt, Carl, 116, 126, 128, 128n,
    129, 129n, 185
Schmidt Plain, 118
Scott, James, 157
sea bear (fur seal), 35
sea beaver (sea otter), 32
sea cat (fur seal), 35
sea dogs (harbor seals), 36
Second Kamchatka Expedition, 58, 75
Serra, Junípero, 174
Shchukin, Nicholas, 57
Shelikhov, Gregory: company of, 4;
    settlement by, 5, 108; expansionist
    plans, 6; shipping needs, 64; death,
    64; on relocation of Okhotsk, 69;
    foreign competition, 75; agricul-
    tural operations, 93–95, 95n; agri-
    cultural hopes, 99, 109; agricul-
    tural failure, 99, 105; attempts at
    foreign trade, 156, 157n
Shelikhov, Natalia, 64
Shelikhov, Paul, 116, 120, 124, 127,
    129, 133, 185
Shields, James, 13, 64
shitiks, 64
Shumagin Islands, 18
"Siberian deliveries," 55
Simpson, Aemelius, 183
Simpson, George, 16, 26, 61n, 66, 167,
    172, 199, 201, 202, 203, 204
Sitka, 26, 103, 103n, 125, 128, 129,
    158, 204
Sitka Bay, 11, 12
Sitkans (see Koloshes)
Slavorossiya, 6, 14, 95, 99, 215
Slavyanka River, 117, 118, 125, 130,
    131n
Slavyansk, 113
Slobodchikov, Sysoy, 210
South Sea Company, 155

South Sea Islands, 156
Speransky, Michael, 61n
Spruce Island (Kodiak Counter), 96,
    99, 108
Stikine, 41
Stikine affair, 23
Stikine River, 23, 25, 200, 201, 201n
Stroganov, Gregory, 179
Stuart Island (Northern District), 17,
    19
Sturgis, William, 34
sumas, 58
Sutter, John, 24n, 51, 118, 139, 139n,
    188
Sutter's Mill, 196

Tamalancia Valley, 117
Tarakanov, Basil, 147, 147n, 148
Tatar Strait, 84
Tebenkov, Michael: northern expedi-
    tion, 16; on Siberian employees,
    26; St. Nicholas Redoubt's brick-
    works, 41; gubernatorial independ-
    ence, 45; shortage of personnel,
    47, 48; Aleut farming, 99; Kodiak
    livestock, 107; colonial citizens,
    108; California trade, 196; multiple
    source of provisions, 205–06; Ha-
    waiian trade, 211
Thompson Co., 167
Three Friends Rancho, 117
Three Saints Harbor, 6, 8, 39, 46, 93,
    99
Tlingit Indians (see Kolosh Indians)
Tokugawa Shogunate, 154
Tomari, 142, 143, 144, 145, 146, 147,
    148, 210
Tomeamea, 142
Tomi-Omi, 142, 143, 144, 148, 210
Torson, Constantine, 84
Transbaikalia, 71

Uda River, 69
Udsk, 69
Ulya River, 69
Unalaska, 7, 8, 9, 39, 100, 101, 103n,
    104, 127
Unalaska Counter, 11, 18, 39, 102

Unalaska Island, 5, 39n, 94, 95, 96, 105, 108, 110n
Unga Island, 41, 99
United American Company, 4, 60, 95
Urak River, 58, 69
Ural Mountains, 55
Urup Island, 7, 14, 16, 19, 28n, 59n, 95, 100, 103
Ust-Maya, 59, 69

Vallejo, Mariano, 118, 124, 130, 185, 188
Vancouver Island, 9, 41, 42, 113
Vasily Rancho, 118n
Vasilyev, Ivan, 16
Veniaminov, Ivan, 15, 106n, 108, 127, 135
Victoria, 28, 41
Victoria, Manuel, 191
Voaga, 144, 145, 148
Von Chamisso, Adelbert, 127, 129, 181, 188
Von Kotzebue, Otto, 122, 127, 129, 181, 188
Von Langsdorff, George, 108, 129, 175, 177, 177n, 188
Von Pahlen, Theodore, 159
Voskresensk, 39
Voyevodsky, Stephen, 25, 41, 197, 215

Waimea, 147
West Indies, 168
Willow Creek (see Dry Creek and Rotchev River)
Woody Island (Kodiak Counter), 42, 96, 108
Wrangel, Ferdinand: settlement by, 17; on incompetence of personnel, 48; Yakutsk-Okhotsk Track, 61; company fleet, 65; Okhotsk beef, 68; Atka livestock, 96; farming at New Valaam, 99; provisionment by Koloshes, 102; shortage of hay on Kodiak, 106; promyshlenniks as gardeners, 108; Aleuts as farmers, 109; Fort Ross, 114–15; California trade, 117; poultry at Fort Ross, 124; lack of fish at Fort Ross, 125; Indian labor at Fort Ross, 128; promyshlenniks, 130; threshing at Fort Ross, 131n; physical environment of Fort Ross, 132; soil exhaustion at Fort Ross, 133; Fort Ross fogs, 135–36; California's attractions, 175; California trade, 189, 191, 191n, 192; decline of California's missions, 194; wheat imports from Chile, 195; British competition, 199–200; prices of American and British goods, 204; provisionment of Kamchatka, 206; monthly rations, 214

Yakutat, 13, 14, 39, 103n, 109, 159
Yakutat Bay, 6, 95, 95n
Yakuts, 26, 48, 57, 58, 61n, 71n, 107, 109n, 164
Yakutsk, 11, 36, 45, 51, 56n, 57, 59, 60, 61, 67, 69, 71, 71n, 73, 82, 164, 197, 202, 212
Yakutsk Track, 57
Yakutsk-Ayan route, 69, 70, 71, 72
Yakutsk-Okhotsk Track, 58, 59, 60, 61, 67, 68, 69, 70, 71, 72, 82n
Yakutsk-Udsk route, 69
yamanina, 13
Yanovsky, Simon, 16, 49, 100, 213, 214, 216
Yarmanka, 58
yasak, 32n
Yenisey River, 56
Young, George, 144
Young, John, 148
Yudoma River, 58, 69
yukola, 18
Yukon River (see Kvikpak River)
Yukon Valley, 37

Zagoskin, Lawrence, 17
Zakharov Bay, 41
zapuskas, 37
Zavalishin, Dmitry, 84, 105, 185
Zubov Islands (see Pribilof Islands)
Zvezdochetov, Basil, 95, 100